The Rocky Mountain
Wild Foods Cookbook

WILD FOODS REGION

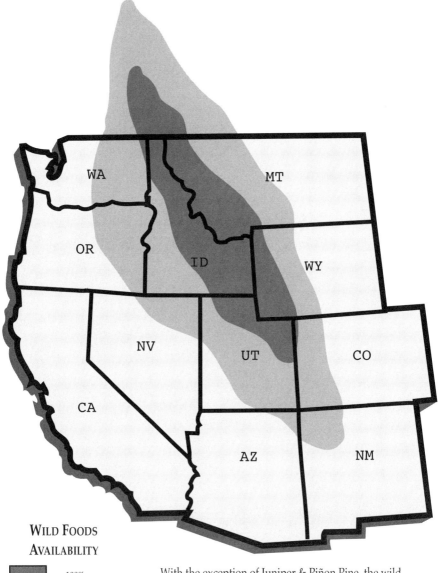

WILD FOODS AVAILABILITY

- 100%
- 50% - 75%
- 50% or less

With the exception of Juniper & Piñon Pine, the wild plants in this book are common throughout the mountain regions of the United States and Canada.

THE ROCKY MOUNTAIN WILD FOODS COOKBOOK

by

Darcy Williamson

Illustrations by the author
Cover Art by Larry Milligan
Cover Design by Teresa Sales

The CAXTON PRINTERS, Ltd.
Caldwell, Idaho
1995

Library of Congress Cataloging–in–Publication–Data
Williamson Darcy.
    The Rocky Mountain wild foods cookbook / by Darcy Williamson ;
illustrations by the author ; cover art by Larry Milligan ; cover design by
Teresa Sales.
        p.   cm.
    Includes bibliographical references and index.
    ISBN 0-87004-367-6
    1. Cookery (Wild foods) 2. Wild plants, Edible--Rocky Mountains
Region.   I. Title.
TX823.W54   1995   95-21282
641.6--dc20   CIP

Lithographed and bound in the United States of America by
The CAXTON PRINTERS, Ltd.
Caldwell, Idaho 83605–3299
160174

To Rob Dow

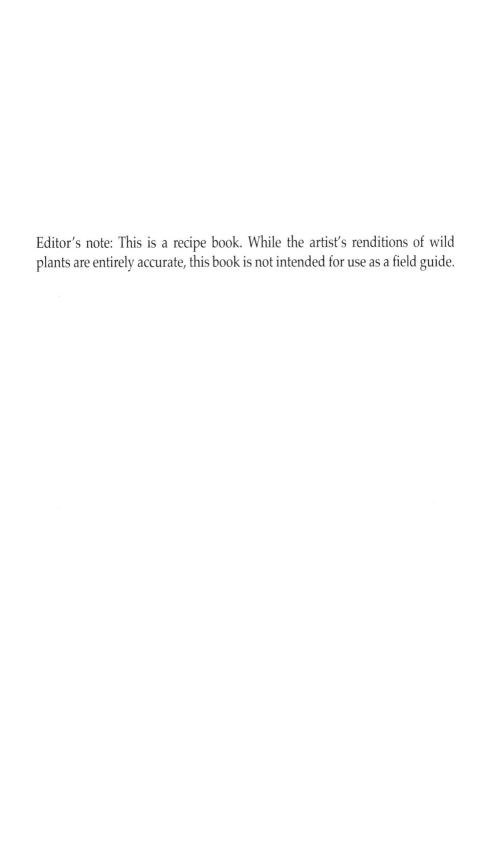

Editor's note: This is a recipe book. While the artist's renditions of wild plants are entirely accurate, this book is not intended for use as a field guide.

TABLE OF CONTENTS

Introduction ix

1   Arrowhead 1
2   Burdock 13
3   Cattail 23
4   Chickweed 34
5   Chokecherry 42
6   Dandelion 50
7   Elderberry 59
8   Fiddlehead 68
9   Fireweed 77
10 Huckleberry 84
11 Juniper 95
12 Lamb's Quarters 104
13 Milkweed 112
14 Miner's Lettuce 121
15 Morel Mushrooms 128
16 Oregon Grape 138
17 Piñon Pine 144
18 Salsify 153
19 Serviceberry 161
20 Sheep Sorrel 170
21 Stinging Nettle 177
22 Watercress 186
23 Wild Currant 193
24 Wild Gooseberry 201
25 Wild Mint 207
26 Wild Plum 214
27 Wild Rose 221
28 Yampa 229

Bibliography 237
Index 239
Color Illustrations ....following 118

INTRODUCTION

I believe that the best part of winter is the anticipation of spring. Shortly after the first carpet of snow has fallen around November, I begin thinking of May, when the first fragrant shoots of Stinging Nettles appear and the tender, pale Dandelion crowns are at their best. I begin longing for the scent of damp earth; the sight of all the shades of green that follow the snow line in its retreat to higher elevations; and of searching for Morels camouflaged among the Trilliums, Lady's Slippers, and last year's pine cones.

As a young girl I was fascinated by learning what foods were found in places other than on the shelves of grocery stores or in someone's labor intensive garden. In the forest near my home lemon-flavored Sheep Sorrel grew in succulent bunches, Miner's Lettuce flourished by a nearby creek and Wild Mint released its heady fragrance along the path that followed the river.

Throughout my adulthood years I expanded my knowledge of wild plants. They provided food when my budget needed stretching, exercise gained in their pursuit, medicine for when I was ill, an alternative to produce grown with pesticides, and exotic ingredients not found on supermarket shelves for the gourmet side of my nature. Though I have gathered and used the wild plants from Oregon to New England and from the Southwest to the Southeast, it is the Rocky Mountains where the edible and medicinal plants are best known to me.

My back yard is the Northern Rocky Mountain range. These mountains form the Continental Divide in western North America, separating the drainage of the Atlantic and Arctic oceans from that of the Pacific Ocean. The head waters of the Arkansas, Platte, Yellowstone, Missouri, Peace, Colorado, Snake, and Columbia Rivers all originate in the Rocky Mountains. *The Rocky Mountain Wild Foods Cookbook* contains twenty-eight plants common to the Northern and Middle Rockies. The Northern Rockies extend approximately 1,000 miles through eastern British Columbia and southwestern Alberta provinces, Canada, into northeastern Washington, northern and central Idaho, and western Montana. The major mountain ranges include the Canadian Rockies, Purcell, Selkirk, Columbia, Pend Oreille, McDonald, Galton, Lewis, Livingston, Flathead, Swan, Mission, Cabinet, Coeur d'Alene, Clearwater, Bitterroot, Big Belt, Garnet, Gallatin, Madison, Snowcrest, Centennial, Beaverhead, Lemhi, Salmon River, Sawtooth, Seven Devils, Boise, Trinity, Smoky, and Lost River.

The Middle Rockies extend 430 miles and occupy the western margin of Wyoming, southeastern Idaho, north–central Utah, and south–central Montana. The major mountain ranges of the Middle Rockies are the Beartooth, Absaroka, Wasatch, Uinta, Snake River, Teton, Wyoming, Gros Venture, Salt, Caribou, Aspen, Bighorn, Shoshone, Owl Creek, Bridger, Pryor, and Bear River.

The Rocky Mountain Wild Foods Cookbook contains recipes and preparation methods relative to healthful and nutritious cooking, but also valuable information about each of the plants featured. Folklore and biological facts are intertwined with information on nutritional and medicinal uses. The wild food harvester can also learn how to identify the plants through detailed descriptions as well as where they may be located within the Rocky Mountains.

As others gain intimate knowledge through the use of the wild plants which live here, so will their respect for the plants' diverse, magnificent and fragile environments grow. It is through such respect that individuals realize that the privilege is not only in benefits gained from these environments but in protecting them as well.

Chapter 1

ARROWHEAD

(Sagittaria latifolia)

Also known as
wappatoo, wapato, duck potato, tule potato, marsh potato.

The starch bearing tubers were a stable food for several Rocky Mountain Indian tribes. Only Camas exceeded Arrowhead as a valued vegetable source. Native American women would gather the aquatic Arrowhead by wading into the water, sometimes breast deep, and digging the tubers from the muddy marsh or pond bottom with their toes. The tubers, once freed from the tangle of roots, would bob to the surface. Tubers were gathered in this manner as long as there was open water. When winter weather became so extreme that the ponds froze over, harvesting ended. The collected tubers were either boiled or roasted in hot ashes; some were dried and pounded into a meal for later use.

Lewis and Clark ate Arrowhead during their expedition in the early 1800s and recorded in their journals: "They [Arrowhead tubers] are nearly equal in flavor to the Irish potato and offer a good substitute for bread."

In the mid to late 1800s the Chinese, who worked the mining areas of the Central Rockies, not only harvested wild Arrowhead tubers but cultivated them, as well. They believed that the tubers bore a resemblance in texture and flavor to the water chestnuts of their homelands.

The Arrowhead was also used as a medicinal plant. Native Americans pressed the raw juice from the tubers and drank the liquid on an empty stomach to increase the flow of urine. Early homesteaders made a concentrated broth, from the cooking liquid of Arrowhead tubers, to be used as a diuretic. In addition to being a valuable food and medicinal plant, Arrowhead tubers are also easily digested, making them suitable food for invalids and convalescents.

Arrowhead is found growing in shallow water in ponds and marshes or along borders of slow moving streams throughout the Rocky Mountain region. The plant grows from a few inches to two or three feet tall. The most common leaf form of the Arrowhead is arrow-shaped with long pointed basal lobes. Though all leaves are not the same shape there are generally enough arrow-shaped leaves in a group to aid identification. When the plants grow submerged, ribbon or lance-like foliage is formed.

Waxy white flowers, usually arranged in whorls of three, grow on their own single stem. The upper flowers generally bear yellow stamens, while pistils are borne on the lower blossoms. The fully opened flowers range from one to one and one-half inches across. Arrowhead blossoms from July to September before fruiting, flattish seeds are formed which are winged on each margin and end in a curved tip.

Potato-like tubers, approximately the size of small hen's eggs, form at the ends of long subterranean runners originating at the base of each plant. The tubers are held in place by a maze of fibrous roots. The tubers can be gathered in quantity by freeing them from the mud with a hoe, rake, or stick.

Arrowhead tubers may be eaten raw, though their flavor is slightly unpleasant owing to its acrid taste. However, it is delicious when cooked or pickled. Campers and backpackers will find the tubers a welcome addition to wilderness fare.

FIELD PREPARATION OF ARROWHEAD

Dig a small pit and line it with stones. Build a fire in the pit and allow it to burn until a good amount of coals have accumulated. Make a well in the center of the coals and add Arrowhead tubers. Rake coals over tubers and allow them to roast.

Small tubers under one inch in diameter will be ready to eat in forty-five minutes; larger tubers, one hour. Peel off outer hull before eating.

ARROWHEAD CHOWDER

Serves 5

  1 large onion, chopped
  1 lb. Arrowhead tubers, scrubbed and quartered
  1 sweet red pepper, seeded and chopped
$1/_4$ cup butter
  1 tsp. salt
$1/_4$ tsp. pepper
  1 quart milk
  1 Tbsp. fresh basil, chopped
  1 Tbsp. flour

Cook Arrowhead, onion, and red pepper in butter until onion is soft. Add remaining ingredients and cook very slowly until heated through. Add flour to $1/_4$ cup water and stir to make a thin paste. Slowly stir into chowder. Heat and stir until thickened. Serve at once.

ARROWHEAD AND CHICKEN STIR-FRY

Serves 6

1 egg white
$1^1/_2$ Tbsp. cornstarch
1 lb. boneless, skinless chicken breast, cut into 1 inch pieces
$1^1/_2$ lb. Arrowhead tubers, scrubbed
$^1/_4$ cup peanut oil
2 cloves garlic, crushed
2 Tbsp. grated fresh gingerroot
1 onion, chopped
1 sweet red pepper, cut into $^1/_2$ inch pieces
6 green onions, cut diagonally into 1 inch pieces
3 Tbsp. soy sauce
1 tsp. sugar
$1^1/_2$ Tbsp. rice vinegar
$^1/_2$ cup chicken broth
1 tsp. sesame oil
1 tsp. cold water

Whisk together egg white and 1 Tbsp. cornstarch, add chicken and let mixture stand for 10 minutes. In large saucepan of boiling salted water cook Arrowhead for 10 minutes, or until they are just tender-crisp. Drain in colander and refresh them under water. Slice tubers to $^1/_4$ inch thick.

Heat a wok over moderately high heat and heat peanut oil until hot but not smoking. Add drained chicken and stir-fry for 1 minute. Transfer it to a bowl. Heat the oil remaining in wok until it is hot and stir-fry the garlic and gingerroot for 30 seconds. Add red pepper and green onions and stir-fry for 2 minutes. Add sliced Arrowhead and stir-fry 1 minute longer.

In small bowl whisk together soy sauce, sugar, vinegar, broth, sesame oil, remaining cornstarch, and cold water. Whisk mixture into hot vegetables and cook until mixture thickens. Serve with rice, if desired.

ARROWHEAD WITH EGG VINAIGRETTE

Serves 4

1 lb. Arrowhead tubers, scrubbed
2 hard-cooked eggs, mashed
1 egg yolk, raw
$^1/_2$ cup olive oil
1 tsp. minced fresh parsley
1 Tbsp. minced fresh basil
1 tsp. minced chives
2 Tbsp. freshly squeezed lime juice
$^1/_2$ tsp. salt
$^1/_4$ tsp. pepper

Boil tubers in salted water until tender. Plunge in ice water and peel off outer layer.

Mash hard-cooked eggs with raw yolk. Add oil, a teaspoonful at a time, while beating vigorously. Add remaining ingredients and mix thoroughly. Pour over Arrowhead and marinate for 3 to 4 hours. Serve on bed of fresh greens.

ARROWHEAD WITH GARLIC DRESSING

Serves 2

$^1/_2$ lb. Arrowhead, scrubbed and steamed until tender
$^1/_2$ cup thinly sliced red onion
3 cloves garlic, crushed
1 tsp. salt
$^1/_2$ tsp. freshly ground pepper
1 cup olive oil
$^1/_2$ cup white wine vinegar
2 tsp. honey
Loose leaf lettuce

Combine garlic, salt, pepper, oil, vinegar, and honey. Mix well. Pour over Arrowhead and onion in bowl. Refrigerate overnight. Serve on bed of lettuce.

ARROWHEAD, LEEK AND CANADIAN BACON SOUP

Serves 6

2 cups thinly sliced white part of leek
$^1/_2$ cup finely chopped onion
10 slices Canadian bacon, chopped
$^1/_4$ cup butter
$1^1/_2$ Tbsp. flour
4 cups beef broth
$1^1/_2$ lbs. Arrowhead tubers, scrubbed
1 cup heavy cream
2 large egg yolks
3 Tbsp. fresh basil, minced
2 tsp. freshly grated lemon rind

In kettle cook leek, onion, and Canadian bacon in butter over medium heat, stirring, until vegetables are softened. Stir in flour and cook, stirring, for 3 minutes. Whisk in the stock, add Arrowhead tubers and bring mixture to a boil. Reduce heat and simmer, covered, for 45 minutes.

In small bowl whisk together cream and yolks. Remove kettle from the heat, stir cream mixture into hot soup. Return to heat and cook over low heat, stirring, until the soup is hot. Do not allow soup to boil. Serve at once garnished with basil and lemon rind.

ARROWHEAD WITH LIME AND DILL

Serves 3

1 lb. Arrowhead tubers, scrubbed
$^1/_4$ cup minced onion
3 Tbsp. butter
3 Tbsp. white wine
$1^1/_2$ Tbsp. fresh lime juice
1 tsp. grated lime rind
1 Tbsp. snipped fresh dill

In steamer set over boiling water steam tubers, covered, for 10 minutes, or until they are just tender. In a skillet cook onion in butter over medium-low heat, until onion is soft. Add the tubers and remaining ingredients. Heat through. Serve at once.

ARROWHEAD PICKLES

6 to 7 pints

5 lb. Arrowhead tubers, steamed 20 minutes
1 lb. brown sugar
1 quart white vinegar
1 tsp. curry powder
3 tsp. cornstarch
$^1/_2$ oz. ground allspice
$^1/_2$ tsp. ground mustard
2 tsp. ground turmeric
$^1/_2$ oz. ground cloves

Scrape outer covering from Arrowhead tubers and soak in brine of $^1/_2$ cup salt to 1 quart water. Allow tubers to stand in brine for 24 hours.

In large kettle boil together vinegar and sugar. Make a paste of cornstarch and spices, adding a little vinegar for moisture. Stir some hot vinegar mixture into paste, then stir paste into vinegar mixture in kettle. Boil until thickened.

Drain and rinse tubers. Pack into sterilized pint jars and pour boiling sauce over the top. Adjust lids and process in boiling water bath for 15 minutes. Allow to age 6 weeks before serving.

ARROWHEAD–TARRAGON SALAD

Serves 8

2 lbs. Arrowhead tubers
6 Tbsp. olive oil
6 Tbsp. cider vinegar
$^1/_2$ cup beef bouillon
$^1/_4$ tsp. paprika
$^1/_4$ cup sliced green onion
1 Tbsp. fresh tarragon

Steam tubers 8 minutes in vegetable steamer. Plunge in ice water and rub off outer layer. Cut tubers in half and add remaining ingredients. Chill for at least 4 hours before serving.

Arrowhead and Watercress Soup

Serves 4

1 1/2 lbs. Arrowhead, scrubbed and chopped fine
2 cups chopped watercress
2 Tbsp. butter
2 cups cream
1 cup water
Salt and pepper to taste

Combine ingredients in kettle and cook slowly for 15 minutes or until heated through. Serve at once.

Arrowhead with Vinaigrette

Serves 4

2 lbs. Arrowhead tubers, outer layer scrubbed clean
1/2 cup olive oil
2 cloves garlic, crushed
1 1/2 Tbsp. white wine vinegar
2 Tbsp. finely shredded carrot
1 1/2 Tbsp. finely minced watercress
1 Tbsp. finely minced chives
2 tsp. finely minced green pepper
1/4 tsp. salt
1/2 tsp. dry mustard
1/4 tsp. pepper

Steam tubers in vegetable steamer for 25 minutes. Meanwhile combine remaining ingredients. Pour over warm tubers. Cool to room temperature. Chill.

CAMPFIRE STEW WITH ARROWHEAD

Serves 3 to 4

Bacon drippings or cooking oil
1 grouse, pheasant, or cottontail
1 medium onion, sliced
$^1/_2$ cup rice
$1^1/_2$ quarts water
1 quart Arrowhead tubers, scrubbed
2 garlic cloves, crushed
2 Tbsp. flour
Salt and pepper to taste

In skillet brown meat and onion in hot drippings or oil. Add garlic and rice. Stir 3 to 4 minutes then add water and Arrowhead. Cover and simmer for 1 hour. Season with salt and pepper. Mix flour with small amount of water to form a thin paste. Stir into stew. Cook until stew has thickened.

CREAMED ARROWHEAD

Serves 2

$^1/_2$ lb. Arrowhead tubers, scrubbed
1 cup heavy cream
$^1/_4$ cup butter
$^1/_4$ tsp. salt
White pepper to taste
Minced fresh basil for garnish
Paprika for garnish

In steamer set over boiling water steam Arrowhead for 7 minutes, or until just tender, transfer them to plate and cool. Cut tubers in half.

In heavy skillet combine Arrowhead, cream, butter, salt, and pepper and cook mixture at a very slow simmer for 40 to 45 minutes, stirring every 5 minutes. Transfer to serving dish and garnish with basil and paprika. Serve at once.

Garlic Puréed Arrowhead

Serves 4

6 large garlic cloves, chopped fine
$^1/_2$ tsp. salt
$1^1/_2$ lbs. Arrowhead tubers, scrubbed
$^2/_3$ cup softened butter, cut into bits
1 cup heavy cream
1 Tbsp. finely chopped cilantro
1 cup fine fresh sourdough bread crumbs

In a mortar with pestle mash garlic with salt to form a paste. In pan with steamer, steam tubers until they are tender. Cool and peel off outer layer. Mash together the tubers and garlic mixture, $^1/_2$ cup butter, cream, cilantro, and salt and pepper to taste until mixture is smooth. Transfer mixture to a baking dish, 12x8x2 inches, smoothing top. Sprinkle with bread crumbs and dot with remaining butter. Bake at 375°F for 25 to 30 minutes or until top is golden.

Millet–Arrowhead Soup

Serves 6

4 quarts chicken, turkey, or vegetable stock
$1^1/_2$ cups millet (available at natural food stores)
2 cups tomato purée
1 large onion, diced
2 cloves garlic, minced
$^1/_2$ green pepper, diced
1 diced carrot
2 cups diced Arrowhead tubers
$^1/_2$ tsp. salt
$^1/_4$ tsp. red pepper flakes

Add millet to stock and simmer over low heat for 1 hour. Add remaining ingredients and simmer 30 minutes longer.

MOLDED ARROWHEAD TOFU SALAD

Serves 6

1 envelope unflavored gelatin
$^1/_4$ cup freshly squeezed lime juice
3 Tbsp. honey
$^1/_2$ cup carrot juice
$^1/_2$ cup boiling water
1 Tbsp. vinegar
1 tsp. onion juice
$^1/_2$ lb. Arrowhead tubers, peeled and chopped
1 cup cubed tofu
1 cup yogurt

Combine gelatin, lime juice, honey, carrot juice, and boiling water in bowl. Stir well. Allow gelatin to soften 10 minutes. Add vinegar and lemon juice. Stir. Chill until partially set.

Blend yogurt, Arrowhead, and tofu into partially set gelatin. Pour into mold. Chill. Unmold on lettuce-lined plate.

NETTLE AND ARROWHEAD SPREAD

2-1/2 cups

2 lbs. young Stinging Nettle shoots
10 Arrowhead tubers
$^1/_2$ cup mayonnaise
1 cup sour cream
$^1/_2$ cup minced onion
$^1/_2$ cup chopped cilantro
  Dash salt
  Pepper to taste

In large kettle, without any added water, cook nettles 10 minutes. Cool. Squeeze out excess liquid. Coarsely chop in food processor. Set aside.

In medium-sized pan cook Arrowhead tubers in water to cover, 10 minutes or until tender-crisp. Drain. Cool. Scrap off outer layer of tubers and coarsely chop.

In bowl toss Nettles with a fork, add Arrowhead, mayonnaise, sour cream, onion, cilantro, salt, and pepper. Mix well, then spoon into serving dish. Serve with whole grain crackers.

SHREDDED ARROWHEAD SALAD

Serves 4

1 lb. Arrowhead tubers, scrubbed
$^1/_4$ tsp. salt
2 Tbsp. peanut oil
1 Tbsp. soy sauce
$^1/_2$ tsp. sesame oil
2 cloves garlic, crushed
$^1/_2$ tsp. honey
   Dash red chili pepper flakes
   Toasted sesame seeds

Shred tubers, using medium-sized grater. Combine remaining ingredients except sesame seeds and toss with Arrowhead. Chill. Serve on a lettuce leaf and garnish with sesame seeds.

VENISON AND ARROWHEAD KABOBS

Serves 4

$^1/_2$ cup peanut oil
$^1/_2$ cup dry red wine
$^1/_2$ cup tarragon vinegar
$^1/_2$ cup soy sauce
2 Tbsp. minced green pepper
4 cloves garlic, crushed
$^1/_2$ tsp. coarsely ground pepper
2 lbs. venison, cut into $1^1/_2$ inch cubes
1 lb. Arrowhead tubers

Combine first 7 ingredients and mix well. Add venison cubes and Arrowhead. Marinate for 3 to 4 hours, stirring occasionally.

Alternate venison and tubers on skewers. Broil about 5 inch from charcoal coals for 15 minutes or until venison is medium rare. Heat marinade to serve with kabobs.

CHAPTER

2

BURDOCK

(Arctium minus)

Also known as
cocklebur, hareburr, hurrburr, turkey burrseed, burr weed, clot-burr,
beggar's buttons, gobo, happy-major, personata, and grass burdock.

It is hard to mistake Burdock. Its clinging burrs hitchhiked with the Roman legions across the Old World, came to America aboard early ships, and attached themselves to coattails and horsetails for transport West. They continued to spread with the trappers and gold seekers to every temperate portion of the Rocky Mountain region and beyond.

Burdock is not native to the United States, for it naturalized during the 1800s. Settlers, familiar with the valuable plant in the Old World, instructed Native Americans in its uses. The Indians soon adapted it to their own purposes, one of which was herbal assistance in their vision quests. They believed that by drinking bitter tea made from unpeeled Burdock roots, visions received would be vividly retained in their minds granting them greater wisdom.

In *The People's Common Sense Medical Advisor*, written by R.V. Pierce, M.D., and published in 1895, Burdock was listed as a valuable treatment for diseases of the blood. A tincture of up to one tablespoon of Burdock taken twenty minutes before meals was recommended. The homeopathic tinctures were imported from French and German pharmacists.

Early homesteaders used chopped Burdock root, steeped in boiling water, not only as a blood purifier but also to aid bladder infections. This tea was used to relieve pleurisy and also to reduce swelling of glands. A wash made by boiling unpeeled roots was used to bathe a variety of skin ailments.

Burdock leaves are believed to neutralize and eliminate poisons in the body system. A poultice of leaves was applied to snake bite. Fresh, bruised leaves were also used as a remedy for poison oak or poison ivy. Crushed, fresh leaves, applied directly, were found helpful in treating acne.

Burdock is a biennial. It prospers throughout most of the United States, growing in profusion around old homesteads, logging regions, and abandoned mining sites. It rarely grows at elevations above 9,000 feet. Whether Burdock is used for culinary purposes or medicinal purposes it is preferable to harvest them in early summer, though they may be gathered up to mid–October.

First year plants bear no flowers or burrs. The young leaves are smooth and velvetlike—green on top and downy gray beneath. These first-year leaves make a suitable potherb when boiled in two changes of water for a total of thirty-five minutes. The tender leaves may also be coarsely chopped and added to salads.

Burdock root is cultivated as a vegetable in Japan but is not often used in the United States. This is probably due to the circumstances of its naturalized habitat. In Japan it is grown in tilled fields where the long roots are easy to extract. Wild Burdock tends to establish itself in rocky areas or in clay-like soil and are difficult to excavate. A slim spade or post hole digger are beneficial tools to have when harvesting Burdock root.

It is the first year roots of the Burdock which are eaten. The roots may reach a foot in length and up to an inch in diameter. A grayish covering protects the cream-colored edible pith. Once harvested the roots need to be completely peeled before using to remove the very bitter outer covering. These plants produce long, thick flower stalks which grow at an astonishingly rapid rate. Rather than bearing only basil leaves as in its first year, the mature plant grows a furrowed, reddish, pithy stem with wooly branches.

The blossoms, which appear from July to October, often reach three-quarters of an inch in diameter and differ in color from light amethyst to white. The flowers mature to prickly ovule carriers which cling tenaciously to fur or clothing. The flower stalks are edible. They need to be picked while the leaves are unfurling, in advance of the expanding of the flower buds. The rind should be peeled from the stalks and the inner core cooked in two changes of water to remove any bitterness.

BRAISED BURDOCK
Serves 4

10 to 12 Burdock roots, peeled
6 Tbsp. butter
1 tsp. sugar
$^1/_2$ cup beef broth
Salt
Freshly ground pepper

Cook Burdock for 45 minutes, changing water twice during process. Drain and rinse well. Melt butter in heavy skillet, and when butter foams and bubbles add Burdock, stirring and cooking over medium heat for several minutes. Sprinkle Burdock lightly with sugar and shake pan so that roots begin to caramelize slightly. When Burdock turns a light brown add the broth. Cover skillet and simmer 10 minutes, shaking pan from time to time. Season to taste with salt and pepper. Serve with the pan juices.

BURDOCK FRITTERS
Serves 4

1$^1/_2$ lbs. Burdock roots, peeled
1 cup milk
2 eggs
$^1/_2$ tsp. baking powder
$^1/_4$ tsp. salt
  Flour
  Oil for deep-frying

Cut Burdock in half lengthwise. Cut each half into 3-inch long pieces. Cook in boiling salted water until tender, changing water twice during cooking. Combine remaining ingredients, adding enough flour to make a batter the consistency of pancakes.

Dip Burdock pieces in batter and fry in deep hot oil (370–390°F) until golden.

BURDOCK GREENS WITH MONTEREY JACK
Serves 4

2 lbs. young Burdock greens
2 Tbsp. butter
2 Tbsp. flour
1 tsp. salt
$^1/_2$ cup milk
$^1/_2$ lb. diced Monterey jack cheese
$^1/_2$ cup fresh bread crumbs
2 Tbsp. melted butter

Cook greens in simmering water for 10 minutes. Drain and rinse. Add greens to fresh water and cook 10 minutes. Drain and rinse. Chop greens coarsely and place in bottom of large kettle; cover with salted water and cook 10 minutes. Drain thoroughly in colander, pressing out liquid.

Melt butter. Blend in flour and salt. Add milk and cook, stirring constantly, until mixture comes to a boil. Add cheese, stirring until cheese is melted and blended.

Place Burdock in greased 2 quart casserole and stir in sauce. Toss bread crumbs with butter and sprinkle over casserole. Bake at 350°F for 25 minutes.

Burdock Mold

$^1/_2$ lb. sliced mushrooms
1 onion, finely chopped
2 Tbsp. vegetable oil
4 cups Burdock flower stems which have been cooked a total of
      35 minutes in two changes of water and cut into 2 inch lengths
1 lemon, halved
2 cups frozen green peas
3 Tbsp. butter
3 Tbsp. flour
$^1/_2$ cup milk
$^1/_2$ cup cream
1 tsp. tarragon
$^1/_4$ tsp. salt
$^1/_4$ tsp. pepper
$^1/_4$ lbs. grated sharp Cheddar cheese
1 package of frozen creamed onions and peas,
      prepared according to instructions on package.

Sauté mushrooms and onion in small skillet and set aside. Squeeze lemon juice over Burdock. Put Burdock in food processor along with peas and pulverize.

Melt butter in skillet. Add flour. Stir in milk and cream and cook until thickened. Add seasoning and cheese and continue stirring until smooth. Add mushroom and onion mixture. Add Burdock and pea mixture. Mix well. Spoon into an oiled ring mold and place in pan of water in oven.

Bake at 350°F for 45 minutes, covered with foil. Unmold on platter, filling center with hot creamed peas and onions.

BURDOCK RELISH

1-1/2 quarts

       5 cups peeled, grated Burdock root
    $^1/_2$ cup cider vinegar
       1 large onion, grated
       2 tart apples, cored and chopped
    $^1/_2$ cup sugar
    $^1/_2$ cup white wine vinegar
    $^1/_4$ cup vegetable oil
       1 Tbsp. water
    $^1/_2$ salt
    $^1/_4$ tsp. pepper

Put grated Burdock in bowl and cover with water. Add cider vinegar and let stand 3 to 4 hours. Drain and rinse. Cook in small amount of water for 10 minutes. Drain and rinse well. Combine with remaining ingredients and let stand overnight. Serve in butter lettuce cups, if desired.

CANDIED BURDOCK

       2 lbs. Burdock flower stalks, peeled and cut into 2-inch lengths
          Water
          Zest of 2 lemons
          Sugar

Simmer peeled flower stalks in water to cover for 10 minutes. Remove from heat and allow to stand overnight. Drain and rinse well. Add water to cover and simmer, again, for 10 minutes. Remove from heat and allow to stand overnight. Rinse well. Add water to cover and zest from the two lemons. Simmer 30 minutes. Measure fruit and liquid and add equal amounts of sugar. Simmer over medium heat 30 minutes. Remove pieces of Burdock from syrup and allow to stand on waxed paper for several hours. Roll in granulated sugar. Store in jar or can with waxed paper dividing each layer of candied Burdock.

CHICKEN CANTONESE WITH BURDOCK
Serves 4

4 Burdock roots, peeled
1 cup pineapple tidbits
$^1/_2$ cup pineapple juice
1 cup sliced celery
1 cup thinly sliced raw carrot
1 onion, chopped
$^1/_2$ cup toasted slivered almonds
$^1/_4$ cup butter
1 Tbsp. cornstarch
2 tsp. fresh grated gingerroot
$^1/_4$ tsp. freshly grated nutmeg
$^1/_2$ cup water
2 Tbsp. soy sauce
2 tsp. fresh lemon juice
2 tsp. chicken bouillon
2 cups cubed cooked chicken
  Hot rice

Simmer Burdock root in salted water for 45 minutes, changing water twice during process. Drain, rinse, and slice roots into $^1/_4$ inch rounds.

Sauté Burdock, celery, carrots, onions, and almonds in butter in large skillet until onions are golden brown. Combine cornstarch, ginger, nutmeg, pineapple juice, water, soy sauce, lemon juice, and bouillon, mixing until well blended. Add to sautéed vegetables and cook until mixture thickens, stirring constantly. Stir in pineapple and chicken. Cover and simmer 10 to 15 minutes. Serve over rice.

CREAM OF BURDOCK SOUP WITH SMOKED STEELHEAD
Serves 6

6 Tbsp. butter
1 lb. young Burdock leaves
$^1/_2$ cup chopped celery
$^1/_2$ cup finely chopped onion
3 cups rich chicken stock
1 bay leaf
1 sprig fresh thyme
5 fresh basil leaves
4 crushed peppercorns
$^1/_2$ cup flour
2 cups cream
Salt and pepper to taste
3 cups smoked steelhead fillets, flaked

Melt 2 Tbsp. butter in heavy large saucepan over medium-low heat. Add Burdock leaves, celery, and onion and cook until vegetables are very tender, stirring occasionally. Add stock and fresh herbs. Bring to boil. Reduce heat and simmer 3 minutes.

Melt 2 Tbsp. butter in heavy saucepan over medium-low heat. Whisk in flour and cook 3 minutes. Gradually whisk in soup and continue cooking 5 minutes, stirring occasionally. Purée soup in blender with 2 cups cream. Strain into bowl. Season with salt and pepper. Chill 2 hours. Ladle into bowls and top each with $^1/_2$ cup smoked steelhead.

GOBO MAKI
20 appetizers

20 3x3 inch thinly sliced pork loin pieces
6 peeled Burdock roots in $2^1/_2$x$^1/_2$ inch lengths
2 Tbsp. sesame oil
1 cup miso broth
1 Tbsp. soy sauce
$^1/_2$ Tbsp. sugar
3 Tbsp. sake

Bring miso to boiling. Add Burdock and simmer for 10 minutes. Set aside and reserve miso. Wrap thinly sliced pork loin around pieces of Burdock, pressing edges together. Add oil to heated skillet and sauté wrapped Burdock root. When pork edges are sealed add reserved miso, soy sauce, sugar, and sake. Cook over medium-high heat until liquid is absorbed and bundles are glazed.

EGG DROP SOUP WITH BURDOCK

Serves 4

    4 Burdock roots, peeled and cut into thin strips
 $^1/_2$ cup flour
$1^1/_2$ Tbsp. water
    8 tsp. chicken bouillon granules
    6 cups boiling water
       Toasted sesame seeds
       Minced chives

Cook peeled roots in water to cover for 10 minutes. Drain; rinse in cold water and cook again in water to cover for 10 minutes. Drain and set aside.

Beat eggs with fork; add flour and water and continue beating until smooth. Dissolve bouillon in boiling water. Add Burdock. Drop egg mixture, in a thin stream, from a spoon into boiling broth. Move spoon slowly back and forth for even distribution. Do not stir soup until egg is cooked. Serve at once garnished with sesame seeds and chives.

PICKLED BURDOCK, CARROTS, AND RED PEPPERS

6 cups

    1 cup white vinegar
    1 cup rice vinegar
    3 cups water
    1 cup sugar
    8 quarter-sized slices fresh gingerroot
    1 Tbsp. dill seeds
    1 Tbsp. celery seeds
    1 Tbsp. pickling salt
    2 tsp. mustard seeds
    1 tsp. Dijon-style mustard
   10 black peppercorns
    4 cloves garlic, peeled
    4 carrots, peeled and cut into $3^1/_2$x$^1/_2$ inch sticks
    1 lb. Burdock root, peeled and cut into $3^1/_2$x$^1/_2$ inch sticks
    2 red bell peppers, cut into $3^1/_2$x$^1/_2$ inch sticks

In saucepan combine vinegar, water, sugar, ginger, and seasonings and bring to a boil. Simmer 3 minutes. Pack vegetables in 4 sterilized pint jars and add a clove of garlic to each. Pour vinegar mixture over vegetables. Adjust and tighten lids. Process in boiling water bath for 10 minutes.

HERBED BURDOCK GREENS

Serves 5

3 slices bacon, cut into slivers
2 medium onions, thinly sliced
2 lbs. Burdock greens
$^1/_2$ cup chopped fresh parsley
1 tsp. dried rosemary leaves
$^1/_2$ tsp. salt
$^1/_4$ tsp. pepper
3 Tbsp. fresh lemon juice

Cook Burdock for 10 minutes; drain and rinse. Cook in fresh water for additional 10 minutes. Drain and rinse.

Cook bacon pieces in large skillet until barely crisp; remove with slotted spoon. Remove all but $1^1/_2$ Tbsp. of drippings; add onion, Burdock, parsley, and seasonings. Cover and cook over medium heat for 10 minutes, stirring once or twice. Add lemon juice and sprinkle with cooked bacon pieces. Serve at once.

JAPANESE STIR-FRY BURDOCK

Serves 4

1 lb. Burdock root, peeled and cut into 2x$^1/_4$ inch long strips
1 cup water
3 Tbsp. rice vinegar
3 Tbsp. sesame oil
3 Tbsp. sake
3 Tbsp. soy sauce
3 Tbsp. sugar
   Dash hot red pepper sauce

Soak Burdock strips in mixture of water and vinegar 15 minutes. Drain. Heat frying pan over high heat. Add oil and stir-fry Burdock root for 3 minutes. Add remaining ingredients and serve while hot.

CATTAIL

(Typha latifolia)

Also known as cat-o'-nine-tail, flag, cossack asparagus, reed mace.

The Cattail, a perennial, aquatic plant, is the most widely known wild vegetable of the Northern Hemisphere. Throughout much of the United States the plant grows in shallow water of marshes, streams, and along the margins of lakes and ponds. It is scattered throughout the Central Rocky Mountain area usually below 8,000 feet. Cattail also thrives in parts of Europe and Asia.

The thick, underground rootstocks of the Cattail yield a flour which contains approximately 80% carbohydrates and about 7% protein. One acre of Cattails could yield as much as 6,000 pounds of flour. The roots grow three to four inches below the soil surface and can be harvested from autumn through early spring, though the roots are richer in starch during autumn. One must be prepared to get wet feet when harvesting Cattail roots. A small spade is sufficient to dislodge the rope-like roots, which will vary from one-half to one inch in diameter. Since geese and muskrat forage on the roots as well, caution should be applied in harvesting only what is needed.

Once gathered, Cattail roots should be rinsed and scrubbed to remove mud. Flour can be prepared by drying the scrubbed roots, pulverizing the core and sifting out the fibers. For immediate use, the roots can be peeled, submerged in a shallow, wide container of water and crushed. The starch settles to the bottom while the lighter root fibers float to the top. The fibers can then be strained off using several changes of water. The flour can be used in its wet state or dried for later use.

In late winter to early spring, enlarged areas at the leading ends of the roots can be gathered. These form the sprouts of the next season's leaves and have a starchy core which is excellent eaten raw or cooked. When the sprouts form, they can be gathered and used as a cooked vegetable or pickled.

Young leaves, emerging from the sprouts, are collected when they are one to two feet high. Pull upward on the cluster of young leaves. The stems will easily break free of the roots. Peel the leaves away to expose the crisp, cream-colored core. The core can be eaten raw, used in a salad, or steamed for twenty-five to thirty minutes. The core is commonly used in Russia as a cooked vegetable—hence the name "Cossack asparagus." The young shoots are more prevalent in the spring but can be found in sufficient numbers throughout the summer and autumn.

The flower spike extends upward through a cluster of tape-like leaves which lightly sheathe the stalk at the base. This spike often reaches seven feet in height and forms a sausage-shaped flower at the top. The immature flower is green, turning brown as it matures. The immature flower spikes can be eaten as a cooked vegetable. Remove their paper-like husks, boil in salted water for a few minutes and nibble the green flowers from the core as one would corn from a cob. The flower spikes reach maturity over a six week period.

The male part of the flower forms at the tip of the spike. This is the pollen producing part of the plant. The loose, yellow pollen forms in early autumn. A large amount of pollen may be collected by shaking the pollen spikes into a plastic bag. This protein-rich pollen can be mixed with flour and made into baked goods. Pollen is best stored in a covered container in the refrigerator for up to one month or placed in freezer containers and stored in the freezer for up to eight months. The people of Bombay harvest Cattail pollen for bread-making.

The Cattail has non–food uses as well. Native Americans used the leaves as a source of rush material for sandals, baskets, chairs, and mats. The leaves are one-quarter to one inch wide and taper gradually to a point. They are collected while still green and hung in bundles to dry. The dried bundles are then soaked in water until soft.

When the flower heads ripen, soft, cottony seeds are formed. Native Americans used the down for padding their cradle-boards. Pioneers used the down for filling pillows and quilts. The down is also useful as insulation in footwear to stave off frostbite and as tinder for starting campfires. Pioneer use of Cattail also included using pounded roots mixed with animal fat as a salve for dressing burns.

DRYING CATTAIL ROOTS

Gather roots from fall to early spring. Scrub roots and arrange in a single layer on a fine screen. Place in sun to dry, turning frequently. Put screen in a dry place at night. Sun-drying takes up to seven days. Roots may also be dried in a dehydrator. Roots can then be stored in a dry place until needed. Grind roots in a food processor, flour mill, or place in a pillow case and pound with a hammer or stone. Sift fibers from starchy flour before using.

CATTAIL BUCKWHEAT PANCAKES

12 pancakes

1 cup buckwheat flour
$^1/_2$ cup all-purpose flour
$^1/_2$ cup Cattail pollen
$2^1/_2$ tsp. baking powder
2 Tbsp. maple sugar
2 eggs
$^1/_3$ cup vegetable oil
$1^3/_4$ cups buttermilk

Put dry ingredients into mixing bowl. Add eggs, oil, and butter-milk. Mix until just blended. Bake on hot lightly-greased griddle.

CATTAIL CORN BREAD

8x8 inch pan

$^1/_4$ cup sugar
1 Tbsp. baking powder
$^1/_2$ tsp. salt
$^1/_2$ cup Cattail pollen
$^1/_2$ cup yellow cornmeal
1 cup all-purpose flour
1 egg
1 cup buttermilk
$^1/_3$ cup vegetable oil

Put dry ingredients in mixing bowl. Add remaining ingredients and mix until ingredients are just moistened. Spoon into oiled 8x8 inch pan. Bake in preheated 425°F oven for 15 to 20 minutes.

CATTAIL FLOUR BATTER BREAD
1 loaf

1 pkg. active dry yeast
$^1/_4$ cup warm water
$^3/_4$ cup milk
1 Tbsp. sugar
2 eggs
1 Tbsp. olive oil
$1^1/_2$ cups Cattail flour
$1^1/_2$ cups all-purpose flour
2 tsp. fennel seed

Dissolve yeast in warm water. Scald milk, then cool to lukewarm. Add milk, sugar, eggs, oil, and Cattail flour to yeast mixture. Beat at high speed for 3 to 5 minutes. Stir in remaining flour. Allow to double in bulk in warm place. Stir well. Put into greased 9x5x3 inch loaf pan, spreading so that dough is even. Brush top with additional olive oil and sprinkle with fennel seeds. Bake in preheated 375°F oven for 50 to 60 minutes.

CATTAIL FLOUR PANCAKE MIX
2 batches

$1^1/_2$ cups Cattail flour
$1^1/_2$ cups all-purpose flour
1 cup buttermilk powder
1 Tbsp. baking powder
1 tsp. baking soda
2 Tbsp. sugar
$^1/_2$ cup oat bran

Combine ingredients and mix well. Divide in half and package each half in quart-size zip-lock bags. To prepare: Combine $2^1/_4$ cups pancake mix with 2 eggs, 1 Tbsp. melted butter, and $1^1/_2$ to 2 cups water (depending on desired consistency). Bake on hot greased griddle. (Each batch makes 24 medium-sized pancakes.)

CATTAIL POLLEN BREAD STICKS
28 sticks

  1 pkg. active dry yeast
$^2/_3$ cup warm water
  2 tsp. sugar
$1^1/_2$ cups sifted flour
$^1/_4$ cup softened butter
$^1/_2$ cup Cattail pollen
  1 egg, unbeaten
  1 Tbsp. cold water
     Coarse salt

Sprinkle yeast into warm water; stir until dissolved. Add sugar, flour, and butter. Beat until smooth, mix in Cattail pollen. Knead dough on lightly floured board until smooth and elastic. Place in greased bowl, cover with towel and let rise in warm place until double in bulk. Punch down. Cut into 28 pieces and roll each into an 8 inch long stick. Place on greased baking sheet 1 inch apart. Beat egg with water. Brush sticks with mixture; sprinkle with coarse salt. Bake in preheated 375°F oven 18 minutes or until golden brown.

SUNSHINE CAKE
9 inch tube pan

 11 egg yolks
  2 cups confectioner's sugar
  1 cup tangerine juice
  1 tsp. vanilla
$1^1/_2$ cups sifted cake flour
$^1/_2$ cup Cattail pollen
  2 tsp. baking powder

Beat egg yolks until light and lemon-colored. Sift sugar three times then beat into the yolks, a little at a time. Stir in juice and vanilla. Sift together cake flour, pollen, and baking powder five times. Fold into egg mixture, mixing just until flour mixture is incorporated. Turn into ungreased 9 inch tube pan and bake at 325°F in preheated oven. When cool, pull cake away from pan with fork. Good served with a cream cheese frosting.

CATTAIL POLLEN–POPPY SEED BISCUITS

16 biscuits

1$^1/_2$ cups all-purpose flour
$^1/_2$ cup Cattail pollen
3 tsp. baking powder
2 Tbsp. poppy seeds
5 Tbsp. butter
2 Tbsp. honey
$^3/_4$ cup buttermilk
Poppy seeds

Sift together flour, pollen, and baking powder. Add poppy seeds. Using pastry blender, cut butter into flour mixture until ingredients are like coarse cornmeal. Stir honey into buttermilk; add to flour mixture and stir until mixture forms a ball and leaves side of bowl. Turn onto floured board and roll to $^1/_4$ inch thickness. Cut with 2 inch biscuit cutter and put on greased baking sheet. Sprinkle tops with additional poppy seeds, pressing seeds lightly into biscuits. Bake in 425°F oven for 10 to 12 minutes.

CATTAIL SHOOT, PEPPER, ANCHOVY SALAD

Serves 4

1 red bell pepper, quartered
6 anchovy fillets, patted dry and minced
2 Tbsp. wine vinegar
$^1/_2$ cup olive oil
5 cups thinly sliced Cattail shoots
$^1/_2$ cup freshly grated Parmesan cheese

Broil red pepper pieces skin side up for 7 to 10 minutes or until skin is blistered and charred. Cool. Peel pepper pieces and cut them into $^1/_4$ inch wide strips. In a small bowl combine anchovies, vinegar, and salt and pepper to taste. Add the oil in a slow steady stream, whisking. Whisk the dressing until well blended, then toss with Cattail shoots, Parmesan and red pepper. Nice served on lettuce leaves.

CATTAIL SHOOT SOUP

Serves 4

  1 cup chopped onion
  3 cloves garlic, chopped
  3 Tbsp. butter
  1$^1/_2$ lbs. peeled Cattail shoots, thinly sliced
  2$^1/_2$ cups chicken broth
  $^1/_2$ tsp. freshly grated nutmeg
  1 tsp. minced fresh basil leaves
  $^1/_4$ tsp. cayenne pepper
  1 cup heavy cream
  $^1/_4$ cup minced fresh parsley leaves
  $^1/_2$ cup wild violet blossoms for garnish, if desired

Cook onion and garlic in butter until onion is softened. Stir in Cattail shoots, broth, nutmeg, basil, and cayenne pepper. Bring to a boil and simmer for 15 minutes. Purée mixture in food processor until smooth. Stir in cream and parsley. Salt and pepper to taste. Chill, covered, at least 3 hours. Serve chilled, garnished with wild violet blossoms.

CATTAIL SHOOTS WITH WILD MINT

Serves 4

  1 lb. trimmed Cattail shoots, cut into 4 inch lengths
  2 cloves garlic, chopped fine
  6 Tbsp. extra-virgin olive oil
  $^1/_2$ cup fresh wild mint leaves, chopped

Steam shoots until tender-crisp. In small skillet cook garlic in oil until pale golden. Toss shoots with garlic mixture, chopped mint, and salt and pepper to taste. Serve warm or at room temperature.

CATTAIL SPROUTS WITH WHOLE WHEAT FETTUCCINE

Serves 6

 2 onions, thinly sliced
$^1/_2$ cup butter
 2 Tbsp. minced garlic
 3 pints well scrubbed Cattail sprouts
$^1/_2$ cup water
$^1/_2$ cup thinly sliced green onions
 2 red bell peppers, cut into thin strips
 1 lb. whole wheat fettuccine
$^1/_2$ cup freshly grated Parmesan cheese

Sauté onions in 3 Tbsp. of butter until onions are golden. Add garlic, sprouts, water, green onions and red peppers, and cook, stirring occasionally, for 20 minutes.

Cook fettuccine in boiling salted water until *al dente*. Rinse in cold water and drain well. Stir pasta into vegetables and keep warm. Melt remaining butter in small skillet and cook over moderate heat until it is browned. Add to pasta–vegetable mixture with the Parmesan and toss well. Serve at once.

CATTAIL SPROUTS AND WILD GREENS SALAD

Serves 5

 5 slices bacon
 3 cups scrubbed sprouts, steamed 5 minutes and chopped fine
 2 tsp. caraway seeds
 3 Tbsp. vegetable oil
 3 Tbsp. white wine vinegar
$^1/_2$ tsp. sugar
 8 cups mixed wild greens (such as Lamb's Quarters, Chickweed, young
      Dandelion greens, Miner's Lettuce, Sheep Sorrel, and Watercress)
      washed and spun dry

Cook bacon in heavy skillet until it is crisp. Drain on paper towels. Heat fat remaining in skillet and sauté sprouts with caraway seeds for 1 to 2 minutes. Remove from heat and stir in oil, vinegar, and sugar. Add wild greens and return to high heat. Cook, tossing, for 1 minute or until greens begin to wilt. Crumble bacon and sprinkle over greens. Serve at once.

CREAMED CATTAIL SHOOTS WITH TARRAGON AND TOMATO

Serves 4

 4 slices Canadian bacon, chopped fine
 1 Tbsp. extra-virgin olive oil
 4 cups thinly sliced Cattail shoots
 1 cup finely chopped seeded tomato
 $^1/_4$ cup finely chopped fresh tarragon leaves
 $^2/_3$ cup heavy cream
 $^2/_3$ cup chicken broth

Cook bacon in olive oil for 2 minutes; add sprouts and cook, stirring occasionally, for 10 minutes. Add tomato, tarragon, cream, and broth. Bring to a boil, then reduce heat and simmer, stirring occasionally, for 5 to 7 minutes or until mixture has thickened. Season to taste with salt and pepper.

HOMESTEAD PUDDING

Serves 6

 3 eggs
 $1^1/_2$ cups sugar
 1 tsp. vanilla
 $^1/_3$ cup Cattail flour
 $2^1/_2$ tsp. baking powder
 $1^1/_2$ cups grated tart apples
 $^1/_3$ cup chopped walnuts

Beat together eggs, sugar, and vanilla until mixture is thick and lemon-colored. Stir together Cattail flour and baking powder. Mix into egg mixture, then fold apples and walnuts into batter. Spread batter into a buttered 8x12 inch baking pan and bake in preheated 325°F oven for 35 to 40 minutes. Serve warm with sweetened whipped cream.

Snake River Moonshine Cake

8x8 inch loaf cake

   2 cups black walnuts
1^1/$_2$ cups dried Wild Currants
   1 cup all-purpose flour
 ^{1}/$_2$ cup Cattail pollen
1^1/$_2$ tsp. baking powder
 ^{1}/$_2$ cup butter
1^1/$_4$ cups sugar
   3 eggs
   2 tsp. freshly grated nutmeg
 ^{2}/$_3$ cup bourbon

Sift together dry ingredients. Cream together butter and sugar. Add eggs, one at a time. Beat in nutmeg and bourbon. Fold in nuts and currants. Grease and flour an 8x8 inch loaf pan. Turn batter into pan and bake in 325°F oven for 60 to 75 minutes. Keeps well wrapped in bourbon-soaked tea towel.

Sprout Pickles

4 pints

   3 lbs. well-scrubbed Cattail sprouts, steamed 10 minutes and cooled
   1 hot red pepper, crushed
   1 tsp. pickling spice
   4 cloves garlic
   1 Tbsp. prepared horseradish
   1 cup white vinegar
   2 cups water
   2 tsp. salt

Pack sprouts in sterilized jars. Combine remaining ingredients and bring to boiling. Pour over sprouts, adjust lids and seal in boiling water bath 10 minutes.

CHAPTER
4

CHICKWEED

(Stellaria media, Cerastium vulgatum, C. arvense)

Also known as satin flower, starwort, tongue-grass, winterweed,
stitchwort, white bird's eye, and pamplinas.

Chickweed, which naturalized from Europe and Asia, now inhabits most areas of the world including Siberia and Tasmania. Several species of Chickweed are common to the Rocky Mountains. It thrives in waste places, along streams, in fertile meadows and in gardens. In the milder areas of the Rockies, Chickweed greens can be found throughout the year, even under light coverings of snow. In harsher areas, fresh greens can be picked from late April through October.

To most people familiar with Chickweed, it is a nuisance which keeps popping up in gardens and lawns. Rather than casting the plant aside as an undesirable, it could be used as an addition to a tossed salad, as greens on a sandwich or as a potherb. Since Chickweed is rich in potash salts, vitamin C, copper, and iron it provides nourishing substances during the times of year when other fresh greens are unavailable. Even the barnyard hen knows the virtues of this common plant, seeking it out and calling excitedly to her chicks when it has been found. Chickens and other small birds thrive on the herb, hence its common name—Chickweed.

Chickweed tea is often used in natural weight loss programs. Its lesser known medical attributes are in soothing stomach ulcers and digestive problems.

An annual, Chickweed has small egg-shaped leaves which grow in pairs on frail pale green stems which grow up to a foot in length. The multi–branched stems most often grow vertical unless the plants are growing in a dense cluster where the fragile stems can support one another. The plants produce small, white, star-shaped flowers having five petals which bloom from May through October. The flowers grow singularly from axils of the leaves. The petals open by mid–morning but remain closed on overcast or rainy days. Not only do the flowers close at night, but the paired leaves fold over the developing buds in the axils and the terminal buds for protection. The lower leaves have leaf stalks which are frequently covered with hairs. The upper leaves lack stalks and attach directly to the stems.

Cooked Chickweed is mild with a slight herbal flavor. When used as a green it is often mixed with stronger flavored plants such as watercress or stinging nettles. Since Chickweed should not be cooked for more than a few minutes, it should be added to other greens after they have cooked to tenderness.

Chickweed is also tasty when eaten raw. For salads and as sandwich greens harvest only the tips of the stems since the lower portions of Chickweed become stringy with maturity.

CHICKWEED AND LAMB'S QUARTERS

Serves 4

$^1/_2$ cup water
4 cups Chickweed greens
3 cups Lamb's Quarters
$1^1/_2$ Tbsp. vinegar
$^1/_2$ tsp. salt
$^1/_4$ tsp. pepper
2 tsp. butter

Simmer Lamb's Quarters with water for 8 minutes. Drain. Add Chickweed and remaining ingredients and heat thoroughly.

CHICKWEED AND MIXED WILD GREENS SALAD

Serves 2

2 cups Chickweed, chopped
1 cup Watercress, chopped
1 cup Sheep Sorrel, stemmed
$^1/_4$ cup green onion tops, minced
$^1/_2$ cup green pepper, diced
$^1/_4$ cup young Dandelion greens, chopped

Mix together greens and toss lightly. Chill. Serve with desired dressing.

CHICKWEED RUSSIAN SANDWICHES

4 sandwiches

$^1/_2$ cup cream cheese, softened
$^1/_4$ cup chopped black olives
$^1/_4$ cup chopped red bell pepper
$^1/_4$ cup mayonnaise
2 cups Chickweed greens
Russian rye bread, thinly sliced

Mix olives and bell pepper with mayonnaise. Spread bread with cream cheese, then mayonnaise mixture. Top with a generous portion of Chickweed, then another slice of bread spread with cream cheese.

CHICKWEED SALAD

Serves 4

1$^1/_2$ lbs. Chickweed
$^1/_2$ tsp. salt
$^3/_4$ Tbsp. honey
$^3/_4$ Tbsp. paprika
$^1/_2$ tsp. dry mustard
1 tsp. soy sauce
2 Tbsp. freshly squeezed lemon juice
$^1/_4$ cup tomato sauce
$^3/_4$ cup sunflower oil
2 Tbsp. cider vinegar

Wash Chickweed. Tear into 2 inch lengths and chill in bowl lined with paper towels. Mix together salt, honey, paprika, mustard, soy, lemon juice, and tomato sauce. Slowly add oil and vinegar alternately while beating with an electric hand mixer. Chill dressing. Add to Chickweed just prior to serving.

CHICKWEED SALAD WITH BEAN SPROUTS

Serves 4 to 5

1 lb. Chickweed
1 lb. mung bean sprouts
8 slices bacon, diced, cooked, and drained
3 hard-cooked eggs, chopped
$^1/_4$ tsp. salt
1 cup olive oil
$^1/_3$ cup honey
$^1/_4$ cup white wine vinegar
1 tsp. salt
$^1/_4$ cup grated onion
1 tsp. Worcestershire sauce

Combine Chickweed, sprouts, bacon, and eggs in salad bowl. Sprinkle with $^1/_4$ tsp. salt. Combine remaining ingredients in quart jar and shake well to make dressing. At serving time sprinkle salad with desired amount of dressing.

CHICKWEED AND SHEEP SORREL GREENS
Serves 4

8 cups Chickweed greens
3 cups Sheep Sorrel
3 slices bacon, fried crisp

Pour $^1/_2$ cup boiling water over Sheep Sorrel greens in pot. Cover and simmer 5 minutes. Add Chickweed and simmer an additional 5 minutes. Drain liquid and season greens with salt and pepper. Top with crumbled bacon.

CHICKWEED WITH SWISS CHEESE
Serves 4

2 quarts chopped Chickweed
2 Tbsp. fresh cilantro, chopped
$^1/_4$ cup butter
$^1/_2$ tsp. paprika
4 eggs
2 cups milk
$1^1/_2$ cups grated Swiss cheese
$^1/_4$ tsp. salt

Sauté Chickweed and cilantro in butter for 5 minutes. Add paprika and beaten eggs to milk then pour over sautéed Chickweed. Add cheese and salt. Pour into greased baking dish. Bake at 350°F for 30 minutes.

EGG SALAD WITH CHICKWEED
Filling for 4 sandwiches

6 hard-cooked eggs, chopped
$^1/_2$ cup finely chopped Chickweed greens
1 tsp. chopped red bell pepper
2 tsp. chopped sweet pickle
1 tsp. prepared mustard
  Mayonnaise to moisten
  Salt and pepper to taste

Mix together ingredients and serve on your favorite bread topped with additional Chickweed greens, if desired.

CHILLED CHICKWEED–VEGETABLE SOUP

Serves 6

 1 cup finely chopped tomatoes
1¹/₂ cups finely chopped Chickweed
 ¹/₂ cup finely chopped green pepper
 ¹/₂ cup finely chopped celery
 ¹/₂ cup finely chopped cucumber
 ¹/₄ cup finely chopped onion
 2 tsp. finely chopped chives
 2 tsp. chopped fresh parsley
 1 clove garlic, crushed
2¹/₂ Tbsp. wine vinegar
 2 Tbsp. olive oil
 1 tsp. salt
 ¹/₂ tsp. coarse pepper
 1 tsp. Worcestershire sauce
2¹/₂ cups tomato juice

Combine all ingredients in glass bowl; stir to mix. Cover and chill several hours. Serve in chilled cups.

GREENS AND BEANS

 Small piece of mutton or bacon fat
 1 lb. Chickweed greens
 ¹/₄ cup chopped onion
 2 cloves garlic, minced
 ¹/₂ cup water
 ¹/₄ tsp. salt
 3 cups cooked pinto beans

Cook fat until crisp. Add Chickweed, onion, garlic, water, and salt. Cook until greens are wilted (approximately 4 minutes) then add beans. Heat through.

MOLDED CHICKWEED–COTTAGE CHEESE SALAD

Serves 6

First layer:

    1 Tbsp. unflavored gelatin

    $^3/_4$ cup tomato juice

    $^2/_3$ cup tomato sauce

    2 tsp. lemon juice

    1 tsp. sugar

    $^1/_4$ tsp. seasoned salt

    1 Tbsp. grated onion

Second layer:

    1 Tbsp. unflavored gelatin

    $^1/_4$ cup cold water

    $^1/_4$ tsp. salt

    $^1/_2$ tsp. paprika

    1 cup chopped Chickweed

    $^3/_4$ cup light cream

    2 cups small curd cottage cheese

To make first layer sprinkle gelatin over tomato juice in saucepan to soften. Heat slowly until gelatin is dissolved, stirring. Add remaining ingredients for first layer, mixing well. Pour into mold and chill until firm.

To make second layer, soften gelatin in cold water for 5 minutes; dissolve in hot water. Add remaining second layer ingredients; mix well. Pour over tomato layer; chill until firm. To serve, unmold on plate lined with lettuce leaves and additional Chickweed greens.

SMOKED SALMON SANDWICH WITH CHICKWEED

    Smoked salmon

    Cream cheese

    Dijon-style mustard

    Chickweed greens

    Bagels

Slice bagels in half lengthwise. Mix mustard to taste with cream cheese. Spread mixture on bagels. Top with slices of smoked salmon and a generous portion of Chickweed greens.

HERBED CHICKWEED

Serves 6

3 slices bacon, chopped
2 medium onions, thinly sliced
2 lbs. Chickweed
1 cup chopped cilantro
2 tsp. minced fresh tarragon
1 tsp. salt
$^1/_4$ tsp. pepper
2 Tbsp. fresh lime juice

Cook bacon in skillet until barely crisp; remove with slotted spoon. Remove all but $1^1/_2$ Tbsp. dripping. Add onions, Chickweed, cilantro, and seasonings to drippings. Cover and cook over medium heat for 6 to 8 minutes, or until wilted. Add an additional squeeze of lime juice, if desired. Sprinkle with bacon pieces.

CHAPTER 5

CHOKECHERRY

(Prunus virginiana, P. melanocarpa, P. demissa)
Also known as choke berry.

During the Lewis and Clark Expedition, Captain Meriwether Lewis fell ill with fever and abdominal pains. He was back to work the following day after taking a tonic of Chokecherry twig tea. Several species of Chokecherries are abundant throughout the Northern Rocky Mountains providing food and medicine for various members of the animal kingdom. Man, however, is the only harvester who cooks the fruit prior to eating it. The fresh fruit contains an astringent which causes the mouth to pucker and the throat to tighten. One early settler wrote in 1634, "chokecherries so furre the mouthe that the tongue will cleave to the roofe, and the throate wax hoarse!"—hence the plant's well deserved name, Chokecherry.

Regional Indians managed to eat the fruit uncooked. They also had a method of leaching acid out of the fresh fruit. A basket was weighted with a few stones and submerged in a shallow stream so that water flowed through the basket. The fruit was then ground in a stone mortar, pits and all, then formed into flattened patties which were sun-dried on flat stones. These patties were later broken up and added to stews and sauces. Some were carried as trail food during hunting expeditions. It is important to note that the pits contain amygdalin, a substance which breaks down in the body to yield deadly cyanide.

Growing as shrubs or small trees, Chokecherries in the Rocky Mountain regions rarely reach fifteen feet in height. Their oval leaves are from two to three inches long and approximately half as wide, abruptly pointed and with sawtooth edges. The small white flowers, in racemes, appear when the leaves are nearly full grown. The dark red to purple fruits, the size of peas, ripen in July and August and contain a large seed. During an abundant season the branches bend with the weight of the fruit which grows in clusters of berry-like drupes. The Chokecherry favors moist ravines and stream banks as their habitat.

Chokecherries do make very palatable wine, jams, jellies, and syrups. Old timers claim that the longer the fruit stays on the tree, the better the flavor. I have found this to be true. When the birds begin to relish them, they have reached their peak. Be quick to harvest at this point since the birds tend to make gluttons of themselves. Leave some berries on the higher branches for the birds.

The best method of extracting the juice is to put the stemmed fruit in a kettle, adding two pints of water for each gallon of Chokecherries. Simmer the fruit in a covered kettle for ten to fifteen minutes. Cool the cooked mass, then pour it into an old, clean pillow case set in a large bowl or pan. Suspend the pillow case over the container to catch the liquid, squeezing and twisting the case to extract as much juice from the pulp as possible. I open a kitchen drawer part way and tie the pillow case to the knob so that the case hangs directly over the collection container. The juice can then be used in numerous recipes.

CHOKECHERRY–APPLE BUTTER

4 pints

   4 cups apple pulp
   $2^1/_2$ cups Chokecherry pulp
   5 cups sugar
   $^1/_2$ tsp. freshly grated nutmeg
   $^1/_2$ tsp. almond extract

To prepare pulp, peel and core apples; pit Chokecherries. Place fruit in kettle and simmer, stirring, 15 minutes. Cool slightly. Put cooked fruit through food mill, discarding seeds. Return to kettle and heat to boiling point, stirring. Add sugar and nutmeg. Allow mixture to return to boiling, stirring until thickened. Add extract. Ladle into hot, sterilized jars, adjust lids and seal in boiling water bath for 7 minutes.

CHOKECHERRY BUTTER

1 quart

   1 quart sieved cooked Chokecherry pulp
   $1^1/_2$ cups brown sugar
   1 tsp. ground cinnamon
   $^1/_4$ tsp. powdered cloves

To prepare Chokecherry pulp, put stemmed Chokecherries in kettle with 1 cup water and cook 15 minutes, stirring frequently. Mash mixture and put through sieve. Measure out 1 quart pulp.

Add sugar and spices to pulp. Put into baking pan and bake in 300°F oven, stirring every 30 minutes, until thick. Ladle into sterilized jars and seal in boiling water bath 10 minutes.

CHOKECHERRY CANDY

$3^1/_2$ Tbsp. unflavored gelatin
 $^1/_2$ cup cold Chokecherry juice
   1 cup boiling Chokecherry juice
   2 cups sugar
      Granulated sugar

To extract juice put 2 quarts stemmed Chokecherries in kettle, add 3 cups water and bring to boiling. Simmer 10 minutes, stirring and mashing berries. Pour into jelly bag and extract juice.

Soften gelatin in $^1/_2$ cup cold juice. Combine 1 cup boiling juice with sugar and stir until dissolved. Boil slowly for 15 minutes. Skim foam. Remove from heat. Pour into chilled 8 inch square pan. Let stand at room temperature for 12 hours. Invert on board which has been sprinkled with granulated sugar. Cut into squares. Roll each in granulated sugar. Remaining juice may be frozen for later use.

CHOKECHERRY DUMPLINGS

   1 quart Chokecherry juice
$1^1/_2$ cups granulated sugar
 $^1/_2$ cup water
   1 cup sifted flour
$1^1/_4$ tsp. baking powder
 $^1/_4$ tsp. salt
   2 Tbsp. granulated sugar
   2 Tbsp. butter
 $^1/_2$ cup milk

To extract juice, simmer Chokecherries in small amount of water, mashing fruit, for 12 minutes. Strain through several layers of cheesecloth and measure 1 quart. Heat juice, $1^1/_2$ cups sugar and water over medium heat until boiling. Meanwhile in bowl combine flour, baking powder, salt and 2 Tbsp. sugar. Cut in butter until mixture is like coarse crumbs. Lightly mix in milk with fork to form a soft dough. Drop dough by spoonfuls into boiling fruit. Simmer uncovered 10 minutes, then cover and simmer 10 minutes longer.

CHOKECHERRY JAM

5 pints

5 cups Chokecherry pulp (see Chokecherry Butter recipe for making
         pulp)
8 cups sugar
1 bottle liquid pectin

In saucepan, boil pulp for 10 minutes. Add sugar and bring to boiling. Boil hard for 2 minutes. Add pectin and boil hard 1 minute. Pour into sterilized jars and seal.

CHOKECHERRY LIQUEUR

2 quarts

7 lbs. Chokecherries, mashed
4 cups sugar
3 cups water
1 tsp. freshly grated nutmeg
1 tsp. freshly grated allspice
2½ cups rum
2 cups brandy

Cook Chokecherries with sugar and water until soft. Strain juice through several layers of cheesecloth. Add spices to juice and bring to boiling; simmer 3 to 4 minutes. Allow to stand over night. Strain again. Add rum and brandy and store in quart bottles or an attractive decanter.

CHOKECHERRY MOUSSE
Serves 2

1 cup cooked Chokecherry pulp (see Chokecherry Butter recipe for making pulp)
$^1/_4$ cup Maraschino liqueur
1 Tbsp. unflavored gelatin
3 egg whites, at room temperature
$^3/_4$ cup sugar
1 pint whipping cream, chilled

Make collar, 2 inch deep, from wax paper and tape it around a 1 quart soufflé dish. Soften gelatin in $^1/_4$ cup warm water and stir in liqueur and Chokecherry pulp. Beat egg whites stiff and add sugar, beating until just smooth. Whip cream stiff, then fold into Chokecherry mixture. Fold in egg whites. Spoon into soufflé dish and chill several hours. With sharp knife, cut around inside of paper collar before removing it. Serve with additional whipped cream, if desired.

CHOKECHERRY SAUCE FOR WILD FOWL

2 cups Chokecherry juice
1 cup Port wine
$^1/_2$ tsp. ground cloves
$^1/_2$ tsp. ground ginger
$^1/_2$ cup currant jelly
1 tsp. arrowroot

Combine juice, wine, cloves, and ginger and bring to boil, stirring. Add arrowroot and stir until thickened. Serve with pheasant, duck, grouse, or goose.

CHOKECHERRY SHERBET

2¹/₂ cups water
1¹/₂ cups sugar
1 cup Chokecherry juice
Dash salt
1 egg white, beaten until soft peaks form

To extract juice, put stemmed Chokecherries into a kettle and cook slowly, mashing fruit, until juice flows. Pour into jelly bag or pillow case and allow juice to drip, squeezing bag gently from time to time.

In saucepan combine sugar and water and boil for 5 minutes. Cool. Add Chokecherry juice and salt. Freeze in ice cream freezer, following manufacturer's directions. When sherbet becomes mushy, add beaten egg white and continue freezing until firm.

CHOKECHERRY SYRUP

7 to 8 pints

6 cups Chokecherry juice
9 cups sugar
1 tsp. almond extract

To extract juice place 8 lbs. stemmed Chokecherries in heavy kettle along with 5 cups water. Cover and simmer 20 minutes. Place in jelly bag or an old pillow case, hang over bucket and allow juice to drip. Gently squeeze out remaining juice.

Pour juice into kettle, add sugar and bring to a boil over high heat, stirring constantly. Reduce heat and simmer, covered, 15 to 20 minutes. Add extract. Ladle into hot sterilized jars, adjust lids and seal in boiling water bath for 7 minutes.

CHOKECHERRY WHIP
Serves 4

1 Tbsp. grated lemon rind
1 cup sugar
1 Tbsp. unflavored gelatin
$1/4$ cup cold water
$1/4$ cup boiling water
3 Tbsp. fresh lemon juice
1 cup Chokecherry juice (see Chokecherry Syrup recipe for extracting
    juice)
1 tsp. pure vanilla extract
4 egg whites, beaten stiff

Stir rind into sugar. Soak gelatin in cold water for 10 minutes, then dissolve in boiling water. Stir in sugar until dissolved. Add lemon juice and Chokecherry juice. Add vanilla. Chill 15 minutes. Fold in whites, then spoon into mold and chill thoroughly. Serve with whipped cream, if desired.

SPICED CHOKECHERRY CORDIAL

3 gallons stemmed Chokecherries
2 sticks cinnamon
4 lbs. sugar
$1/2$ cup fresh lime juice
2 quarts vodka

Put Chokecherries in large kettle and simmer for 12 minutes, mashing fruit. Strain through several layers of cheesecloth. Add cinnamon and sugar to juice. Simmer over medium heat for 30 minutes. Add lime juice. Cool. Remove cinnamon and add vodka to juice; mix well. Bottle and cork or cap securely.

CHAPTER
6

DANDELION

(Taraxacum officinale)

Also known as swine's snout, Irish daisy, and puff ball.

The Dandelion is native to Europe and Asia, but since it was deliberately carried from place to place for cultivation it has naturalized throughout the temperate regions of the world. As a potherb the plant became popular in Europe and America during the nineteenth century. During World War II the roasted, ground taproots were used as a coffee substitute and the bright yellow flower petals were chopped and added to spreads to simulate the color of butter.

The Dandelion is one of the first wild perennials to appear in spring in the Rocky Mountains. The toothed leaves grow from a thick taproot which often reaches two feet in length. The yellow, pollen-laden flowers appear a few weeks after the first leaves have developed. The solitary blossoms growing on hollow stems exude a milky juice when picked and the flowers mature to a fluffy, down-like puff ball. The round seed head contains a cluster of as many as two hundred narrow seeds each bearing a parachute of hairs at the apex.

The Dandelion, often referred to as a weed, abundantly grows in lawns, gardens, meadows, wooded areas and along road sides. The greens are more nutritious than spinach. They contain bitter glycosides, vitamin A, one of the vitamin B complex, vitamin C, vitamin D, calcium, potassium, and iron. As an added bonus, the leaves contain photosterols which prevent the body from accumulating cholesterols. Parts of the Dandelion can be harvested from early spring to late autumn.

The English word for Dandelion comes from the French *dent de lion*, meaning lion's tooth, in reference to the jagged shape of the leaves. The tender young leaves appear as early as March in mild winter areas and make an excellent salad green or potherb. It is important to gather the young leaves before the flower buds develop. Be certain to harvest the greens well away from any areas which may have been sprayed with pesticides. As the plant matures the leaves take on an unpleasant bitter taste due to the glycosides. The best salad greens are found in areas unexposed to bright sunlight. These are lighter in color and have a milder flavor. Some people cover developing young Dandelions with cardboard or paper bags for five to seven days to assure an abundance of bleached Dandelion salad greens.

After gathering the greens they should be rinsed in cold water, drained well, and stored in a damp dish towel in the refrigerator until used. They will keep up to six days.

During early spring the entire plant may be pulled up exposing the long taproot. The outer leaves can then be stripped away and the heart of the plant severed from the root. This tender heart can be used in omelets or cooked with the young leaves as a vegetable. The root can be scrubbed clean, roasted, and ground to be used as a coffee substitute.

During late spring or early summer mature leaves can be gathered, bundled with light string, and hung in a warm airy place to dry. Once the leaves have dried, crumble them and store the herb in tightly covered containers. This makes a good substitute for tea by steeping two teaspoons of dried leaves in a cup of boiling hot water.

The blossoms, which are most abundant in May, also produce a valuable wild food. The petals can be plucked from the green flower base and used in biscuits, muffins, and wine. These petals are best gathered in the early afternoon hours while the flowers are in full bloom (they close on cloudy days and at night). The flavor and freshness of the petals are at their best when used within three to four hours of harvesting.

During late autumn, Dandelion taproots may be dug and planted in a wooden crate of prepared soil. The crate can then be stored in a basement, root cellar or other cool, dark place. With regular watering, the roots will produce a good supply of tender, blanched leaves throughout the winter.

Buttermilk Pancakes with Dandelion Flowers

12 medium-sized pancakes

1 cup whole wheat flour
$^1/_2$ cup all-purpose flour
Dash salt
$1^1/_2$ tsp. baking soda
1 egg
$1^1/_2$ cups buttermilk
$^2/_3$ cup Dandelion flower petals
2 Tbsp. melted butter

Sift together dry ingredients. Beat together egg and milk, then stir into dry ingredients along with petals. Stir in butter. Bake on hot, lightly greased griddle.

DANDELION CREPES

1 dozen

Filling:

    1$^1/_2$ lbs. young Dandelion greens

      1 quart boiling water

      3 Tbsp. butter

    $^1/_4$ cup finely chopped onion

    2$^1/_2$ Tbsp. all-purpose flour

      1 cup warm milk

Crepes:

    $^3/_4$ cup all-purpose flour

        Dash salt

      1 Tbsp. extra-fine sugar

      1 tsp. baking powder

      2 eggs

    $^3/_4$ cup milk

    $^1/_4$ cup water

      1 tsp. freshly grated lemon rind

    1$^1/_2$ cups grated sharp Cheddar cheese

Cook greens in water for 20 minutes. Drain well and chop greens coarsely. Melt butter in saucepan; stir in onion and 2$^1/_2$ Tbsp. flour. Slowly stir in milk. Cook over medium heat 10 minutes. Fold in greens. Keep warm.

Sift together $^3/_4$ cup flour, salt, sugar, and baking powder. Beat together eggs, milk, water, and rind. Pour into dry ingredients and mix lightly. Cook as thin pancakes over medium heat. Stack and keep warm.

Place a spoonful of filling on each crepe. Roll in jelly-roll fashion. Place crepes in shallow baking dish, sprinkle with cheese and place under broiler until cheese melts. Serve at once.

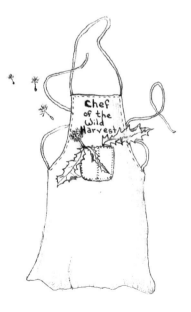

DANDELION DUCHESS SOUP

Serves 4

1$^1/_2$ cups young Dandelion greens
1$^1/_2$ Tbsp. butter
$^1/_2$ cup finely chopped onion
1$^1/_2$ Tbsp. flour
3$^1/_2$ cups milk
2 Tbsp. freshly grated Parmesan cheese
2 egg yolks
1 cup sour cream
$^1/_2$ tsp. celery salt
Pepper to taste

Boil greens in $^1/_2$ cup water for 10 minutes. Drain well. Melt butter in saucepan and sauté onion until tender. Blend in flour. Slowly stir in milk. Cook until mixture thickens slightly. Beat together Parmesan, yolks, and sour cream. Add to soup along with greens. Heat through; season with celery salt and pepper.

DANDELION FLOWER BISCUITS

1-1/2 dozen 2 inch biscuits

1$^1/_2$ cups whole wheat flour
$^1/_4$ cup all-purpose flour
$^1/_2$ cup Dandelion flower petals
Dash salt
2 tsp. baking powder
2 Tbsp. butter
$^3/_4$ cup buttermilk

Sift together flours, salt, and baking powder. Cut in butter until mixture resembles cornmeal. Stir in petals and buttermilk. Stir vigorously 3 minutes. Turn dough onto lightly floured board. Form into ball, then roll $^1/_4$ inch thick. Cut with 2 inch biscuit cutter. Bake at 425°F for 12 minutes on lightly oiled baking sheet.

DANDELION GREENS

Serves 4

$^1/_2$ lb. young Dandelion greens
$^1/_2$ cup water
$^1/_4$ tsp. salt
     Dash pepper
$2^1/_2$ Tbsp. butter
  1 lime, quartered

Cook greens in water over medium heat for 12 minutes. Drain. Add salt, pepper, and butter and heat with greens until butter melts. Serve hot with wedges of lime.

DANDELION GREENS SOUTHERN STYLE

Serves 6

$1^1/_2$ lbs. young Dandelion greens
$^1/_4$ tsp. salt
$^3/_4$ cup chopped ham
$^1/_4$ tsp. freshly grated nutmeg
  2 tsp. fresh lemon juice
$^1/_2$ cup chopped green onion

Combine greens, salt, and cooked ham in heavy saucepan, adding a small amount of water. Steam until greens are wilted, tossing occasionally. Reduce heat and cook until just tender. Add nutmeg, lemon, and green onion. Toss well and serve at once.

Dandelion Salad with Guacamole Dressing

Serves 4

4 cups young light green Dandelion greens
8 radishes, sliced
1 cup watercress, chopped
1 small head lettuce, torn into bite-sized pieces
2 ripe medium avocados
2 cloves garlic, crushed
1 Tbsp. fresh lime juice
   Dash salt
1 Tbsp. finely chopped cilantro
2 Tbsp. minced onion
$^1/_4$ cup sour cream

Cut greens into small pieces. Add radishes, watercress, and lettuce. Place remaining ingredients into blender or food processor and pulse on and off to chop fine. Serve over greens.

Dandelion–Sheep Sorrel Salad

Serves 6

5 cups lightly packed young light green Dandelion greens
3 cups lightly packed Sheep Sorrel leaves
1 Tbsp. tarragon vinegar
2 tsp. water
$^1/_2$ tsp. sugar
3 Tbsp. extra-virgin olive oil

In bowl, toss together Dandelion and Sheep Sorrel greens. Chill. In small bowl beat together remaining ingredients and toss with salad.

DANDELION ROOT COFFEE

2 lbs. scrubbed Dandelion roots

Cut roots into $^1/_2$ inch sections. Place in single layer on a cookie sheet and dry in 225°F oven for 4 to 5 hours or until roots are brittle and brown inside. Store in tightly covered container. Grind as needed and brew using $^1/_4$ less Dandelion coffee as you would regular coffee.

FREEZING DANDELION GREENS

2 lbs. young Dandelion greens
3 quarts boiling water to which has been added 2 tsp. salt

Pour boiling water over rinsed and drained Dandelion greens. Let water and greens sit 5 minutes. Drain well. Pack greens in quart-sized freezer bags and freeze. May be used in any recipe calling for cooked Dandelion greens.

TUNA AND DANDELION GREEN SALAD

Serves 4

$1^1/_2$ quarts shredded young Dandelion greens
1 can tuna in spring water, well drained
8 anchovy fillets
$^1/_2$ cup sliced green olives with pimento
1 hard-cooked egg, chopped
$^1/_2$ cup diced Swiss cheese
$^1/_2$ cup diced green pepper
$1^1/_2$ Tbsp. finely chopped fresh basil
Vinaigrette dressing

Combine all ingredients, except dressing and toss well. Add dressing just prior to serving.

DANDELION WINE

        2 gallons fresh Dandelion petals (no stems or green parts)
        8 unpeeled oranges, finely chopped
        4 unpeeled lemons, finely chopped
    $1^1/_4$ gallons water
        3 lbs. sugar

Place Dandelion blossoms (no green stuff!) and fruit in crock. Boil $1^1/_4$ gallons water and pour over ingredients in crock. Stir well, then cover crock and allow to stand 24 hours. Strain liquid, squeezing pulp as dry as possible. Discard solids.

Return liquid to clean crock and add sugar. Stir well to dissolve sugar. Cover crock and allow to stand for two weeks, stirring occasionally. Skim scum from surface of liquid, cover crock and allow to stand two weeks longer without stirring. Skim again. Siphon liquid into glass jugs and fit a balloon over tops of jugs. When wine is clear, and fermenting action has ceased siphon into decorative bottles; cork. Allow to age 8 months.

SCALLOPED DANDELION GREENS

Serves 4

        6 cups young Dandelion greens
    $^1/_4$ cup water
        4 hard-cooked eggs, diced
        1 cup milk
    $1^1/_2$ Tbsp. butter
    $1^1/_2$ Tbsp. all-purpose flour
    $1^1/_4$ cups grated sharp Cheddar cheese

Simmer greens in water 10 minutes in covered pot. Drain well. Make white sauce by melting butter in saucepan. Stir in flour, then slowly add milk and cheese. Cook over low heat, stirring, until sauce thickens and cheese has melted. Add eggs, pour over greens in baking dish and bake at 400°F for 15 to 20 minutes.

ELDERBERRY

(Sambucus glauca, S. cerulea)

Also known as elder, boretree, tree of music, sweet elder.

The name Elderberry encompasses some thirteen species of deciduous shrubs native to or naturalized in North America. Several naturalized species were brought from Europe by settlers. Elderberry is also native to west Asia and North Africa.

Early settlers believed that this member of the honeysuckle family could not be struck by lightning so Elderberry bushes were planted near the house. Since Elderberry was also considered a plant of spiritual powers it was believed to protect those living in the house from sickness and evil spirits. A twig was often carried close to the body as a charm of good health and luck.

Some Indian tribes called the Elderberry "the tree of music." They made flutes from branches cut in the spring and dried with the leaves left on. The core of soft, white, pith was then removed and holes were bored into the wood with a hot stick. The generic name *Sambucus* most likely came from the Greek *sambuke*, another instrument made from Elderberry wood.

Lewis and Clark first reported the Elderberry as an "alder" with "pale, sky blue" berries. Elderberry bushes or trees reach six to fifteen feet in height. They prefer rich soil and are found growing along fence rows, roadsides, ravines and streams. In areas where the Elderberry grows in abundance, it often forms impenetrable thickets because of its habit of sending up numerous erect stems to form a tangled mass.

The young stems have greenish bark covering a narrow cylinder of wood that surrounds a soft, white core. In older stems the bark becomes grayish-brown and the woody layer thickens. As many a pioneer child knew, the hollowed stems make fine pea shooters. Hunters have bugled elk with whistles made from Elderberry stems.

The leaves of the plant are composed of five to eleven leaflets, oval with sharply acute tips and serrated edges. They are arranged in opposite pairs on the leaf stalks. White to cream-colored flowers appear from May through July and grow in flat terminal cymes which are between four to seven inches in diameter.

These flat-topped bouquets are made up of hundreds of small fragrant flowers shaped like five-pointed stars. The flower clusters, called Elder Blow, are used to make a sweet-smelling wine and can also be coated with batter to be fried as fritters. Individual flowers are good in muffins, pancakes, and tea. Pick the flowers when they're in full bloom and use the harvested blossoms within twenty-four hours since they deteriorate quickly. I find the flowers eaten fresh off the bush have more pleasurable flavor than the fresh, raw berries.

Early farmers considered the appearance of the first green immature berries as a signal that it was time to sow their wheat. The berries, which fruit from late summer to early autumn, are borne in great umbels and turn from green to dark blue with a whitish bloom. Each berry averages one quarter inch in diameter and contains three tiny seeds. Elderberries are rich in calcium, iron, potassium, thiamine, niacin, vitamin A, and vitamin C. Since the ripe berries are rich in such essentials they were made into wines and syrups by pioneers and taken to prevent colds. Elderberries contain about 450 calories and nine grams of protein per pound.

Elderberry fruit is best gathered in the autumn after the first frost since this is when their flavor is at its peak. The berries lack an acid tartness and are therefore of poor quality when eaten raw. In fact, the fresh fruit has been known to cause nausea when eaten in abundance. The flavor is brought out by cooking, and the fruit's musky taste compliments jams, jellies, chutneys, preserves, and wine. Gather the ripe berries on a dry day and separate them from the stems before extracting their juice.

To extract the juice of the Elderberry, place stemmed fruit in a large pan and add one quart of water to each six quarts of fruit. Simmer, mashing the berries as they cook, for ten to fifteen minutes. Strain the juice through a clean pillow case or cheesecloth, discarding solids. The juice may be frozen or canned for later use.

Though the fresh fruit may be added to pancakes, muffins, or pies, the preferred way to use the fruit is dried. The simplest method of drying Elderberries is to tie a few cluster stems together and suspend them over newspaper in a moisture free area for seven to eight days. Store the dried berries in tightly covered containers.

The branches of the Elderberry are hollow and therefore quite brittle. When harvesting the clumps of flowers or berries, gently bend the branch and cut the base of the fruit bearing umbel, letting the cluster drop into a bucket or basket. It is not wise to cut the branches or chop down the shrub because, according to Danish folklore, a spirit, the *Hylde–Mikoer* (elder-tree mother) lives in Elderberry plants. She will haunt any person who destroys her home.

ELDERBERRY ANGEL PIE

4 egg whites
$^1/_4$ tsp. cream of tartar
1 cup sugar
6 egg yolks
$^2/_3$ cup sugar
   Dash salt
$^1/_2$ cup Elderberry juice
$1^1/_2$ Tbsp. freshly grated lemon rind
1 cup heavy cream, whipped

Heat a 9 inch pie plate slightly in 300°F oven, then grease lightly with vegetable oil. Beat whites until soft peaks form. Add cream of tartar and beat until uniform bubbles begin to form then gradually add sugar and beat until mixture stands in soft peaks. Spread evenly in prepared pan. Set in preheated 300°F oven and bake 1 hour. Turn off oven and leave the door slightly ajar until meringue shell is completely cool.

Beat yolks slightly in top of double boiler. Add sugar, salt, Elderberry juice, and rind. Place over slowly boiling water and cook and stir until thick. Remove from heat and chill. Whip cream until stiff. Spread half of it on the shell, leaving a margin of about 1 inch. Spread filling on the cream and top with remaining cream. Chill pie overnight.

ELDERBERRY CORDIAL

1-1/2 gallons

$3^1/_2$ gallons stemmed Elderberries
4 lbs. sugar
$^1/_2$ cup fresh lime juice
2 quarts brandy

Mash berries and extract juice. Strain through several layers of cheesecloth. Add sugar and berry juice and simmer over medium heat for 35 to 40 minutes. Add lime juice. Cool. Add brandy and mix well. Pour into attractive bottles; cork and cap securely.

ELDERBERRY JELLY

6 8-oz. glasses

3 lbs. Elderberries, stemmed
$^1/_4$ cup lemon juice
4 cups sugar
1 pkg. powdered pectin

Place berries in saucepan and crush. Heat slowly until juice begins to flow. Cover and simmer 10 to 15 minutes. Place in jelly bag and squeeze out 3 cups juice. Add lemon juice. Mix pectin with juices and bring to hard boil over high heat. Add sugar and boil hard 1 minute. Remove from heat and pour into sterilized jars. Adjust lids and seal in boiling water bath for 7 minutes.

ELDERBERRY SAUCE

$1^1/_2$ cups Elderberry juice
1 cup sugar
1 tsp. freshly squeezed lemon juice
1 Tbsp. grated lemon rind
$2^1/_2$ tsp. cornstarch
1 Tbsp. butter

Combine ingredients in saucepan and cook over moderate heat, stirring, until mixture thickens. Serve over ginger bread, waffles, pancakes, or ice cream.

ELDERBERRY SLUMP

Serves 4

2 cups Elderberry juice
$^1/_2$ cup sugar
1 cup water
1 cup all-purpose flour
$2^1/_2$ tsp. baking powder
$^1/_2$ cup milk

Combine Elderberry juice, sugar, and water. Bring to boil and simmer for 10 minutes. Mix together flour and baking powder, then quickly stir in milk to make dumpling dough. Drop spoonfuls of dough into liquid, cover and simmer 10 minutes. Serve with whipped cream or vanilla ice cream.

ELDERBERRY SOUFFLE

Serves 4

1   cup Elderberry juice
4   Tbsp. Chambord liqueur
2   egg yolks
$^1/_3$ cup sugar
6   egg whites
2   tsp. cream of tartar
2   tsp. sugar

Combine Elderberry juice with liqueur. Beat egg yolks and sugar in a bowl over simmering water until thick. Slowly beat in Elderberry mixture. Remove from heat. Beat egg whites with cream of tartar until very thick, adding the 2 teaspoons of sugar at the end. Fold the beaten egg whites into the Elderberry mixture by hand, using a spatula. Spoon into a 1 quart soufflé dish which has been buttered and sprinkled with a layer of fine sugar. Bake on bottom rack of oven at a preheated 375°F for 20 minutes.

ELDERBERRY SYRUP

4 pints

3   quarts stemmed Elderberries
5   cups sugar
3   inch piece stick cinnamon
$1^1/_2$ Tbsp. whole cloves
1   cup brandy

Mash berries and strain to extract juice. Measure 2 pints juice. In large kettle combine juice, sugar, and spices. Simmer gently 15 minutes. Cool. Strain syrup through several layers of cheesecloth. Add brandy to strained syrup. Mix well. Bottle in attractive containers and cap or cork. If a thicker syrup is desired, cook an additional 10 minutes before adding brandy.

ELDERBERRY TAPIOCA

Serves 4

  2 cups water
$^1/_2$ cup quick cooking tapioca
$^3/_4$ cup sugar
  3 cups Elderberry juice
  1 Tbsp. fresh lemon juice
    Whipping cream

Boil 2 cups water in top of double boiler over direct heat. Combine sugar and tapioca, then gradually stir into boiling water. Return to boil, then place over rapidly boiling water in bottom of double boiler. Cook and stir 5 minutes. Stir in Elderberry juice and lemon juice. Cook a few minutes longer. Remove from heat, pour into serving bowl and chill. Serve with whipped cream.

ELDER BLOSSOM FRITTERS

Serves 4

$1^1/_2$ cups all-purpose flour
$1^1/_2$ tsp. baking powder
  3 eggs
$^2/_3$ cup orange juice
    Oil for deep frying
    Elder blossom umbels
    Confectioners' sugar

Sift together flour and baking powder. Beat eggs well; add to orange juice. Stir in flour mixture and blend well. Holding stem, dip umbels into batter and deep fry at 375°F until golden brown. Drain on paper towels. Dust with powdered sugar and serve at once.

ELDER BLOSSOM MUFFINS

6 muffins

1 cup whole wheat flour, sifted
2 tsp. baking powder
$^1/_4$ cup sugar
$1^1/_2$ cups Elder blossoms, stems removed
2 Tbsp. butter
1 egg beaten
$^1/_2$ cup buttermilk
$^1/_2$ cup orange juice

Sift together flour, baking powder, and sugar. Stir in blossoms. Add remaining ingredients and stir until just moistened. Fill greased muffin tins $^2/_3$ full and bake in preheated 400°F oven for 25 minutes.

ELDER BLOSSOM PANCAKES

Serves 3 to 4

1 cup all-purpose flour
Dash salt
1 tsp. baking powder
2 Tbsp. powdered sugar
2 eggs
1 cup buttermilk
1 tsp. grated lemon rind
$^1/_4$ cup water
2 cups Elder blossoms, stems removed
2 Tbsp. clarified butter

Sift together dry ingredients. Beat eggs and add to milk, rind, and water, then stir into dry ingredients. Mix lightly. Heat a little clarified butter in skillet. Pour spoonfuls of batter onto skillet and sprinkle blossoms over pancakes. Bake until bubbles form and begin to break. Turn and bake until golden. Repeat with remaining butter and batter.

SPICED ELDERBERRIES

4 pints

    5   quarts stemmed Elderberries
$2^1/_2$ tsp. ground cloves
$2^1/_2$ tsp. ground cinnamon
  $^1/_2$ cup apple juice
  $^1/_2$ cup cider vinegar
   14   cups sugar
    1   bottle liquid pectin

In saucepan combine Elderberries with spices, apple juice, and vinegar. Bring to boiling over medium heat, stirring constantly. Lower heat and continue cooking, covered, 10 minutes. Add sugar and mix well. Bring to boiling and boil hard for 2 minutes, stirring carefully. Remove from heat and stir in pectin. Stir and skim alternately for 5 minutes. Ladle into hot sterilized jars, adjust lids and seal in boiling water bath for 7 minutes.

CHAPTER
8

FIDDLEHEAD

(Pteretis pensylvanica)

Also known as ostrich fern.

Fiddleheads are the name of the developing fronds produced by the ostrich and similar ferns, rather than the name of the plant itself. Ferns are by far the most abundant and familiar of the pteridophytes. Although there are an estimated four thousand kinds of ferns throughout the world, only forty-five are known to grow in North America. The ostrich fern abounds in the cool, moist, acid-rich soil along Rocky Mountain streambeds.

These perennial plants have roots, stems, and leaves but do not reproduce by flowers and seeds. They are the highest form of flowerless plants and also the "old men" of the planet, having lived here approximately three hundred forty-five million years.

The reproduction sequence of the ostrich fern is typical of ferns, but is so unusual among the plant kingdom that it warrants description. The fern includes an alternation of a sexually reproducing plant and an asexually reproducing one. The terminal portion of the frond bears spots on its undersurface that look like small brown seeds. Each spot consists of a stalked spore-sac whose capsule is filled with microscopic spores. These spores are single-celled, asexual reproductive structures. The spores fall to the ground and, under the right conditions, germinate into a heart-shaped, green plant slightly larger than a dime, which matures and develops a male and a female sex organ. When moisture is present, the sperm from the male organ swims to the female organ to fertilize the single egg. The fertilized egg remains in place and develops into an embryonic asexual plant which develops a root, stem, and small frond. In time the frond matures into an adult fern capable of producing spores and repeating the cycle. This system of reproduction is called "alternation of generation."

The stem, or rhizome, of the fern is a thickened, horizontal underground organ which produces a few erect leaves each year. The leaves, or fronds, borne on stemlike stalks are subdivided into many small leaflets. The fronds occur in dense clumps. Paper-like scales which cover the center stalk are a pale brown to cinnamon color. Fronds have a midrib to which the major leaf divisions are attached. Leaflets vary from four to six inches in length and gradually become shorter toward the base of the frond. The many sterile fronds are pinnately compound and two to four feet high. Sterile frond leaflets have deeply indented edges. Fertile fronds are much shorter (eight to twenty inches high) and are found in the center of clumps of sterile fronds. Leaflets on fertile fronds are narrow and covered with the small brown spore bodies. The curled up tips of young fronds are known as

Fiddleheads. Fiddleheads derive this unusual name because their tightly curled tops resemble the head of a violin.

The underground stem is black, scaly, and heavily branched. In early spring the young fronds (Fiddleheads) are frequently surrounded by the persistent, dried remains of the previous year's fronds. The developing Fiddleheads have stout, rapidly tapering stalks which are covered with the paper-like, brown to cinnamon colored scales.

Fiddleheads should be collected when they are less than five to six inches high and the fronds are still tightly curled. Break off the Fiddleheads as close to ground level as possible. The scales that cover the Fiddleheads can be rubbed off by hand, but are more easily removed by first soaking them in cool water for ten minutes. Take care to remove all scales including those that are on the coiled leafy tip. Ostrich fern Fiddleheads may be eaten raw but when the fronds unfurl the fern is no longer palatable.

Fiddleheads are a delicacy when canned. In fact, in the Northeastern states such as Maine and Massachusetts where Fiddleheads are more commonly eaten, cans of Fiddleheads grace the shelves of supermarkets. To can, cover de-scaled Fiddleheads with boiling water and allow them to stand for five minutes. Drain. Pack Fiddleheads upright in pint jars, leaving one-half inch of headroom. Add one-half teaspoon of salt to each pint. Pour boiling water over Fiddleheads, leaving one-half inch of headroom. Adjust lids. Pressure can at ten pounds (240°F) for twenty minutes.

To freeze Fiddleheads, pour boiling water over them and allow to stand five minutes. Drain well, then pack in freezer containers. Frozen Fiddleheads keep up to eight months.

For a winter supply of fresh Fiddleheads, transplant ostrich fern crowns after the first frost to a wooden crate filled with loamy, acid-rich soil. Water the soil well and keep crate in a cool basement or cellar.

BATTER FRIED FIDDLEHEADS

Serves 4

1 lb. Fiddleheads
$^1/_4$ tsp. pepper
1 tsp. fresh lime juice
1 cup all-purpose flour
$^1/_4$ cup sugar
$^1/_4$ tsp. salt
2 tsp. baking powder
1 egg, well beaten
$^1/_2$ cup milk
1 Tbsp. melted butter
   Cooking oil

Steam Fiddleheads in small amount of water for 8 minutes. Drain on paper towels. Sprinkle with pepper and lime juice. Sift together dry ingredients. Combine egg and milk, then gradually add to dry ingredients while stirring batter smooth. Stir in melted butter. Dip Fiddleheads into batter, drop into oil heated to 375°F, cook until golden. Drain and serve immediately.

DILLED FIDDLEHEAD PICKLES

5 pints

3 lbs. Fiddleheads
3 cups cider vinegar
3 cups water
6 Tbsp. salt
10 heads dillweed
10 small garlic cloves
   Mustard seeds

Rub scales off Fiddleheads under cool running water. Rinse and drain. Pack Fiddleheads in 10 sterilized $^1/_2$ pint jars. Add a head of dillweed, a clove of garlic and $^1/_4$ tsp. mustard seed to each jar.

Bring vinegar, water, and salt to boiling. Boil until salt has dissolved. Pour boiling mixture over Fiddleheads. Adjust lids and process in boiling water bath 7 minutes.

FIDDLEHEAD BURGOO

Serves 10

  7 lbs. shin of beef
  5 lb. stewing hen
  6 potatoes, cut into large cubes
  8 carrots, cut into thick slices
  5 turnips, cut into large cubes
  1 bunch celery, cut into 1 inch pieces
  5 onions, sliced
  3 cups canned tomatoes
  2 lbs. fresh or frozen green beans
  2 lbs. frozen peas
  2 lbs. frozen lima beans
$1^1/_2$ lbs. frozen corn
  1 head cabbage, shredded
$1^1/_2$ lbs. Fiddleheads
  1 cup chopped cilantro
$1^1/_2$ tsp. red pepper flakes
  1 bell pepper, cut into strips
  3 Tbsp. fresh thyme leaves
     Salt and pepper to taste

Put beef and hen in large 12 to 15 quart pot and cover with water. Add 1 Tbsp. salt. Bring to boil and simmer 5 minutes, skimming when necessary. Cover and simmer until beef and hen are very tender; remove meat and fowl from broth and cut into bite-sized pieces. Return meat and fowl to broth, bring to boil and add vegetables. When mixture comes to a full rolling boil add seasonings. Simmer, covered, 45 minutes. Serve in warmed bowls with a good crusty bread.

FIDDLEHEADS WITH CHEESE

Serves 4

$1^1/_2$ lbs. Fiddleheads
$^1/_2$ cup grated sharp Cheddar cheese
$^1/_4$ cup grated Swiss cheese
$^1/_4$ tsp salt
Dash freshly grated pepper
1 Tbsp. butter

Cut Fiddleheads in 2 inch pieces and steam in small amount of water for 8 minutes. Drain well and layer in baking dish. Sprinkle with cheeses, salt, and pepper. Dot with butter. Bake at 350°F for 15 minutes.

FIDDLEHEAD CHOWDER

Serves 4

$1^1/_2$ lbs. Fiddleheads, cut into 1 inch pieces
2 cups sliced celery
1 red bell pepper, diced
$^1/_2$ cup chopped onion
$^1/_2$ cup butter
1 cup canned tomatoes, chopped
$^1/_4$ tsp. salt
1 tsp. brown sugar
$^1/_4$ tsp. Gumbo filé
$4^1/_2$ cups boiling water

Sauté Fiddleheads, celery, pepper, and onion in butter for 5 minutes. Add tomatoes to boiling water along with vegetables and seasoning. Simmer gently for 45 minutes.

FIDDLEHEADS IN CREAM
Serves 5 to 6

2 lbs. Fiddleheads, cut into 2 inch pieces
   Salt and freshly ground pepper
$^1/_4$ cup butter
1 Tbsp. fresh dill
$^3/_4$ cup heavy cream
2 Tbsp. chopped parsley

Steam Fiddleheads with small amount of water. Drain. Return to pan and add butter, salt, and pepper. Shake well over medium heat. Add dill and cream and toss with Fiddleheads. Spoon into heated serving dish and sprinkle with parsley.

FIDDLEHEADS WITH EGG MUSTARD SAUCE
Serves 4

$1^1/_2$ lbs. Fiddleheads
$^1/_2$ tsp. salt
3 Tbsp. butter
3 Tbsp. all-purpose flour
2 cups milk
$1^1/_2$ cups plain yogurt
$^1/_3$ cup Dijon-style mustard
3 Tbsp. lemon juice
1 tsp. freshly grated lemon rind
4 hard-cooked eggs, chopped
$^1/_4$ tsp. freshly ground pepper

Steam Fiddleheads with small amount of water until tender-crisp. Drain. Melt butter in saucepan, then blend in flour. Gradually add milk, then stir in yogurt and cook slowly, stirring, until thickened. Remove from heat and add remaining ingredients. Serve over steamed Fiddleheads.

FIDDLEHEADS WITH MORELS
Serves 4

1 lb. Fiddleheads
$1^1/_4$ lbs. Morel mushrooms
$^1/_4$ cup butter
2 Tbsp. olive oil
1 tsp. freshly ground pepper
Salt
$^1/_2$ cup buttered bread crumbs

Steam Fiddleheads with small amount of water until tender-crisp. Drain and set aside. Cut Morels in half and cook in dry skillet over moderate heat until most of the liquid cooks out. Drain. Add butter and oil; sauté mushrooms 7 to 8 minutes. Season with salt and pepper. Add Fiddleheads and heat through. Spoon into heated serving dish and top with bread crumbs.

FIDDLEHEADS, ORIENTAL STYLE
Serves 2

$^1/_2$ lb. Fiddleheads
1 cup water
$^1/_4$ cup sliced water chestnuts
$^1/_4$ cup soy sauce
$1^1/_2$ tsp. freshly grated gingerroot
2 Tbsp. toasted sesame seeds

Steam Fiddleheads with small amount of water until tender-crisp. Drain. Return to pan and add water chestnuts, soy sauce, and gingerroot. Heat a few minutes. Serve with a sprinkling of sesame seeds.

FIDDLEHEADS PARMESAN

Serves 4

1 lb. Fiddleheads, cut into 2 inch pieces
2 cloves garlic, minced
$^1/_4$ cup olive oil
$^1/_4$ tsp. salt
 Dash pepper
$^1/_3$ cup freshly grated Parmesan cheese

Sauté Fiddleheads and garlic in oil until Fiddleheads are tender-crisp. Season with salt and pepper, then toss with Parmesan. Serve at once.

SHRIMP–FIDDLEHEAD GUMBO

Serves 6

2 Tbsp. butter
2 onions, finely chopped
2 lbs. Fiddleheads, cut into $^1/_2$ inch pieces
3 lbs. shrimp, peeled
3 cloves garlic, minced
3 quarts water
 Salt and pepper
$^1/_2$ tsp. Gumbo filé
 Cooked rice

In skillet cook onions until they are lightly browned. Add Fiddleheads and garlic, cook slowly over low heat for 1 hour, stirring occasionally. Add water a cup at a time, stirring after each addition. Salt and pepper to taste. Add shrimp, cover and cook slowly 20 minutes. Sprinkle with Gumbo filé and serve over rice.

FIREWEED

(Epilobium angustifolium)

Also known as willow-herb, willow weed, firetop,
burntweed, pilewort, deerhorn, and blooming Sally.

Fireweed, a member of the evening primrose family, springs up as if by magic in burns, clear cuts, and misused forest lands, covering scarred terrain with an unexpected burst of color. It is abundant in the Rocky Mountains from 5,000 feet to timberline growing along roadsides, in meadows, and by riverbanks. Fireweed prefers rich, cool soil but will accept poor, sandy ground when necessary. It often forms spectacular, dense patches spreading from underground stems.

The plant is also common in Europe, Asia, and North America. It grows from Greenland to Alaska, south to North Carolina, Kansas, and Southern California. In Europe and Asia the young shoots are used like asparagus; Canadians and northern Europeans favor the young leaves and stems as potherbs. Fireweed is used as a tea adulterant in England. It has held a place of importance in the United States as a honey and forage plant. In bygone days, Rocky Mountain Indians would split the older stalks and eat the sweet, glutinous, vitamin C–rich pith. Fireweed is also an astringent and is used in domestic remedies as an intestinal medicine.

Young Fireweed shoots can be found during spring growing at the base of last year's plants, which remain as erect brown stalks bearing the previous year's spent seed pods. These young shoots are best when collected between four and six inches high. They are good used raw in a mixed green salad, cooked as a vegetable, or used in casseroles. The shoots are somewhat glutinous and can make a decent substitute for okra.

The stems of Fireweed grow from two to five feet tall. The lower part is covered with many lance-shaped alternative leaves, reddish in color. The leaves are four to six inches long with veins joined in loops near the edge of the leaf. The tender leaves can be stripped from the stems and used as a potherb. The young leaves also make an acceptable salad when mixed with other wild or domestic greens. The mature leaves make a good herbal tea when dried and used as one would commercial tea.

The rapidly blooming, single-stemmed perennials start their decorative flowering from the base and ascend slowly. The bottom portions of the numerous spikes may be heavy with long seed-packed pods, the center graced with flowers, and the tip still in bud. The blooming begins in late June and continues throughout September. The lilac-purple spires are made up of numerous flowers each having four sepals and four petals. The petals are from one-half to three-quarters of an inch long.

When the flower spikes appear and begin to bud, the spikes can be gathered and used raw in tossed salads or cooked. Once the buds bloom, the blossoms make colorful garnishes or additions to mixed green salads and gelatin molds. Fireweed flowers can usually be found in their continuing journey up the stem until frost.

The fruit pods are two to three inches long, slender, and stand out rigidly from the stem. The masses of pods, filled with tightly layered seeds, break open at maturity to release hundreds of hair-tufted parachutes. These wind borne seeds often form a thin, downy covering along roadsides, burns, and newly logged areas in the autumn—the promise of another grand color show to take place in unlikely locations the following season.

BRAISED FIREWEED

Serves 6

 2 lbs. young Fireweed shoots
 4 Tbsp. bacon drippings
 $^1/_2$ tsp. salt
 $^1/_2$ tsp. freshly ground pepper
 2 tsp. chopped fresh dill
 $^1/_2$ cup beef or chicken stock

Melt bacon drippings and add Fireweed; sear over high heat until lightly browned. Reduce heat and add remaining ingredients, cover and simmer 5 minutes. Remove cover and cook down liquid over high heat for 2 to 3 minutes. Serve hot.

CURRIED FIREWEED

Serves 4

 $1^1/_2$ lbs. young Fireweed shoots
 3 Tbsp. butter
 3 Tbsp. flour
 $^1/_2$ tsp. garlic salt
 $^1/_2$ tsp. paprika
 3 tsp. curry powder
 $1^1/_2$ cups milk
 2 hard-cooked eggs, sliced

Steam Fireweed shoots until tender-crisp. Melt butter in saucepan. Stir in flour and seasonings. Slowly pour in milk, stirring constantly, until thickened. Serve over drained Fireweed shoots. Top with hard-cooked egg slices.

FIREWEED ALMANDINE

Serves 6

1$^1/_2$ lbs. young Fireweed shoots
$^3/_4$ cup butter, melted
$^1/_3$ cup fresh lime juice
$^2/_3$ cup toasted slivered almonds

Steam Fireweed until tender-crisp. Drain. Put shoots in serving dish. Stir lime juice into melted butter; heat through. Pour over Fireweed and sprinkle with almonds.

FIREWEED IN BUTTERMILK BATTER

Serves 4

1 lb. young Fireweed shoots
1 egg
1 cup buttermilk
1 cup all-purpose flour
$^1/_2$ tsp. baking soda
$^1/_4$ tsp. salt
   Oil for deep-frying

Beat together egg and buttermilk; add dry ingredients and beat well. Heat oil to 375°F. Dip shoots in batter and deep-fry until golden brown. Serve at once.

FIREWEED WITH CHEDDAR AND PARMESAN

Serves 6

$^1/_4$ cup butter
$^1/_4$ cup flour
$^3/_4$ cup chicken broth
$^3/_4$ cup milk
$^1/_2$ cup grated Cheddar cheese
$^1/_4$ cup grated freshly Parmesan cheese
    Salt and pepper to taste
2 lbs. young Fireweed shoots
2 Tbsp. freshly grated Parmesan cheese

Melt butter in saucepan; blend in flour. Add chicken broth and milk and cook, stirring constantly, until mixture is thick and bubbly. Add Cheddar, $^1/_4$ cup Parmesan, salt, and pepper; stir until cheese melts.

Steam young Fireweed shoots with small amount of water until tender-crisp. Drain. Put in serving dish and pour cheese sauce over top. Sprinkle with 2 Tbsp. Parmesan.

FIREWEED WITH ORANGE SAUCE

Serves 4

$1^1/_2$ lbs. young Fireweed shoots
3 Tbsp. butter
3 Tbsp. flour
$1^1/_4$ cups fresh orange juice
1 tsp. grated orange rind
    Salt to taste

Steam shoots with small amount of water until tender-crisp, drain. Meanwhile melt butter in small saucepan; blend in flour and cook a few minutes. Add orange juice, rind and salt. Cook until thick and smooth. Drain Fireweed and serve with orange sauce.

FIREWEED PURÉE

Serves 6

2 lbs. young Fireweed shoots
  Salt
6 Tbsp. melted butter
1 tsp. coarsely ground pepper
$^1/_4$ tsp. freshly grated nutmeg
$^1/_4$ cup heavy cream
$^1/_2$ cup freshly grated Parmesan cheese

Cut shoots into 2 inch pieces and simmer in lightly salted water until shoots are tender. Drain well. Purée Fireweed in a food processor. Season with butter, pepper, nutmeg, and cream. Spoon into baking dish, sprinkle with Parmesan and bake at 375°F for 15 minutes.

FIREWEED WITH TOMATOES

Serves 5 to 6

$1^1/_2$ lbs. young Fireweed shoots, cut into 2 inch lengths
$^1/_2$ cup olive oil
2 onions, coarsely chopped
4 cloves garlic, crushed
2 cups canned Italian plum tomatoes
  Salt and pepper to taste
1 tsp. ground coriander
  Lemon wedges

Sauté onions and garlic in olive oil until onions are slightly browned. Add Fireweed and cook 3 minutes. Add tomatoes and seasonings. Cover pan and simmer 20 minutes. Serve hot with lemon wedges.

Spring Lamb–Fireweed Soup

Serves 6

2 lamb shanks
4 cups water
2 cups carrot juice
1 large onion, sliced
$^1/_4$ cup fresh chopped parsley
2 bay leaves
$^1/_2$ tsp. powdered cloves
1 tsp. salt
$^1/_2$ tsp. whole peppercorns
1 cup cracked wheat
3 cups young Fireweed shoots, cut into 2 inch pieces
$^1/_2$ lb. Morel mushrooms, halved

Combine lamb shanks with water, carrot juice, onion, parsley, bay, cloves, salt, and peppercorns in Dutch oven. Bring to boil; reduce heat and simmer, covered, 2-$^1/_2$ hours. Remove shanks from stock; dice meat. Strain broth, discarding solids. Return meat to broth and chill overnight. Next morning skim fat and discard. Add remaining ingredients to soup, bring to boil and simmer 30 minutes.

Stir-Fried Fireweed

Serves 4

$1^1/_2$ lbs. young Fireweed shoots, cut into 2-1/2 inch pieces
4 Tbsp. olive oil
2 tsp. sesame oil
$^1/_2$ cup chicken broth
2 tsp. black bean paste
2 cloves garlic, crushed
2 tsp. freshly grated gingerroot

Heat oil in skillet or wok until it just begins to smoke; add shoots, toss and cook quickly for 2 to 3 minutes. Reduce heat, add remaining ingredients, cover skillet or wok and allow to steam until just tender. Serve with soy sauce, if desired.

CHAPTER
10

HUCKLEBERRY

(Vaccinium globlare, V. membranaceum)

Also known as
bilberry, blueberry, whortleberry, and deerberry.

The most complete history of Huckleberries in America was prepared by Henry David Thoreau. He found references to Huckleberries as early as 1615 in Champlain's journals. It was the English author, John Lawson, who first used the word "Huckleberry" while writing about finding the berries in North Carolina in 1709.

The Huckleberries of the Rocky Mountains have defied cultivation and continue to grow where they please, usually preferring the steep slopes of forests and mountains at elevations of 3,500 to 7,000 feet. They favor moist, deep, acid rich soil.

These low, highly branched members of the heath family grow two to four feet tall and produce one of the most sought after wild berries of the Northwest. Huckleberries have shallow roots and reproduce by rhizomes. The leaves have small teeth along the margins, are oval to oblong in shape, and grow alternately along the branches. Delicate white to pink urn shaped blossoms, approximately one-quarter of an inch long, appear in June, ripening to small bluish-black berries during late July through early September. The berries average one-quarter of an inch in diameter, are rich in sugar, and contain large quantities of vitamin B.

Some of the ways the sweet to tart berries can be used are raw, cooked into sauce, made into pies, added to muffins and pancakes, or preserved as jams, jellies, and syrups. Huckleberries also contain a pigment believed to kill or inhibit the growth of bacteria, and have thus been used for treating intestinal maladies caused by microorganisms.

Patience is required in gathering a significant amount of berries since they grow singularly among the branches rather than in clusters. A pail or other container which could not be easily overturned is a wise choice of equipment. Experienced pickers often take small containers to collect the fruit and empty them regularly into the larger receptacle. A favorite patch may produce sweet berries one year and tart berries the next. The flavor differences correlate to the amount of water the bushes get from winter snow pack or summer rain showers.

There are several popular methods of preserving a bumper crop of Huckleberries. One is home canning. To can Huckleberries, fill clean hot pint jars with berries which have been rinsed and sorted. Shake the jars gently to settle fruit and produce a firmer pack. Make a syrup by mixing together two cups of sugar and four cups of water in a saucepan. Heat over medium-high heat until sugar dissolves and mixture comes to a boil. Pour over berries in jars, leaving a quarter of an inch of headroom. Process in boiling water bath for ten minutes.

A good method for freezing the fruit is to spread the berries in a single layer on a cookie sheet. Freeze solid before storing berries in freezer containers. These berries have been known to hold their flavor up to two years frozen. Use frozen berries as you would fresh.

To dry berries, spread the rinsed and sorted berries on cheesecloth which has been stretched over a wooden frame. Dry in the sun for four to five days. Store berries in a tightly covered container.

During spring, before flowers appear, Huckleberry leaves may be collected and dried for tea. The leaves make an interesting beverage when mixed with mint or an assortment of other dried herbs.

Huckleberry leaf tea has been widely used in Europe to lower or modify blood sugar levels. Two cups of tea taken daily on a regular basis has been known to alleviate hyperglycemia.

Chilled Huckleberry Soup

Serves 6

3 cups Huckleberries
3 cups apples, peeled, cored, and cut in chunks
$^1/_3$ cup freshly squeezed lemon juice
$^3/_4$ cup white wine
$^1/_4$ cup honey
2 cups plain yogurt
$^3/_4$ cup sour cream

Topping:
$^3/_4$ cup sour cream
$1^1/_2$ Tbsp. freshly squeezed lemon juice
3 Tbsp. prepared horseradish

Purée Huckleberries, apple, lemon juice, wine, and honey in food processor or blender. Add yogurt and $^3/_4$ cup sour cream; blend. Chill. Combine topping ingredients and chill. Serve soup in chilled bowls topped with a tablespoon of horseradish mixture.

HUCKLEBERRY–APPLE CRISP

2 cups Huckleberries
2 cups tart apples, peeled and sliced
1 Tbsp. lemon juice
$^1/_2$ cup packed brown sugar
1 cup all-purpose flour
$^3/_4$ cup sugar
1 tsp. baking powder
1 egg, slightly beaten
$^1/_2$ cup butter
$^1/_2$ tsp. cinnamon

Butter $1^1/_2$ quart baking dish. Put in Huckleberries and apples. Sprinkle with lemon juice and brown sugar. Mix next four ingredients, stir in egg and mix until crumbly. Sprinkle over fruit. Top with melted butter and cinnamon. Bake at 350°F for 45 minutes. Serve warm or at room temperature.

HUCKLEBERRY BUTTERMILK PANCAKES

1 cup all-purpose flour
3 tsp. baking powder
1 egg
$1^1/_4$ cups buttermilk
$^1/_2$ cup Huckleberries
2 Tbsp. melted butter

Sift dry ingredients together. Beat together egg and buttermilk. Pour over dry ingredients and blend until smooth. Add melted butter and Huckleberries. Bake on hot, lightly oiled griddle.

HUCKLEBERRY CAKE

1$^1/_2$ cups cake flour
$^1/_2$ cup sugar
2 tsp. baking powder
$^1/_4$ cup plus 2 Tbsp. milk
1 egg
3 Tbsp. butter, melted
1$^1/_2$ cups Huckleberries
1 tsp. almond extract

Sift together dry ingredients. Beat together milk, egg, butter, and extract. Stir milk mixture into dry ingredients and mix until all particles are just moistened. Stir in berries. Pour into an 8x8 inch cake pan and bake in 375°F preheated oven for 50 minutes. Cool before cutting.

HUCKLEBERRY CHEESECAKE

9 inch pie

1 graham cracker crust, unbaked
12 oz. pkg. cream cheese
2 eggs
$^1/_2$ cup sugar
1 tsp. vanilla
2 cups Huckleberries
$^1/_2$ cup sugar
1$^1/_2$ Tbsp. cornstarch
$^1/_4$ cup fresh lemon juice

Beat together cream cheese, eggs, $^1/_2$ cup sugar and vanilla until fluffy. Pour into crust and bake in preheated 350°F oven for 25 minutes or until set. Cool. Simmer berries with sugar and lemon juice in saucepan for 5 minutes. Thicken with cornstarch. Pour over pie. Chill overnight.

HUCKLEBERRY CHOCOLATES

$2^1/_2$ cups sugar
$^3/_4$ cup water
$^1/_4$ tsp. cream of tartar
$^1/_4$ cup Huckleberry jam
    Dipping chocolate
    Candy molds

Combine sugar and water. Bring to boiling over medium-low heat, stirring constantly. Add cream of tartar. Cover pan and steam for 3 minutes. Remove cover. Cook mixture to soft ball stage (238°F) without stirring. Pour onto cooled surface. Blend mixture with spatula until smooth. Cover and let stand $^1/_2$ hour. Cut into pieces with knife and place pieces in bowl. Cover with damp cloth and allow to stand 2 to 3 days. With a spatula work the jam into fondant.

Test dipping chocolate to assure that it is compatible with molds and removes easily. Heat chocolate until just melted. Coat molds with solid layer of chocolate. Chill until hard. Fill each mold with fondant and cover with final layer of chocolate sealing edges carefully.

HUCKLEBERRY DRESSING

1 cup

3 Tbsp. Huckleberry vinegar
2 tsp. honey
1 tsp. cardamom
$^1/_2$ cup olive oil
$^1/_4$ cup Huckleberry jam

Whisk together vinegar, honey, and cardamom. Add oil in a slow steady stream while whisking mixture. Stir in jam. Allow to stand at room temperature for at least 1 hour to blend flavors. Great with tossed greens or fresh fruit salad.

HUCKLEBERRY JAM

4 pints

6 cups Huckleberries
1 cup water
6 cups sugar
Juice of 1 lemon
2 tsp. grated lemon rind
1 pkg. powdered pectin

In saucepan combine berries and water. Bring to boiling. Add sugar and boil hard 2 minutes. Add juice, rind, and pectin. Boil hard 1 minute longer. Remove from heat and pour into hot, sterilized jars, adjust lids and seal in boiling water bath 7 minutes.

HUCKLEBERRY NUT BREAD

2 loaves

2 cups flour
1 tsp. baking powder
Dash salt
1$^{1}/_{2}$ cups Huckleberries
$^{1}/_{2}$ cup chopped walnuts
$^{1}/_{2}$ cup maple syrup
2 eggs, beaten
$^{3}/_{4}$ cup butter, melted

Sift together first three ingredients. In separate bowl beat together syrup, eggs, and butter. Fold in berries and nuts. Mix with the dry ingredients. Butter two bread loaf pans and line with waxed paper. Butter paper. Spoon Huckleberry mixture into pans. Bake at 325°F for 60 to 70 minutes. Cool.

HUCKLEBERRY PIE

9 inch pie

Pastry for two 9 inch crusts
4 cups Huckleberries
1$^{1}/_{4}$ cups sugar
3 Tbsp. flour
1 Tbsp. butter

Mix together Huckleberries, sugar, and flour in mixing bowl. Line pie plate with pastry. Fill with berries and dot with butter. Adjust top crust. Bake at 450°F oven for 10 minutes, then reduce heat to 350°F and bake 40 to 50 minutes longer. Cool completely before serving.

HUCKLEBERRY PUDDING WITH LEMON SAUCE
Serves 6

     2 cups flour
$1^1/_2$ cups sugar
     2 tsp. baking powder
$^1/_2$ tsp. freshly grated nutmeg
$^1/_2$ tsp. cinnamon
     1 tsp. grated lemon peel
$^3/_4$ cup butter, softened
     2 eggs
$^3/_4$ cup milk
$2^1/_2$ cups Huckleberries

Mix together first six ingredients. Cut in butter with pastry cutter until the size of peas. Add eggs and milk, then mix thoroughly. Pour into greased and floured 9x9x2 inch pan and top with Huckleberries. Bake in preheated 350°F oven for 1 hour and 15 minutes. Serve warm with lemon sauce.

Lemon Sauce:
$^1/_2$ cup sugar
     1 Tbsp. cornstarch
$^1/_4$ cup cold water
     1 egg yolk
     3 Tbsp. lemon juice
     1 tsp. grated lemon rind
     2 Tbsp. butter

Combine sugar and cornstarch in saucepan. Stir in cold water and mix well. Gradually stir in boiling water. Cook, stirring, over medium heat for 10 minutes or until clear and fairly thick. Blend together egg yolk and lemon juice, then gradually stir into sauce. Add lemon rind and butter.

HUCKLEBERRY SYRUP

2 pints

- 4 cups Huckleberries
- 4 cups sugar
- 1 cup water
- 2 tsp. lemon juice
- $^1/_4$ tsp. freshly grated nutmeg

Combine all ingredients in saucepan and simmer over medium heat, stirring frequently, until syrup has thickened slightly (approximately 15 minutes). Pour into attractive bottles and cork.

HUCKLEBERRY TORT WITH BOURBON FILLING

- 1 cup unsalted butter
- 1 cup sugar
- 4 eggs
- $^1/_2$ tsp. vanilla
- 1 cup sifted cake flour
- 6 rounds of baking parchment 7 inches across

Filling:
- 1 Tbsp. cream
- 1 egg white
- 1 Tbsp. butter
- 1 lb. confectioners' sugar
- 4 eggs
- $^1/_4$ cup bourbon
- 1 quart Huckleberries

Cream together butter and sugar until light. Beat in eggs one at a time. Beat in vanilla. Sift flour over mixture and lightly fold into butter mixture. Place parchment papers on baking sheets and spread a very thin layer of batter on each. Bake in preheated 375°F oven for 3 to 5 minutes. Cool slightly, then remove from papers.

Combine cream, egg white, butter, and confectioners' sugar. Mix until very light. Beat in eggs and bourbon. Reserve 1 cup of mixture. Mix Huckleberries with bulk of mixture and spread filling between cake layers. Chill reserved mixture until it reaches spreading consistency, then spread on top layer of tort.

HUCKLEBERRY TRUFFLES

       6 oz. semi–sweet chocolate
    $^1/_2$ cup whipping cream
       2 cups confectioners' sugar
       1 egg white
    $1^1/_2$ Tbsp. rum
       1 cup Huckleberries
          Cocoa powder

In heavy saucepan combine chocolate and cream. Heat over low heat until chocolate has melted. Remove from heat. Combine Huckleberries with confectioners' sugar and egg white. Mix well with wooden spoon. Stir in chocolate and rum and mix to combine well. Chill until just firm enough to handle. Form into balls and roll in cocoa powder. Chill.

HUCKLEBERRY WAFFLES

Serves 4

    $1^1/_2$ cups cake flour
    $^1/_4$ cup oat bran
       2 tsp. baking powder
       1 Tbsp. sugar
       3 eggs, separated
    $^1/_4$ cup butter, melted
    $1^1/_2$ cups milk
    $1^1/_2$ cups Huckleberries

Sift together flour, bran, baking powder, and sugar. Beat egg yolks. Add to butter. Stir into dry ingredients until dry particles are just moistened. Beat egg whites stiff. Fold into batter along with Huckleberries. Bake on preheated waffle iron.

SOUR CREAM HUCKLEBERRY MUFFINS

$1^1/_2$ cups flour
2 Tbsp. granulated sugar
2 tsp. baking powder
1 tsp. baking soda
$1^1/_2$ cups Huckleberries
1 egg, slightly beaten
2 Tbsp. butter, melted
$^3/_4$ cup sour cream

Sift together first four ingredients. Mix together egg, butter, and sour cream. Blend into dry ingredients until dry mixture is just moistened. Fold in Huckleberries. Spoon into buttered muffin tins and bake in preheated 350°F oven for 25 to 30 minutes.

UNCOOKED HUCKLEBERRY PIE

1 baked graham cracker crust
2 cups Huckleberries
$^1/_2$ cup confectioners' sugar
2 cups whipped cream

When pie is to be served, fill crust with berries. Sprinkle with powdered sugar and top with whipped cream.

Chapter 11

JUNIPER
ROCKY MOUNTAIN

(Juniperus scopulorum)
Also known as Rocky Mountain red cedar and river Juniper.

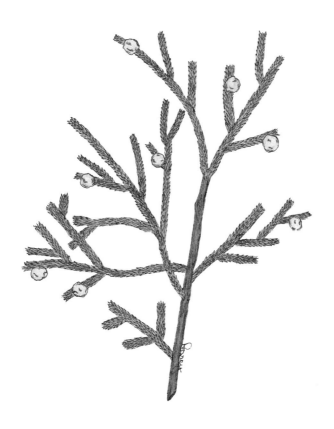

A member of the cypress family, Juniper has long been associated with ritual cleansing. It was not only burned in Asian temples as part of regular purification rites, but also used by Native Americans during their spiritual quests. Juniper ranges from the Arctic Circle to Mexico, as well as being widely distributed in Europe and Asia. There are approximately fifteen species of this aromatic shrub or tree native to North America, all producing edible berry-like cones.

The Rocky Mountain Juniper is an evergreen tree growing up to twenty feet tall and one and a half feet in diameter with a straight trunk, narrow, pointed crown and slender branches of gray-green foliage. Its thin, fibrous and shedding bark is grayish on the tree's exterior and reddish-brown underneath. The tree is found growing on dry, sandy or gravel-like soil such as limestone and lava, preferring moist canyons in the semi–arid areas. It ranges from 3,000 to 9,000 feet in elevation. Juniper is found in open woodlands at the lower border of trees in the northern part of the Central Rockies. It is also found among the Piñon pines in foothills located in the southern portion of the Central Rockies. The fragrant wood is used for cedar chests, fenceposts, timber, and fuel.

Legend has it that Juniper planted beside the front door will keep witches from entering the house; the only way for a witch to get past the tree is by correctly counting its leaves. A close look at the leaves would convince even the most optimistic individual of the enormity of such a task. The pointed scale-like leaves grow in alternating pairs forming slender wings one-sixteenth of an inch long and are so closely pressed to the twig that they nearly obscure it. The Rocky Mountain Juniper flowers from April through June. Male and female flowers grow in whorls and are on separate plants; male flowers being yellow and female, green. Although Juniper does not begin flowering and yielding cones until it is about ten years old, it continues its production for nearly three hundred years.

The aromatic cones are round, approximately one-fourth of an inch in diameter, bluish-black and covered with a white, waxy bloom. Often referred to as "berries" the cones are soft, juicy and have a sweet resinous flavor. These "berries" are usually two-seeded, mature the second year, and are found the year around intermingled with the immature green cones.

The vitamin C–rich Juniper "berries" have numerous uses; the most common being a flavoring ingredient in the Dutch invention called gin. In fact, the name gin is derived from the Dutch word *jenever,* which means

Juniper. The French flavor the appetite stimulating Juniper in their stews; Germans add the "berries" to sauerkraut and cabbage dishes; United States cooks frequently add the aromatic seasoning to wild game and fowl; Native Americans eat them raw or add the dried, ground cones to their breads. Various forms of wildlife also feed on the berry-like cones.

A few fragrant, green branches tossed on the outdoor grill will give meat and vegetables a subtle Juniper flavor. After harvesting Juniper "berries" dry them on a flat screen in a ventilated place until they become brittle. Store them in tightly covered jars. The dried "berries" will keep their flavor for several years.

The inner bark of the Juniper trunk was sometimes peeled off and eaten by Native Americans during acute food shortages. Ashes derived from burning green Juniper branches was used in baking bread and flat cakes.

ALSATIAN STEW

Serves 6

  1 lb. small red potatoes, halved
  1 lb. cubed veal
  1 lb. cubed pork
  3 cloves garlic, crushed
  1 bay leaf
10 Juniper berries, crushed
  1 tsp. salt
  2 cups dry white wine
$^1/_4$ cup melted butter

In 3 quart casserole combine ingredients and mix well. Cover and bake in 375°F oven for $1^1/_2$ hours.

BELGIUM RED CABBAGE

Serves 4

1 medium-sized red cabbage, shredded
3 tart apples, cored and diced
$^1/_4$ cup butter
$^1/_4$ cup currant jelly
5 Juniper berries
3 whole cloves
$^1/_4$ cup apple cider
$^1/_2$ tsp. salt
2 tsp. red wine vinegar

Sauté apples in butter for a few minutes. Add cabbage and continue to sauté 2 minutes longer. Add remaining ingredients. Mix well and simmer, covered, 1 hour. May be served warm or cold.

FOIL ROASTED QUAIL WITH JUNIPER

Serves 3

3 quail, dressed
8 Juniper berries, crushed
1 medium onion, cut into thirds
  Salt and pepper
3 strips bacon
  Heavy duty foil

Sprinkle birds inside and out with salt, pepper, and Juniper. Place a piece of onion in the cavity of each bird. Wrap a bacon strip around each and place each on square of foil. Wrap foil tightly around birds, pinching edges together to seal tightly. Place wrapped birds over hot coals and allow to bake 2 hours, turning once.

INDIAN FLAT BREAD
1-1/2 dozen

$^2/_3$ cup green Juniper ashes
1 cup whole wheat flour
$^1/_2$ cup cracked wheat
$^1/_2$ tsp. salt
   Cooking oil or bacon drippings

Burn the green Juniper, not the branch part, until you get $^2/_3$ cup of ash. Mix with flour, cracked wheat, and salt. Add water to form a stiff dough. Knead briefly, pinch off pieces of dough the size of walnuts. Flatten each piece as thinly as possible between palms of hands. Fry each flattened piece, one at a time, in hot oil or drippings in skillet over moderate heat until crisp and lightly browned.

JUNIPER CHICKEN
Serves 3 to 4

$^1/_2$ cup peanut oil
$^1/_2$ cup burgundy
8 Juniper berries, crushed
2 Tbsp. honey
2 Tbsp. tomato paste
2 Tbsp. molasses
1 Tbsp. Worcestershire sauce
$^1/_4$ tsp. salt
$^1/_2$ tsp. curry powder
2 cloves garlic, crushed
$1^1/_2$ lbs. chicken pieces

In bowl combine all ingredients except chicken. Add chicken and allow to stand at room temperature for 2 hours. Cook over medium-hot coals to desired doneness, brushing several times with marinade.

JUNIPER GRAVY FOR WILD GAME

12 whole Juniper berries
4 cloves garlic, crushed
3 beef bouillon cubes
1¼ cups water
1½ Tbsp. bacon drippings
1 Tbsp. flour

In small pan add Juniper, garlic, bouillon, and water. Simmer, covered, 10 minutes. Mix drippings with flour, blending well. Drop small amounts into simmering sauce, stirring well. Cook and stir until gravy has thickened.

JUNIPER MARINADE FOR WILD GAME

1 quart

10 Juniper berries
3 cups dry white wine
1¼ cups olive oil
3 onions, sliced
5 cloves garlic, crushed
1½ tsp. celery salt
2 bay leaves
3 Tbsp. chopped cilantro
4 peppercorns

Mix together all ingredients. Place meat in bowl just large enough to hold it. Pour marinade over meat. Marinate in refrigerator for 2 days, turning occasionally. Broil or grill meat to desired doneness.

LEG OF LAMB WITH JUNIPER SAUCE

Serves 6

6 lb. leg of lamb, boned, rolled and tied
3 cloves garlic, cut into slivers
$^1/_2$ cup beef broth
$^1/_2$ cup Burgundy wine
1 Tbsp. crushed Juniper berries
2 Tbsp. butter

Lightly salt lamb. Cut small gashes in meat and insert slivers of garlic. Bake in 325°F oven for $1^1/_2$ to 2 hours, basting frequently with sauce made from broth, wine, Juniper, and butter simmered together for 15 minutes.

LEG OF PORK WITH JUNIPER

Serves 8

1 leg of pork (approximately 12 lbs.), skin removed
5 cloves garlic, crushed
15 Juniper berries, crushed
10 peppercorns, crushed
10 allspice berries, crushed
2 Tbsp. fresh thyme leaves
$^1/_2$ tsp. freshly grated nutmeg
1 bay leaf, crushed
4 strips lime zest
1 onion struck with 4 cloves
   Olive oil
   Red wine
4 Tbsp. butter
4 Tbsp. flour

Rub all herbs and spices into the pork, place in large bowl or crock, and cover with red wine. Add lime zest and onion. Refrigerate for 7 days, turning several times daily. Dry roast and rub with olive oil. Place in roasting pan and bake at 300°F, allowing 25 minutes per pound of meat. Baste every half hour with heated marinade.

Transfer leg to a hot platter, strain the juices in pan and remaining marinade; boil down to 2 cups.

Melt butter in saucepan, add flour and cook for a few minutes until mixture begins to brown. Stir mixture into the 2 cups pan dripping/marinade. Serve sauce with roast.

Navajo Juniper Corn Bread

$^1/_2$ cup Juniper ashes
$^1/_2$ cup boiling water
$^1/_2$ cup whole wheat flour
$2^1/_2$ cups cornmeal
$^1/_2$ tsp. salt
$1^3/_4$ cups boiling water
    Heavy duty aluminum foil

Burn green part of Juniper (not branch), until you get $^1/_2$ cup ashes. Mix with $^1/_2$ cup boiling water.

In saucepan bring $1^3/_4$ cups water and salt to boiling. Add ash mixture and stir. Mix flour with cornmeal and stir into ash mixture. Cool. Knead until dough is soft and firm. Shape into a loaf and wrap in foil. Place on bed of hot coals in campfire or in an oven heated to 350°F. Bake for 1 hour, turning frequently if baking over coals.

Pauper's Bread

$^1/_2$ cup whole wheat flour
$^1/_2$ cup barley flour
$^1/_2$ cup Juniper ash
$^1/_2$ tsp. salt
$1^1/_2$ tsp. baking powder
  2 Tbsp. honey
$^1/_3$ cup milk
  1 egg
  2 Tbsp. melted butter

Burn green Juniper (not branch) until you get $^1/_2$ cup of ashes. Sift ashes together with flour, salt, and baking powder. Add honey, egg, milk, and butter. Mix well. Turn onto floured board and pat into a $^1/_2$ inch thick circle. Place on buttered 9 inch pie plate. Bake at 425°F for 15 minutes.

ROAST GROUSE WITH JUNIPER BUTTER

Serves 2

    4 Tbsp. butter, softened
    2 tsp. crushed Juniper berries
 1¹/₂ tsp. freshly grated lemon zest
    1 grouse, rinsed and patted dry

In small bowl blend together 2 Tbsp. butter with the Juniper and lemon zest. Loosen skin covering breast meat of grouse and insert butter mixture, smoothing it by rubbing outside of skin. Rub remaining butter over bird, place bird in roasting pan and bake at 425°F for 45 to 60 minutes, basting with juices every 10 minutes. Let stand for 5 minutes before cutting and serving.

CHAPTER 12

LAMB'S QUARTERS

(Chenopodium album, C. berlandieri)

Also known as pigweed and goosefoot.

Lamb's Quarters is a native of Europe and Asia but has naturalized all over North America except in the extreme north. The generic name, *Chenopodium*, is Greek for goose foot. The leaves, broad and somewhat triangular at the base and narrowing toward the tip in a series of blunt teeth, resemble the shape of the feet of geese.

The erect, multi–branched annual has green leaves which are coated with a white, waxy powder that acts as a water repellent. The one to four inch leaves grow on long leaf stalks alternately on the stems. The plant averages from one to two and one half feet tall. Lamb's Quarters can be found growing in rich soil in waste areas, cultivated fields, pastures, and along stream banks.

When six to ten inches high, the succulent, tender plants make a very desirable potherb or non–bitter salad green. As the plant matures the individual leaves can be gathered and cooked like spinach. Since Lamb's Quarters lose a great deal of bulk when cooked, an ample supply should be collected. Young shoots begin making their appearance during early May in most Rocky Mountain areas and the plants continues to put up new shoots through most of the summer.

Older plants bear tiny inconspicuous green flowers, lacking petals, which are crowded on small spikes interspersed with the leaves. After flowering the spikes are covered with small, black lackluster seeds that are almost flat and have convex faces *(C. album)*. *Chenopodium berlandieri* have seeds with surfaces roughened with minute pits. Without examining the seeds under a magnifying glass it would be difficult to tell the two plants apart.

The seeds were commonly used by Indians as a source of meal for bread and gruel. Seeds are extremely abundant and it is frequently possible for the modern day harvester to gather several quarts in an hour by rubbing them from the spikes into a container. The husks are winnowed out before the seeds are ground into flour. Lamb's Quarters seeds are quite hard and are most easily ground with a coffee grinder or food processor. Because of the black hulls, the flour produced is very dark. This flour is good mixed with wheat flour for making pancakes, muffins, and waffles. Porridge produced by boiling the seeds until they are soft, can be eaten as a breakfast cereal or emergency food. The tiny seeds are available from the time they dry and darken in autumn until well into winter.

CREAMED LAMB'S QUARTERS WITH ONIONS
Serves 4

1$^1/_2$ lbs. Lamb's Quarters
14 small white onions, peeled
$^1/_4$ cup butter
3 Tbsp. flour
1$^1/_2$ cups milk
$^1/_2$ cup sour cream
Salt and pepper to taste

Steam Lamb's Quarters until wilted. Cook onions in boiling, salted water until tender. Combine with drained Lamb's Quarters. Make the sauce by melting butter in skillet, then slowly stirring in milk until smooth. Stir in sour cream and add salt and pepper to taste. Cook until thickened, then pour over Lamb's Quarters and onions in serving dish. Serve at once.

LAMB'S QUARTERS SICILIANI
Serves 4

1 lb. Lamb's Quarters
4 cloves garlic, crushed
3 Tbsp. olive oil
5 anchovy fillets, minced
2 tsp. lime juice

Cook greens in covered pan with $^1/_2$ cup water for 8 minutes. Drain well in colander. Sauté garlic in oil for 5 minutes. Add Lamb's Quarters and cook, stirring, for 3 minutes longer. Stir in anchovies and serve sprinkled with lime juice.

LAMB'S QUARTERS WITH HAZEL NUTS
Serves 6

2 lbs. Lamb's Quarters
4 Tbsp. butter
$^2/_3$ cup chopped toasted hazelnuts
1$^1/_2$ Tbsp. soy sauce
Pepper to taste

Melt butter in large skillet, add Lamb's Quarters and sauté, stirring, until wilted. Toss with hazelnuts, soy sauce, and pepper. Heat a few minutes longer, then serve.

LAMB'S QUARTERS AND GREEN ONION TART

Serves 4 to 5

Rich pastry for a 9 inch tart
3 cups chopped Lamb's Quarters
2 cups chopped green onions
5 Tbsp. butter
4 eggs, lightly beaten
1$^1/_2$ cups light cream
$^1/_4$ tsp. salt
$^1/_4$ tsp. freshly ground pepper
$^1/_4$ tsp. freshly grated nutmeg

Line pan with pastry and flute edges. Line shell with foil and fill with rice or beans. Bake at 425°F for 10 to 12 minutes or until lightly browned. Remove foil and beans or rice. Sauté Lamb's Quarters and onions in butter for 3 to 5 minutes. Lightly beat eggs, then beat in the cream. Season with salt, pepper, and nutmeg. Spoon Lamb's Quarter mixture into tart shell and pour egg mixture on top. Bake at 350°F for 25 to 30 minutes.

LAMB'S QUARTERS SOUP

Serves 4

1 onion, chopped
2 Tbsp. butter
1 Tbsp. flour
2 cups chicken stock
3 cups packed chopped Lamb's Quarters
3 Tbsp. snipped Sheep Sorrel
$^1/_4$ cup heavy cream
1 Tbsp. fresh lime juice
Pinch freshly grated nutmeg

In saucepan cook onion in butter over moderately low heat until onion has softened. Add flour and cook, stirring, for 3 minutes. Whisk in stock and bring mixture to a boil, whisking. Add Lamb's Quarters and Sheep Sorrel and simmer mixture for 10 minutes. Purée in batches in food processor or blender. Transfer to a heated bowl and stir in cream, lime juice, nutmeg, and salt and pepper to taste. Divide into four bowls and serve at once.

LAMB'S QUARTERS–PIÑON SALAD

Serves 4

2 pints Lamb's Quarters, coarsely chopped
$^1/_2$ tsp. salt
2 Tbsp. toasted Piñon nuts
$^1/_2$ cup chopped sweet onion
Juice of 2 lime
$^1/_4$ cup olive oil

Toss Lamb's Quarters with salt and Piñon nuts. Mix remaining ingredients in small bowl, pour over greens and toss to mix.

LAMB'S QUARTERS WITH POT LIKKER

Serves 8

1 lb. salt pork
$1^1/_2$ quarts water
3 lbs. Lamb's Quarters
Salt and pepper to taste
$^1/_2$ tsp. hot pepper sauce

Boil salt pork in water for $1^1/_2$ hours. Add greens and simmer for 15 minutes. Remove greens and chop coarsely; season with salt, pepper, and hot pepper sauce. Serve on platter with slices of salt pork and some of the pot likker. Good with corn bread.

LAMB'S QUARTERS SEED GRIDDLE CAKES

$^2/_3$ cup all-purpose flour
$^1/_3$ cup finely ground Lamb's Quarter seeds
1 tsp. baking powder
$^1/_4$ tsp. salt
1 Tbsp. sugar
1 egg, beaten
$^3/_4$ cup milk
3 Tbsp. melted butter

Combine dry ingredients. Mix together egg and milk, then beat into dry ingredients, forming a smooth batter. Add melted butter; mix well. Drop batter onto hot greased griddle. Bake, turning cakes when they are browned on the underside and puffed and slightly set on top.

Lentil Stew with Lamb's Quarters

Serves 6

$1^1/_2$ cups lentils, rinsed
1 large onion, sliced
2 carrots, sliced
1 bay leaf
1 tsp. salt
2 cups water
4 cups chopped Lamb's Quarters
$1^1/_2$ lbs. Polish sausage, cut into 3 inch pieces

Combine all ingredients, except sausage and Lamb's Quarters in Dutch oven or kettle. Bring to a boil over high heat then reduce heat and simmer 30 minutes. Add sausage and Lamb's Quarters and cook for 20 more minutes.

Wilted Lamb's Quarter–Watercress Salad with Bacon

Serves 2

$^1/_2$ lb. Lamb's Quarters
$^1/_4$ lb. Watercress
3 Tbsp. olive oil
$1^1/_2$ whole mustard seed
$^1/_2$ cup chopped onion
$1^1/_2$ Tbsp. balsamic vinegar
2 slices bacon, cooked until crisp and crumbled

Wash greens and spin dry. Put into large bowl. In skillet heat oil with the mustard seeds for 3 to 4 minutes. Add onion and cook, stirring, until onion is softened. Remove skillet from heat, stir in vinegar, and bring mixture to a boil. Drizzle immediately over greens, add bacon, toss and serve.

LAMB'S QUARTER SEED DROP BISCUITS

$1^1/_2$ cups all-purpose flour
$^1/_2$ cup finely ground Lamb's Quarter seed
2 tsp. baking powder
3 Tbsp. sugar
$^1/_4$ tsp. salt
$^1/_4$ cup butter
$^1/_2$ cup milk
1 egg, beaten

Combine dry ingredients in bowl. Cut in butter using two knives or pastry cutter. Beat together milk and egg, then add to flour mixture and stir until dry ingredients are just dampened. Then stir briskly until mixture forms a soft dough that clings to the sides of the bowl. Drop from a teaspoon onto greased skillet. Cover with lid or aluminum foil and bake at 350°F for 25 to 30 minutes or until biscuits are done.

LAMB'S QUARTERS WITH BASIL

Serves 6

2 lbs. Lamb's Quarters
3 green onions, chopped
$^1/_2$ cup fresh basil, chopped
2 Tbsp. butter

In large saucepan add $^1/_3$ cup water to Lamb's Quarters and onions. Cover and steam for 10 minutes. Drain. Add basil and butter. Toss to mix. Serve at once.

OAT BREAD WITH LAMB'S QUARTER SEED

2 loaves

    2 pkgs. active dry yeast
 $^1/_2$ cup lukewarm water
$1^1/_3$ cup warm milk
    1 cup hot water
 $^1/_4$ cup butter
 $^1/_3$ cup molasses
    2 tsp. salt
    6 cups all-purpose flour
    2 cups finely ground Lamb's Quarter seeds
$2^1/_2$ cups uncooked rolled oats
    2 Tbsp. melted butter
    1 Tbsp. milk

Combine yeast and warm water in small bowl; set aside 5 minutes.

Combine warm milk, hot water, and $^1/_4$ cup butter and stir until butter melts. Stir in molasses, salt, and yeast mixture.

Gradually add 2 cups flour, then stir in Lamb's Quarter seeds, mixing well. Add oats and remaining flour. Turn dough onto floured surface and knead until smooth and elastic. Place dough in greased bowl, turn so that top is greased. Cover and let rise in warm place until double in bulk. Punch down, divide in half, and shape each half into a loaf. Place each loaf in greased bread pan and let rise in warm place until double in bulk. Bake in preheated 350°F oven for 40 to 45 minutes.

CHAPTER
13

MILKWEED

(Asclepias speciosa)

Also known as lechones and silkweed.

The Milkweed *(Asclepias)* are plants for all seasons—sources of food, fiber, and medicine. They were named for the Greek god, Aesculapius, son of Apollo and Coronis, and patron of physicians.

Asclepias speciosa is a grayish, velvety native perennial with erect leafy stems growing from thick spreading root stalks. The plant averages two to four feet in height. Milkweed leaves are four to eight inches long, opposite and oval in shape with conspicuous veins extending from the midrib to the leaf edge. In late June or early July rounded umbels of sweet smelling star-like flowers appear. Each flower is about three-quarters of an inch wide with five reddish sepals, five stamens, and five pinkish petals each with an upright hood and an inward curving horn. These are followed by warty seed pods averaging three to four inches long. When mature the pods split down one side to release the small flat seeds attached to long, silky hairs. All parts of the plant oozes a milky sap when injured. Milkweed prefers dry gravel-like slopes or roadsides, fields, and waste places with sandy soil.

Properly prepared, Milkweed is one of the most enjoyable wild foods. Almost every part of the plant can be eaten. The harvest period extends from early spring to mid–summer.

In the spring young shoots may be gathered and cooked like aspara-gus, changing the cooking water once to remove any bitterness. The shoots should be gathered while less than eight inches high, otherwise they may be tough. A week later young leaves form. They can be collected from spring until the flower buds form in summer. They make an excellent potherb, but should be cooked in two changes of boiling water to remove the bitterness.

When the flower buds appear they can be harvested through the sum-mer and into early autumn. They have a grayish, woolly appearance before cooking, but turn a bright green when boiled and resemble broccoli. As with the leaves, the buds need to be cooked in two changes of boiling water. Native Americans made a sweet, thick, brown syrup from the opened flower buds.

When the pale green seed pods form they can be boiled and served like okra. The pods should be collected when firm, before they feel elastic when pressed between the fingers. The pods are somewhat mucilaginous and act as a natural thickener when added to soups, stews, and gumbos. It is best to precook the pods in two changes of boiling water before mixing them with other foods. They may also be blanched in two changes of boiling water, drained, and frozen for later use.

Native Americans and early homesteaders found numerous uses for Milkweed. The sap from the leaves and stems was collected and dried in the sun, making an acceptable substitute for chewing gum. Fresh sap was used as a healing application to cuts and wounds. Warts were cured by repeated applications of the milky juice. The sap also contains a latex that will yield rubber. The fibers of the stalks were used to make cordage and fishing line. The stalks were harvested when dry, pounded to remove the woody parts, then the fiber was cleaned by hand.

During World War II, scientists with the US Department of Agriculture experimented with the downy Milkweed seeds to see if it could take the place of kapok, a down harvested from a silk-cotton tree of the East Indies, Africa, and tropical America. The Milkweed substitute for kapok was then widely used by the US Navy and Air Force in flotation devices.

MILKWEED BUD CHOWDER

Serves 5

$^1/_2$ lb. lean bacon, cooked and crumbled
$^1/_4$ cup bacon drippings
$^1/_2$ cup diced onion
$^1/_2$ cup diced celery
 3 medium potatoes, peeled and cubed
 2 carrots, peeled and sliced
 1 lb. Milkweed buds
 1 cup water
 1 quart milk
 2 Tbsp. fresh chopped dillweed
 1 cup shredded Swiss cheese
    Salt and pepper to taste

Place Milkweed in saucepan, cover with boiling water and continue to boil for 5 minutes. Drain; rinse and repeat boiling process. Drain well. Sauté onion in drippings. Add celery, potatoes, Milkweed, 1 cup water, and salt and pepper to saucepan. Bring to boil, reduce heat, then cover and simmer gently 30 minutes. Stir in milk, cheese and dillweed. Heat, stirring, until cheese melts. Serve garnished with crumbled bacon.

CREAM OF MILKWEED SOUP

Serves 4

2 cups milk
2 cups cream
3 Tbsp. butter
3 Tbsp. flour
2 cups Milkweed shoots
$^1/_4$ tsp. salt
$^1/_4$ tsp. pepper
2 Tbsp. fresh tarragon
$^1/_8$ tsp. cayenne pepper

Simmer Milkweed shoots in salted water for 10 minutes. Drain; repeat procedure. Rinse in cold water and drain well. Cut shoots into $^1/_2$ inch pieces. Melt butter in large skillet; stir in flour. Mix together milk and cream, then slowly stir into butter/flour mixture. Cook 5 minutes, stirring continuously. Add Milkweed and seasoning. Heat, but do not boil. Serve at once.

BEER BATTERED MILKWEED

Serves 4 to 5

1 lb. Milkweed buds
12 oz. can dark beer
1 cup all-purpose flour
$^1/_2$ tsp. baking powder
1 tsp salt
$^1/_4$ tsp. hot pepper sauce
    Oil for deep-frying

Cover Milkweed buds with cold water and bring to boiling. Turn off heat and allow to stand 10 minutes. Drain and rinse well. Chill buds. Pat dry just before using.

Make batter by sifting together flour, baking powder, and salt. Add beer and stir well. Add pepper sauce and allow to stand 20 minutes. Heat oil to 375°F. Dip buds into batter and deep-fry until golden on all sides. Serve at once with choice of dipping sauce or soy sauce.

CREOLE GUMBO WITH MILKWEED PODS

Serves 4

6 slices lean bacon, cut into small pieces
18 young Milkweed pods
1 large onion, thinly sliced
1 green pepper, finely chopped
3 cloves garlic, crushed
Flour
3 cups chicken broth
$1^1/_2$ cups diced celery
$1^1/_2$ cups canned tomatoes, chopped
2 tsp. fresh thyme
1 bay leaf
1 Tbsp. Worcestershire sauce
Salt and pepper
3 cups peeled shrimp
Filé
Boiled rice

Cover pods with boiling water and let stand 15 minutes. Drain and rinse well. Repeat.

Cook bacon in skillet for 3 minutes, then add Milkweed pods, onion and green pepper. Sauté 5 minutes. Add garlic, sprinkle with flour and stir well. Stir in broth, celery, tomatoes, thyme, bay leaf, Worcestershire sauce, and salt and pepper to taste. Cover and simmer 1 hour, then add peeled shrimp. Cook 10 minutes. Add a little more chicken broth if mixture seems too thick. Serve in bowls with a sprinkling of filé and a spoonful of boiled rice.

MILKWEED WITH ALMONDS

Serves 6

2 lbs. Milkweed shoots, cut into 2 inch pieces
Salt
2 cups blanched almonds, toasted
$^1/_2$ cup butter

Simmer Milkweed in salted water for 10 minutes. Drain; repeat procedure. Rinse in cold water and drain well. In skillet sauté almonds in butter until heated through. Salt lightly, then add Milkweed, stirring and cooking until Milkweed is heated. Serve at once.

MILKWEED BUDS WITH SESAME SEEDS

Serves 4

$1^1/_2$ lbs. Milkweed flower buds
$^1/_4$ cup butter
$^1/_4$ cup water
1 Tbsp. soy sauce
1 cup thinly sliced water chestnuts
3 Tbsp. toasted sesame seeds

Cover buds with boiling water, boil for 5 minutes. Drain, then repeat procedure. Rinse cooked buds in cold water. Combine butter, water, and soy sauce in frying pan. Bring to boil; stir in water chestnuts. Add cooked buds, cover and simmer for 12 minutes. Remove from heat and stir in sesame seeds. Serve at once.

MILKWEED WITH CORN AND TOMATOES

Serves 4

2 cups Milkweed buds, shoots (in 2 inch pieces), or pods
4 Tbsp. butter
$1^1/_2$ cup chopped onion
1 green pepper, seeded and chopped
2 cups canned Italian plum tomatoes
2 cups fresh corn kernels or drained whole kernel corn
Salt and pepper to taste

Cook Milkweed in salted water for 10 minutes. Drain and rinse. Add fresh water to Milkweed and simmer for 5 minutes. Drain and rinse.

Sauté onion in butter 3 to 4 minutes; add Milkweed, green pepper, and tomatoes and cook 20 minutes. Add corn and season to taste with salt and pepper. Serve in heated dish.

MILKWEED PIE

Serves 6

Baked 9 inch pie shell
4 cups Milkweed buds
3 Tbsp. butter
3 Tbsp. flour
1 cup milk
1 chicken bouillon cube
$1/4$ cup minced onion
Salt and pepper to taste
4 hard-cooked eggs
$1/2$ cup grated sharp Cheddar cheese

Cook Milkweed buds in boiling salted water 5 minutes. Drain and rinse well. Again cook in boiling salted water 5 minutes. Drain and rinse. Melt butter; blend in flour. Add milk and cook, stirring constantly, until mixture bubbles and is thickened. Add bouillon cube, onion, salt, and pepper. Stir until bouillon cube is dissolved. Remove from heat and add Milkweed buds. Chop 3 eggs and add to creamed mixture. Turn into baked pie shell. Sprinkle with grated cheese. Bake at 350°F for 7 to 10 minutes, or until cheese melts. Remove from oven. Cut remaining egg into 6 wedges; arrange on center of pie, petal-fashioned. Serve at once.

MILKWEED SHOOTS IN MUSTARD SAUCE

Serves 4

1 lb. Milkweed shoots, in 4 inch lengths
2 Tbsp. butter
1 Tbsp. flour
1 Tbsp. Dijon-style mustard
1 cup milk
$1^1/2$ tsp. freshly squeezed lemon juice

Simmer shoots in water to cover for 10 minutes. Drain and rinse. Return shoots to pan with 1 cup salted water and simmer for 10 minutes longer. Meanwhile melt butter in small skillet. Stir in flour and mustard and cook until thickened. Remove from heat and add lemon juice. Serve sauce over drained Milkweed shoots.

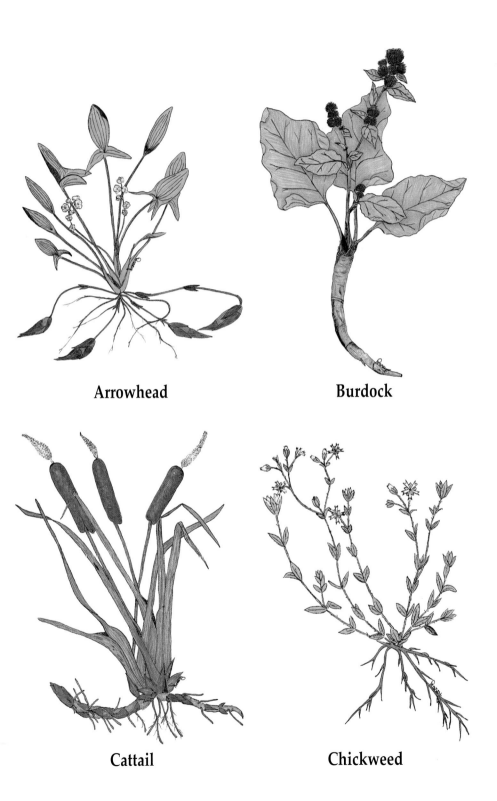

Arrowhead

Burdock

Cattail

Chickweed

Chokecherry

Dandelion

Elderberry

Fiddlehead

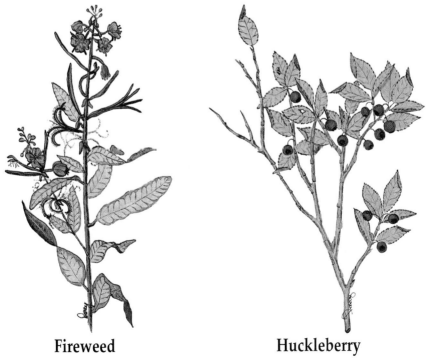

Fireweed　　　　　　　　**Huckleberry**

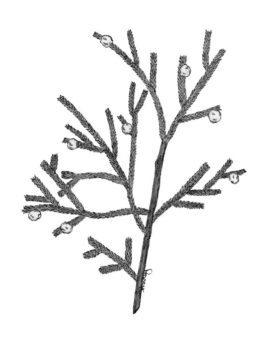

Juniper

Lamb's Quarters

Milkweed

Miner's Lettuce

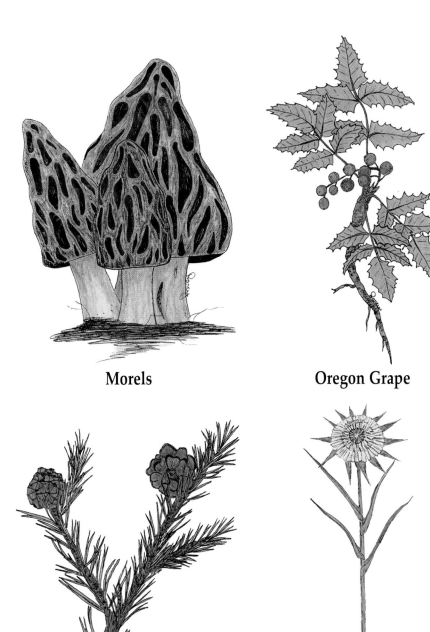

Morels

Oregon Grape

Pinon Pine

Salsify

Serviceberry

Stinging Nettle

Sheep Sorrel

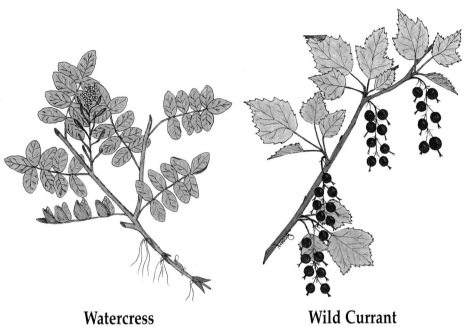

Watercress

Wild Currant

Wild Gooseberry

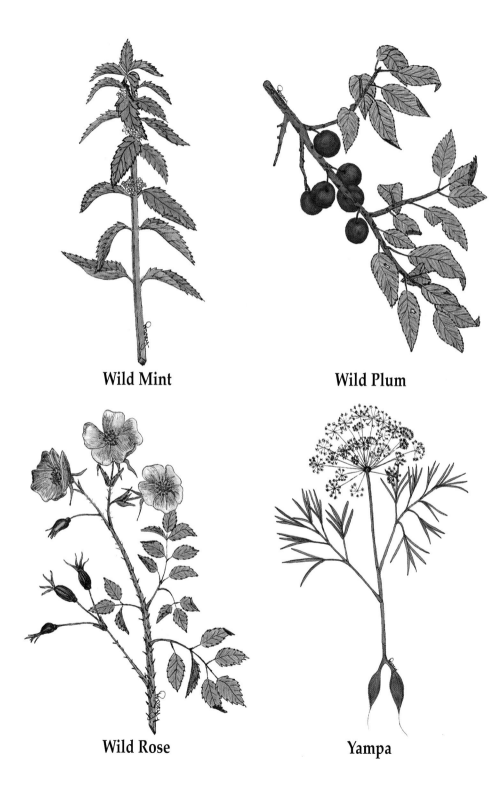

Wild Mint

Wild Plum

Wild Rose

Yampa

MILKWEED TEMPURA WITH GINGER SAUCE

1¹/₂ lbs. Milkweed buds, picked just as they begin to show pink
  1 cup all-purpose flour
1¹/₂ Tbsp. cornstarch
  1 egg yolk
 ¹/₂ tsp. rice vinegar
  1 cup water
   Vegetable oil for deep-frying

Sauce:
  1 cup chicken broth
  2 Tbsp. soy sauce
  1 Tbsp. honey
  1 tsp. freshly grated gingerroot
  1 Tbsp. sherry
  2 tsp. cornstarch

With wire whisk beat together flour, cornstarch, yolk, vinegar, and water. Heat oil to 325°F. Dip Milkweed buds in batter and deep-fry until golden brown. Make sauce of broth, soy, honey, ginger, sherry, and cornstarch, by heating together in saucepan until thickened.

SAUTEED MILKWEED

Serves 4

1¹/₂ lbs. Milkweed shoots, buds or pods
1 green pepper, seeded and cut into julienne strips
1 red pepper, seeded and cut into julienne strips
2 cloves garlic, crushed
¹/₂ cup olive oil
¹/₂ tsp. salt
1¹/₂ Tbsp. freshly squeezed lime juice

Cook Milkweed in two changes of water for 10 minutes each. Drain well and pat dry. Heat olive oil in skillet and add Milkweed, peppers, and garlic. Cover and let steam for 10 to 12 minutes. Add salt and lime juice; heat through, then serve at once.

Chapter 14

MINER'S LETTUCE

(Montia perfoliata)

Also known as Naiad spring beauty,
winter purslane, Indian lettuce, and Spanish lettuce.

This succulent native North American member of the purslane family has been introduced into Europe where it is cultivated under the name of winter purslane. It was also introduced into Cuba as a cultivated plant. In both foreign environments this North American plant escaped from the fields and naturalized in the wilds. An odd and dainty plant, Miner's Lettuce grows larger and coarser when cultivated.

Miner's Lettuce starts as a whirl of basal leaves through which several stems push their way upward four to eight inches. The fleshy basal leaves vary greatly in shape. Some are narrow while others are nearly round. Approximately two-thirds of the way up, each of its several stems grows a single pair of leaves so united as to form a disk or cup, completely encircling the stem. Above this, on a continuation of the stem, are clusters of pink or white flowers. Each flower has two sepals and usually five petals ranging from one-eighth to one-quarter of an inch long. Small shiny black seeds develop from the blossoms.

Miner's Lettuce prefers moist stream banks, slopes, and partially shaded areas. It thrives during the spring months when weather is cool and moist. During the summer, heat dehydrates the plants and they most often perish unless they happen to be growing along shaded stream banks.

Miner's Lettuce was a well-known native food to the Rocky Mountain Indians and early settlers. Because it is high in vitamin C, the plant has been accredited with preventing scurvy among the miners during the California gold rush—hence its name, Miner's Lettuce. Aside from using the plant as a food source, Native Americans made a strong tea of the fresh herb and drank it as a remedy for constipation.

The ideal time to collect Miner's Lettuce is during th early spring while the plant is abundant. Stems, leaves and newly formed flowers all make a refreshing salad green. They can also be cooked as a potherb.

GREEN RICE

Serves 6

3 cups cooked rice
2 cups chopped Miner's Lettuce
2 eggs, well beaten
1 cup milk
2 tsp. Worcestershire sauce
$^1/_2$ tsp. salt
1 Tbsp. grated onion
$^1/_4$ cup butter
$^1/_2$ cup sharp grated Cheddar cheese

Toss rice with Miner's Lettuce. Add eggs, milk, Worcestershire, salt, and onion. Toss gently to mix. Pour into buttered 2 quart baking dish and sprinkle cheese on top. Bake at 325°F for 35 minutes.

MINER'S LETTUCE WITH CELERY SEED DRESSING

Serves 6

8 cups Miner's Lettuce
1 small can mandarin oranges
1 ripe avocado, diced
$^1/_3$ cup honey
$1^1/_2$ tsp. dry mustard
$^1/_2$ tsp. salt
1 Tbsp. celery seed
2 Tbsp. grated onion
$^1/_4$ cup white wine vinegar
$^3/_4$ cup olive oil

Combine Miner's Lettuce, mandarin oranges, and avocado in serving bowl. Chill. Blend remaining ingredients in food processor; serve with chilled salad.

MINER'S LETTUCE–MUSHROOM SALAD

Serves 4

2 cups Miner's Lettuce
2 cups sliced fresh mushrooms
$^1/_2$ cup sliced radishes
$^1/_2$ cup sliced green onions
$^1/_4$ tsp. dry mustard
$^1/_4$ tsp. salt
    Dash cayenne pepper
$^1/_4$ tsp. paprika
$^1/_4$ tsp. honey
1 small clove garlic, crushed
2 Tbsp. fresh lemon juice
$^1/_4$ cup safflower oil

Combine Miner's Lettuce, mushrooms, radishes, and onions. Chill. Combine remaining ingredients in jar and shake well. Pour over salad just prior to serving.

MINER'S LETTUCE–ROAST BEEF SALAD

Serves 2

1 cup cooked cold roast beef, cubed
2 hard-cooked eggs, sliced
1 cup cherry tomatoes, halved
4 anchovy fillets, minced
4 cups Miner's Lettuce, in bite-sized pieces
    French salad dressing
    Miner's Lettuce for lining salad plates

Mix together beef, eggs, tomatoes, and anchovies. Place on salad plates lined with crisped Miner's Lettuce. Serve with French dressing.

Miner's Lettuce Salad

Serves 4

  6 cups Miner's Lettuce
 1/2 cup grated Monterey Jack cheese
  2 hard-cooked eggs, grated
 1/4 cup sliced water chestnuts
 1/4 cup olive oil
 1/4 cup fresh lime juice
1 1/2 tsp. honey
  1 tsp. salt
  1 clove garlic, crushed
 1/4 tsp. freshly ground pepper

Mix Miner's Lettuce, cheese, eggs, and water chestnuts in serving bowl. Chill. In food processor blend remaining ingredients. Just prior to serving toss salad with dressing.

Miner's Lettuce Salad with Peanuts

Serves 4

  8 cups torn Miner's Lettuce
  1 medium cucumber, thinly sliced
1 1/2 cups dry roasted peanuts
 1/4 cup cider vinegar
  3 Tbsp. minced Wild Mint
  1 cup olive oil
  1 Tbsp. minced chives
 1/2 tsp. salt
 1/4 tsp. pepper

In bowl, toss together Miner's Lettuce and peanuts. Chill. Mix remaining ingredients in jar and shake vigorously; add cucumber and marinate, refrigerated, for at least 1 hour. Just before serving, toss cucumbers with Miner's Lettuce and peanuts, dressing salad with desired amount of marinade mixture.

Miner's Lettuce with Spicy Lime Dressing

Serves 8

12 cups Miner's Lettuce
$1/3$ cup fresh lime juice
 2 cloves garlic, minced
$1/8$ tsp. ground cardamom
$1/2$ tsp. ground cumin
$1/2$ tsp. dry mustard
$1/2$ tsp. paprika
 1 tsp. honey
$2/3$ cup olive oil
$1/4$ cup minced cilantro

Put Miner's Lettuce in serving bowl and chill. Combine remaining ingredients and beat until well blended. Pour over Miner's Lettuce and toss.

Miner's Lettuce Spring Mold

Serves 6

 2 cups chopped Miner's Lettuce
 3 oz. pkg. lemon-flavored gelatin
 1 cup boiling water
$1/2$ cup cold water
 3 Tbsp. fresh lime juice
$1/2$ cup mayonnaise
$1/2$ cup diced celery
$1/2$ cup small curd cottage cheese
    Dash salt
 2 Tbsp. minced Watercress
 2 Tbsp. minced cilantro
    Miner's Lettuce

Dissolve gelatin in hot water. Add cold water and mayonnaise and beat well. Chill until gelatin begins to set. With electric mixer whip gelatin. Mix together remaining ingredients and fold into gelatin. Spoon into lightly oiled mold and chill until firm. Unmold on bed of Miner's Lettuce.

MINER'S LETTUCE AND TOMATO SALAD

Serves 4

3 cups fresh Miner's Lettuce, torn
4 ripe tomatoes, chopped
4 green onions, sliced
1 ripe avocado, peeled and mashed
1 Tbsp. freshly squeezed lime juice
$^1/_4$ cup mayonnaise
$^1/_4$ tsp. vegetable salt
   Dash pepper
$^1/_2$ tsp. chili powder
$^1/_4$ tsp. cumin seed
1 clove garlic, crushed
   Dash cayenne pepper

Toss together Miner's Lettuce, tomatoes, and onions. Combine remaining ingredients and blend until smooth. Add dressing to salad just prior to serving.

MINER'S LETTUCE–YOGURT SALAD

Serves 4

$1^1/_2$ lbs. torn Miner's Lettuce leaves
$^2/_3$ cup minced onion
1 Tbsp. olive oil
2 cups yogurt
$^1/_4$ tsp. salt
$^1/_4$ tsp. pepper
2 cloves garlic, crushed
2 tsp. chopped Wild Mint
2 Tbsp. chopped roasted cashews

Combine Miner's Lettuce with onion. Heat oil in skillet. Add Miner's Lettuce–onion mixture and cook until Miner's Lettuce wilts. Remove from heat and cool. Add yogurt, salt, pepper, and garlic. Top with Wild Mint and cashews.

Chapter
15

MOREL MUSHROOMS
(Morchella angusticeps, spp.)
Also known as
black Morel, sponge mushroom, and pine cone mushroom.

Morels are fleshy mushrooms in the class *Ascomycetes,* the sac fungi. These prized culinary delicacies are the best known wild mushrooms in Europe and the United States. Gathering Morels for food, as with any wild fungi, can be dangerous. They are easy to identify, but it is best for the novice to go Morel hunting with someone who has knowledge of them. Though Morels contain niacin and vitamin D, plus traces of several important minerals, including sodium, calcium, and iron, they are not very digestible and should not be eaten raw or in large quantities. It is also inadvisable to eat Morels or other wild mushrooms while consuming more than a moderate amount of alcoholic beverages since stomach upset may occur.

The edible and choice Morel features cone shaped heads consisting of pits which vary from oval to elongated. When young the whole head is grayish to tan, but the ridges and eventually the whole head becomes black. The honey-combed cap is three-quarters to one and five-eighths inches wide and three-quarters to two inches high. The buff colored stalk has an elastic texture and hollow center. The stalk is two to four inches long and three-quarters to one and five-eighths inches thick. There is no free margin of the head to hang down as a skirt. Since there is no veil or vulva, the spores are borne on the exposed surface of the cap.

Morcella angusticeps is often the first true Morel to appear in the spring, usually late April through May. It closely resembles other excellent varieties, *M. elata* and *M. conica.* In regions with cold winters Morels develop slowly, taking several weeks to attain full size. As a result, the Morel season can span a couple of months or longer, moving up in elevation as the snow melts.

Morels are located among mountain conifers, in recently logged or burned areas, on hillsides, and along hiking trails. They are very abundant over the forested areas of the Rocky Mountain region and are by far the most popular edible fungi of the snowbank mushroom flora.

Look for Morels when the Lady Slippers begin to bloom and the Trilliums have begun to turn from white to pink. They blend well with their surroundings and it takes experience to spot them regularly. When gathering Morels, avoid all that appear unusually soft to the touch or those which have brownish colored stems since these are signs of over maturity. Small white worms often infest older mushrooms, but if the flesh is still firm the Morels can be salvaged. Soaking them in salted, cold water for a couple of hours will destroy these pests. Morels should be cut at ground level with a sharp knife, rather than be pulled from the ground since this action destroys some of the mycelia that could have continued producing mushrooms for a number of years.

Morels may be dried, frozen, or canned; drying being the preferred method of preserving. The best way that I have found for drying wild mushrooms is to string the whole or halved mushrooms with a darning needle and heavy thread. Tie ends together and hang them in a warm dry area for three to five days. Since mushrooms are ninety percent water, a great deal of shrinkage will occur. Keep dried Morels in air tight containers until you are ready to use them in soups, stews, or casseroles.

BAKED MORELS WITH SOUR CREAM

Serves 4

    2 Tbsp. butter
    2 Tbsp. flour
    2 cups milk, scalded
 1$^1/_2$ lbs. Morels, halved lengthwise
    1 small can minced pimento
    2 tsp. Dijon-style mustard
    2 cups sour cream
 $^1/_2$ cup dry bread crumbs
       Salt to taste

Cook Morels in dry skillet 10 minutes; drain and set aside. Melt butter in saucepan over low heat. Stir in flour. Slowly add scalded milk, stirring carefully until thickened. Add Morels and salt and cook slowly 5 minutes. Stir in mustard, half the pimento, and sour cream. Pour into buttered casserole dish, cover with crumbs, and dot with remaining pimento. Bake at 325°F for 20 minutes.

CHICKEN WITH MOREL MUSHROOM SOUP

Serves 4

8 chicken backs
$^1/_2$ cup chopped celery leaves
1 onion, chopped
$1^1/_2$ quarts water
$^1/_2$ tsp. salt
1 lb. Morel Mushrooms, halved
3 Tbsp. butter
3 Tbsp. flour
$^1/_4$ cup sherry
1 cup cream

In kettle simmer chicken, celery, onion, and water, uncovered, 2 hours. Strain, discarding onion and celery. Set backs aside. Sauté Morels in butter 10 minutes. Remove mushrooms and set aside. Slowly add flour to pan drippings. Add broth, a small amount at a time. Cook until smooth and thickened. Skin chicken backs and dice meat into soup; add mushrooms, sherry, and cream. Serve at once.

DRIED MORELS AND RICE

Serves 4

$1^1/_2$ cups white rice
1 cup dried Morels
$^1/_2$ cup butter
$^1/_4$ cup olive oil
2 cloves crushed garlic
2 shallots, chopped fine
2 cups rich chicken broth
1 cup water
$1^1/_4$ cups dry white wine
Salt and pepper to taste

Soak Morels in hot water 20 minutes. Drain and chop. Sauté garlic, onion and mushrooms in 2 tablespoons butter and $^1/_4$ cup olive oil for 5 minutes. Add chicken broth and rice and cook over low heat, uncovered, for 45 minutes, stirring occasionally and adding water as needed. Add remaining water and wine, then cover. Reduce heat to simmer and allow to stand 30 minutes without stirring. Add remaining butter then salt and pepper to taste.

CREAMED MORELS AND OYSTERS

Serves 4

1 cup fresh oysters
$^1/_3$ cup melted butter
3 Tbsp. flour
2 cups Morels, halved
$1^1/_2$ cups cream
2 egg yolks, slightly beaten
Salt to taste
1 tsp. onion juice
1 tsp. freshly squeezed lime juice

Drain liquid from oysters and reserve. Heat oysters in skillet until edges begin to curl. Set aside. Place oyster liquid in pan along with lime and onion juice; add cream. Stir together.

Melt 3 Tbsp. butter in saucepan; slowly stir in flour. Add cream mixture, a little at a time, stirring and cooking over low heat until thickened. Add yolks all at once, stirring continuously.

Cook morels in dry skillet over high heat for a few minutes. Drain liquid. Add remaining butter and sauté 5 minutes. Add to sauce along with oysters and salt to taste. Cook slowly over low heat until heated through. Serve over toast, noodles, or baked potatoes.

CRAB STUFFED MORELS

12 appetizers

12 large Morels
1 sweet onion, finely chopped
3 Tbsp. butter
1 Tbsp. flour
$^1/_2$ cup crab meat
2 Tbsp. sherry
1 Tbsp. chopped parsley
Salt and pepper to taste

Sauté onion in butter until soft. Mix together flour and sherry, then stir into butter mixture. Stir in parsley, salt, and pepper. Carefully stir in crab meat. Stuff Morels with mixture and place on oiled baking sheet. Bake at 350°F for 15 minutes. Serve at once.

FETTUCCINE WITH MORELS

Serves 5 to 6

$^1/_2$ cup butter

$1^1/_2$ cup cream

1 lb. Morels

$^2/_3$ cup freshly grated Parmesan cheese

Salt and pepper to taste

1 lb. cooked fettuccine

Cook Morels in dry skillet over high heat two to three minutes. Drain liquid. Set mushrooms aside. Melt 2 Tbsp. butter over moderate heat, add cream and salt and pepper to taste. Bring to boil. Add Morels and simmer, covered, 10 minutes. Stir in Parmesan and toss with warm fettuccine.

MOREL FRITTERS

Serves 4

2 cups chopped Morels

2 Tbsp. butter

$^1/_2$ cup flour

$^1/_2$ tsp. baking powder

1 egg, beaten

$^1/_2$ cup milk

Salt and pepper to taste

Oil for deep-frying

In skillet sauté mushrooms in butter 10 minutes. Drain. Mix remaining ingredients, except oil. Add to sautéed mushrooms. Drop by spoonfuls into hot cooking oil (325°F) and fry until golden brown. Drain on paper towels and serve at once.

MOREL PATE

Serves 12

$^1/_2$ cup butter
1 cup finely chopped green onion
1 cup chopped sweet onion
1 cup chopped celery
1 Tbsp. chopped garlic
2 lbs. Morels, thinly sliced
2 Tbsp. dried sweet basil, crumbled
1 tsp. salt
$^1/_2$ tsp. freshly ground pepper
12 oz. softened cream cheese, cut into cubes
$^3/_4$ cup fresh sour dough bread crumbs
3 eggs, lightly beaten
2 cups Piñon nuts, toasted
Crackers

In large skillet sauté green onion, onion, celery, and garlic in butter until vegetables are softened and golden. In separate skillet cook Morels over high heat 5 minutes. Drain liquid. Add mushrooms to onion mixture along with basil, salt, and pepper. Cook, stirring occasionally, until liquid has evaporated. Stir in cream cheese, stirring until mixture is well combined. Remove from heat and cool slightly.

In food processor purée mixture (in two batches) until smooth. Add bread crumbs and eggs and purée until smooth. Stir in Piñon nuts. Pour into buttered glass 9x5x2$^1/_2$ inch pan, wrap completely with waxed paper and then foil; bake in preheated 350°F oven for 1$^1/_2$ hours. Cool in oven then refrigerate, unwrapped, overnight. Loosen paté and invert onto serving dish.

Morel, Piñon, and Currant Stuffing

Stuffs a 12 to 14 lb. turkey

  2   cups minced onion
1¹/₂ cups chopped celery
 ¹/₂ cup butter
1¹/₂ lbs. Morels, sliced lengthwise
 ¹/₂ cup dried Wild Currants
  1   tsp. crumbled dried sage
  1   tsp. crushed Juniper berries
 ¹/₂ cup toasted Piñon nuts
 10   slices white bread cut into ¹/₂ inch cubes and toasted

In large skillet cook onion and celery in butter until vegetables are softened. Add Morels and cook until tender, stirring occasionally, and until all but ¹/₂ cup liquid is evaporated. Stir in Currants, sage, and Juniper. Add salt and pepper to taste and cook mixture, stirring, for 1 minute. Transfer mixture into large bowl and add Piñon nuts and toasted bread. Toss to mix, then stuff turkey.

Morel Stuffed Lamb Chops

Serves 6

  6   thick lamb chops, with pockets cut
  1   lb. Morel mushrooms, quartered
 ¹/₂ cup butter
  4   green onions, finely chopped
      Salt and freshly ground pepper to taste

In dry skillet cook mushrooms over high heat until liquid has cooked out. Drain liquid, reserving for later use in soup or gravy. Add butter and cook until mushrooms begin to brown. Add green onions and cook a few minutes longer. Salt and pepper to taste. Stuff chops with mushroom mixture and broil 6 inches from heat, turning several times, until chops reach preferred doneness.

RICOTTA STUFFED CHICKEN BREASTS WITH MOREL SAUCE

Serves 4

- 4 whole chicken breasts, boned and halved
- 2 cups Ricotta cheese
- $1/4$ cup finely chopped fresh basil
- $1/2$ cup olive oil
- $1/4$ cup butter

Sauce:

- 1 lb. Morels, sliced
- $1/2$ cup butter
- 2 cloves garlic, minced
- $1^1/2$ Tbsp. flour
- $1^1/2$ cups Morel cooking liquid
  Salt and pepper to taste

With meat mallet or tenderizer, pound chicken breasts until flattened. Mix basil with Ricotta and place $1/2$ cupful on half of chicken breasts. Top with another breast and pound edges together; tuck edges under. Repeat with remaining breasts. Sauté breasts in skillet in mixture of olive oil and butter for 20 to 25 minutes, browning both sides. Meanwhile prepare sauce.

Put Morels in dry skillet and cook on medium-high heat until liquid has cooked out. Pour liquid off, reserving $1^1/2$ cups. Remove Morels to platter. Melt butter in skillet and add Morels and garlic. Sauté until mushrooms are lightly browned. Sprinkle flour over mushrooms, then stir in reserved liquid. Cook until thickened. Serve over browned breasts.

SAUTEED MORELS WITH PIÑON NUTS

Serves 4

- 3 Tbsp. olive oil
- 1 cup minced onion
- 1 lb. Morels, sliced lengthwise
- $1^1/2$ cup Piñon nuts
  Salt and pepper to taste

Sauté onion and Morels in oil 10 minutes over moderately-high heat. Drain. Add Piñon nuts and seasonings; heat. Serve at once.

ROTELLE WITH MOREL SAUCE

Serves 4

1 cup finely chopped onion
2 Tbsp. butter
$1^1/_2$ lbs. Morels, thinly sliced
2 tsp. Worcestershire sauce
$^1/_2$ cup cream
1 Tbsp. fresh lemon juice
1 lb. rotelle pasta
$^1/_2$ cup minced fresh basil leaves

Cook onion in butter until softened; add Morels and cook, stirring occasionally, until liquid has evaporated from the Morels and they are browned lightly. Stir in Worcestershire sauce, cream, and lemon juice. Cook for 2 to 3 minutes then season to taste with salt and pepper.

Cook rotelle in pot of salted water until pasta is *al dente*. Reserve 1 cup cooking water and drain the pasta well. Transfer to large bowl and add the Morel mixture and basil. Toss mixture, adding enough reserved cooking liquid to thin sauce to desired consistency. Serve at once.

SUN-DRIED MORELS IN OLIVE OIL

Cut large Morels in half, leave smaller mushrooms whole. Place on screen and dry in sun. If nights are cool, bring screens indoors at night. When mushrooms are dried (three to five days depending on temperatures) blanch quickly in boiling water and drain well. Pack in sterilized jars. Add a clove of garlic to each jar and fill to $^1/_2$ inch from top of jar with a fine quality olive oil. Adjust lids and seal in boiling water bath for 15 minutes.

WILD RICE AND MOREL SOUP

Serves 4

6 oz. box wild rice
3 onions, finely chopped
$1^1/_2$ cups dried Morels
2 quarts beef broth
Salt and pepper to taste

Pour boiling water over rice and allow to stand overnight. Pour off water the following morning and rinse under cool water. Soak Morels in warm water 20 minutes then chop into coarse pieces. Combine with rice and remaining ingredients in soup pot and bring to a boil. Reduce heat and simmer gently $1^1/_2$ hours.

CHAPTER
16

OREGON GRAPE

(Mahonia repens)

Also known as Rocky Mountain grape,
holly-leaved barberry, creeping barberry, and trailing mahonia.

Oregon Grape is not a grape, but a member of the barberry family, though the ripe fruits resemble small grapes. There are more than one hundred species of *Mahonia*. The genus was named to honor Bernard M. Mahon, a distinguished early American horticulturist of Philadelphia who died in 1816.

This hardy low growing perennial, which seldom exceeds a foot high, blooms from late April into May—two to three weeks after the snow leaves the foothills. The blossoms are in fragrant, bright yellow clusters that form on the ends of the leaf covered stems. The flowers are approximately one-half inch wide with six sepals, and six stamens lying against the petals.

The pinnately compound leaves resemble holly, complete with ten or more spiny teeth on the edges of each of the five to nine leaflets. If exposed to a lot of sunlight the thick, leathery leaves are tinged with red; those growing in the shade have a deep green color. The leaves oxidize to glowing crimson and golden yellow in the autumn.

The pea-sized dark blue berries, which ripen in early September, have a powdery blush and grow in clusters of three to ten. The fruit has a slightly bitter but not unappetizing taste. The vitamin C–rich berries make excellent jelly, wine, and flavoring for soup. Oregon Grape jelly is a gourmet condiment to use with meats, particularly game. The fruit rarely goes to waste since it is a favorite snack for a variety of wildlife.

The main stems of the Oregon Grape seldom rise more than an inch or two and are actually above ground extensions of the many slender, creeping roots that form interconnected colonies. The irregular, knotty rootstock has a brownish bark with yellow wood underneath. This wood makes an excellent dye.

The bitter tasting root is one of our most versatile Rocky Mountain herbs. Native American medicine men and women not only used the dried rootstock as a dye, but also to cure a wide variety of ailments including ulcers, heartburn, rheumatism, kidney disorders, and skin conditions. Early settlers learned of the root's healing powers from the Indians and its popularity as a medicine boomed in the 1800s. It was listed in official pharmacopoeias until 1950.

Look for Oregon Grape growing on slopes in pine mulch and loose, rocky outcroppings. It prefers ponderosa to lodgepole stands.

To prepare Oregon Grape juice for use in recipes add one cup of water per one pound of stemmed berries in a large kettle. Simmer over medium-high heat until the berries break open and juice begins to flow. Pour the mixture into a jelly bag or strain through several layers of cheesecloth, squeezing out excess juice and discarding solids. The juice may be frozen or bottled for later use.

FROSTED OREGON GRAPE COOLER

4 tall drinks

2   cups French vanilla ice cream
1   cup lemon sherbet
2   cups Oregon Grape juice
2   cups ginger ale

Whirl ice cream, sherbet, and Oregon Grape juice in blender until just blended. Stir in ginger ale and pour into chilled glasses.

OATMEAL PANCAKES WITH OREGON GRAPE SYRUP

Serves 4

Syrup:

1   lb. Oregon Grapes
1   cup water
$1^1/_4$ cups sugar
$^3/_4$ cup light corn syrup

Pancakes:

2   cups old-fashioned rolled oats
$^1/_2$ cup whole wheat flour
$^1/_3$ cup sugar
1   tsp. baking powder
1   tsp. baking soda
2   cups buttermilk
2   eggs
    Oil for griddle

In heavy saucepan combine Oregon Grapes and water. Simmer, stirring occasionally, for 20 minutes. Strain mixture through several layers of cheesecloth, squeezing hard on the solids to extract all the juice. Combine juice with sugar and corn syrup and simmer 3 to 5 minutes. Cool slightly before serving.

In large bowl mix together oats, flour, sugar, baking powder, and soda. Whisk eggs into buttermilk, then whisk into dry ingredients until well mixed. Allow to stand at room temperature for 1 hour. Cook on hot, lightly oiled griddle. Serve with warm syrup.

OREGON GRAPE FREEZER JAM

4 cups sieved Oregon Grapes
$^1/_2$ cup water
6$^1/_2$ cups sugar
1 pkg. pectin
1 cup water

Add $^1/_2$ cup water to Oregon Grapes and simmer for 10 minutes. Add sugar and stir well. Bring 1 cup water to boiling and add pectin. Boil hard 1 minute. Stir pectin mixture into berry mixture until all is well combined. Allow to stand for two days at room temperature then spoon into sterilized jars, leaving $^1/_2$ inch head space and freeze.

OREGON GRAPE GLAZE

for ham, pork, or poultry

$^1/_2$ cup catsup
$^1/_2$ cup Oregon Grape juice
3 drops hot pepper sauce
2 Tbsp. grated onion
2 Tbsp. melted butter
$^1/_4$ cup honey
2 tsp. freshly squeezed lemon juice
2 tsp. dry mustard

Combine all ingredients, blending well. Brush on meat last 20 minutes of baking or grilling time.

OREGON GRAPE JELLY

      4 lbs. Oregon Grapes
      1 cup water
    $^1/_4$ cup fresh lime juice
      1 pkg. pectin
    $4^1/_2$ cups sugar

Wash and crush Oregon Grapes. Add 1 cup water and simmer, covered for 15 to 20 minutes. Pour into jelly bag or old pillow case and squeeze out juice. Measure 3-$^1/_2$ cups juice and put in kettle. Add lime juice and pectin; boil hard 1 minute. Add sugar and boil hard 2 minutes. Ladle into sterilized jars, adjust lids, and process in boiling water bath for 7 minutes.

OREGON GRAPE ICE CREAM

      4 eggs
    $2^1/_2$ cups sugar
      4 cups Oregon Grape juice
      2 cups heavy cream
      1 pint whipping cream
      1 pint half and half
      1 tsp. almond extract

Beat eggs until light. Add heavy cream to eggs, then beat in sugar. Add whipping cream. Cook over double boiler until thickened; or cook on high in microwave for 5 minutes, stir well and cook for 5 minutes longer. Add Oregon Grape juice and half and half, mixing well. Freeze in ice cream freezer following manufacturer's directions.

OREGON GRAPE LIQUEUR

2 pints

4 cups ripe Oregon Grapes, stemmed
1 fifth of vodka
3 cups sugar
1 cup water

Mash berries slightly, put in gallon jug or bottle and pour vodka over berries. Cover and allow to stand 1 month. Siphon clear liquid into large bowl. Combine water and sugar in saucepan. Bring to boiling. Boil hard for 1 minute. Cool completely. Stir sugar syrup into Oregon Grape liquid. Pour into pint bottles and cap or cork securely (there should be a generous glass leftover for yourself!).

OREGON GRAPE SHERBET

3 cups Oregon Grape juice
2 cups sugar
$^1/_2$ cup freshly squeezed lime juice
   Dash salt
1 egg white

Boil together Oregon Grape juice and sugar for 5 minutes. Cool. Add lime juice. Freeze in ice cream freezer following manufacturer's directions. Meanwhile beat egg white until soft peaks form; add dash of salt. When sherbet begins to turn mushy, add white and continue freezing until firm.

OREGON GRAPE VINEGAR

3 pints

2 cups Oregon Grape juice
$^1/_2$ cup sugar
4 cups white vinegar
$2^1/_2$ cups dry white wine

Combine juice and sugar and bring to a boil. Reduce heat and simmer 3 minutes. Cool. Combine with vinegar and wine. Allow to stand overnight. Bring mixture to boiling and boil, uncovered, 4 minutes. Cover and cool completely. Strain through several layers of cheesecloth. Pour into decorative bottles and seal. Store in dark place. Keeps up to 3 years.

CHAPTER
17

PIÑON PINE

(Pinus edulis)

Also known as
Colorado Piñon pine, two–leaf Piñon and Rocky Mountain nut pine.

The seeds, or nuts, of the Piñon are a well-known food source containing sixty to sixty-two percent fat; also carbohydrates, protein and small amounts of phosphorus, iron, niacin, and thiamine. One pound of nuts contains approximately 3,000 calories. Male members of some Native American tribes would not allow their pregnant wives to eat the nuts since the weight gained often made delivery more difficult.

These small, bushy, resinous trees of the pine family grow fifteen to thirty feet high and are one to two feet in diameter. They have short trunks and compact, rounded, spreading crowns. The branches are low, often sweeping to the ground. Native Americans used Piñon ashes, derived from burning the green portion of these branches, mixed with meal made from wild grains. This mixture was then moistened with water and baked or fried.

The fragrant evergreen needles normally grow two to a bundle, though sometimes there are three or one. They are three-quarters to one and one-half inches long, stout and light green in color. The needles have good yields of vitamin A and C, making them an emergency source of antiscorbutic when brewed as a tea.

The bark is gray to reddish brown in color, rough and furrowed. As with all pines, the Piñon has a life-sustaining edible inner bark, or cambium, rich in vitamin C. The tender, fleshy, mucilaginous cambium is best cut from the south side of the trunk. When it has been scraped or sliced off it can be eaten raw, dried and ground into meal, or cooked during any time of the year as an emergency food. The Piñon flowers in the spring and coats everything with thick, yellow pollen. The pollen fertilizes the female stigmas of blossoms and the cones begin to form. These cones are edible when young. The woody, globular-shaped cones are approximately two inches in diameter. They are brownish-yellow in color, resinous and have thick, blunt cone scales. The cones mature the second year, producing large, slightly flattened, wingless, thick-walled seeds. The seeds ripen during the months of October and November developing on the scales of the cones. These seeds contain what are commonly referred to as Piñon "nuts."

Though the nuts were at one time an important Native American food source and remain a wild commercial crop in areas where they are abundant, the Piñon is not a dependable crop-producing tree. Only once in every seven to eight years is there a bumper crop in any one area. One can, however, make a fairly accurate estimate of the prospect for next years crop by observing the number of immature cones on the trees.

At one time Piñon nuts took the place of wheat for some Indian tribes. They were also devoured by a wide variety of wildlife including jays, deer, bear, and pack rats. Since there was such a demand for the high calorie food it often took considerable cunning to store enough away for the long winter months. Pack rats built elaborate nests of sticks and twigs and stored their gathered nuts in piles within the nests. Native Americans would often tear the pack rats' nests apart in search of the cache, frequently gleaning a quart or more per raid.

Aside from grinding the Piñon nuts into meal to be baked or cooked as porridge, Native Americans made oil from the nuts. They were shelled then put in a shallow container, covered with water and simmered over a slow fire for twenty-four hours. The liquid was then cooled and the oil was skimmed from the top of the water.

The modern day forager need not resort to raiding the nests of pack rats. There are two successful methods of gathering the nuts. One is to gather the unopened, brown cones; place them in a burlap sack and hang the sack in a warm place until the cones have fully opened. Shake the sack and scoop out the nuts which have fallen to the bottom. Second, in the autumn as cones are opening, spread a large canvas on the ground beneath the tree. Shake the tree to bring down the nuts.

Some of the nuts are aborted, leaving an empty seed. To separate the empty seeds from those which contain nuts, dump the crop in a bucket of water and stir vigorously. The seeds that remain floating can then be skimmed off and discarded.

After seven to eight months raw nuts begin to turn rancid. Roasting permits longer storage. To roast nuts place them in a cast iron skillet and shake over heat until a sampled nut has reached the desired consistency and taste. A simple method of shelling the Piñon nuts is to place them, warm from the skillet, between two damp dish towels. Roll vigorously with a rolling pin or a large bottle. Separate the nut meats from the shells.

Piñon pines are found at elevations of 4,000 to 7,500 feet, in the southern end of the Middle Rocky Mountains. They grow in large stands or are mixed with Juniper trees. Like the Juniper, Piñon grows on dry, rocky foothills, mesas, plateaus, and lower mountain slopes. Unfortunately, many of the stands that recently existed on public lands have been cut down by the Forest Service to encourage the growth of grasses to provide more grazing for cattle.

BRANDIED BLUE CHEESE–PIÑON SPREAD
2 cups

6 oz. Blue cheese, at room temperature
2 pkg. (16 oz. each) Cream cheese at room temperature
$^1/_3$ cup good quality brandy
$1^1/_2$ cups toasted Piñon nuts

Crumble Blue cheese. Combine with remaining ingredients and mix well. Pack into small crocks or decorative jars. Keeps up to 4 weeks refrigerated.

ESCAROLE SALAD WITH PIÑON NUTS
Serves 2

4 cups loosely packed, bite-sized pieces escarole
$^1/_4$ cup Piñon nuts
2 Tbsp. olive oil
1 lime, halved
2 Tbsp. minced fresh cilantro

Put escarole in salad bowl. In small skillet cook Piñon nuts in olive oil until nuts are golden. Drizzle nuts and oil over escarole. Toss. Squeeze lime juice over salad, season with salt and pepper, sprinkle with cilantro and toss again. Serve at once.

GOURMET CHEESE BALL WITH PIÑON

$^1/_4$ lb. Blue cheese, crumbled
1 tsp. dried celery leaves
2 tsp. dried chives
3 (8 oz. each) Cream cheese, softened
3 Tbsp. sherry
$^1/_2$ tsp. Worcestershire
$^1/_8$ tsp. garlic powder
$1^1/_2$ cups toasted Piñon nuts

Combine all ingredients, except Piñon nuts, in mixing bowl. Beat with electric mixer until smooth. Chill in refrigerator until mass is workable. Form into a ball. Wrap in plastic wrap and chill overnight.

Remove wrap. Press Piñon nuts onto surface of cheese ball.

GROUND LAMB KABOBS WITH PIÑON

Serves 4 to 5

2 lbs. ground lamb
2 crushed garlic cloves
1 cup Piñon nuts
$^1/_2$ cup chopped cilantro
$^1/_2$ tsp. salt
1 tsp. freshly ground pepper
$^1/_4$ cup dry bread crumbs
2 eggs

Mix ingredients well. Mold around skewers, brush with olive oil and broil over coals or in a broiling oven until medium rare. Great served in pita with cucumber–yogurt sauce or with broiled eggplant and tomatoes.

HUMMUS WITH PIÑON NUTS

4 cups

5 garlic cloves
$^1/_2$ tsp. salt
2 lbs. canned chick peas, drained and rinsed
$^1/_2$ cup tahini
$^1/_4$ cup fresh lime juice
$^1/_2$ cup olive oil
$^1/_4$ cup fresh parsley leaves
$^1/_4$ cup Piñon nuts, toasted
   Pita loaves, cut into eighths

Mash together garlic and salt to form a paste. Purée chick peas in food processor along with garlic paste, tahini, lime juice, $^1/_4$ cup olive oil, and $^1/_2$ cup water until hummus is smooth.

In cleaned food processor purée parsley with remaining olive oil. Put hummus in serving dish and drizzle parsley oil over top. Sprinkle with Piñon nuts. Serve hummus with wedges of pita.

LEBANESE LAMB AND RICE

Serves 4

1 lb. lamb, chopped
$^1/_2$ lb. cup butter
1 large onion, finely chopped
$^1/_4$ tsp. Chinese five spice
   Salt and pepper to taste
1 cup rice
4 Tbsp. butter
3 cups chicken broth
$^1/_2$ cup Piñon nuts

Sauté lamb and onion in $^1/_2$ cup butter, stirring occasionally until onion is golden. Add seasoning.

Sauté rice in 4 Tbsp. butter until golden, and add to lamb and onion. Add chicken broth, cover and cook over low heat until rice has absorbed all liquid. Toast Piñon nuts in dry skillet over medium-high heat until golden. Add to lamb mixture just before serving.

PIÑON–BLUE CORNMEAL GRIDDLE CAKES

12 4 inch griddle cakes

1 cup buttermilk
$^1/_4$ cup blue cornmeal
2 tsp. butter
$^3/_4$ cup all-purpose flour
$^1/_?$ cup Piñon nuts, toasted
1 tsp. honey
$1^1/_2$ tsp. baking powder
1 egg, beaten lightly
   Butter
   Honey or maple syrup

Combine buttermilk with 1 cup water and bring to boiling. Slowly stir in cornmeal. Whisk in butter and honey; remove from heat.

In bowl combine flour, Piñon nuts and baking powder, mixing to blend. Whisk in egg and milk mixture. Batter should be consistency of thick cream.

Bake batter, $^1/_4$ cupfuls per griddle cake, on lightly greased griddle until golden brown on underside. Turn and bake to a golden brown. Serve with butter and honey or syrup.

Piñon Brottorte

Serves 6

6 eggs, separated
1 cup sugar
1¹/₄ cup fine dry bread crumbs
1 tsp. baking powder
1 tsp. cinnamon
1 toasted ground Piñon nuts
¹/₄ cup lemon juice
1¹/₂ tsp. grated lemon rind

Sauce:
³/₄ cup dry sherry
3 whole cloves
2 cinnamon sticks
¹/₄ cup sugar

Beat egg yolks until thick and lemon-colored. Gradually beat in half the sugar. Combine other ingredients and fold into yolks. Beat whites until foamy, then slowly add other half of the sugar, beating until soft peaks form. Gently fold into yolk mixture, then turn into an 8 inch springform pan that has bottom buttered. Bake in preheated 350°F oven for 1 to 1¹/₄ hours. Mix remaining ingredients and simmer for a few minutes. Remove spices and pour sauce over hot cake. Cool before removing from pan.

Pesto

8 cloves garlic
³/₄ cup firmly packed chopped fresh basil
2 Tbsp. minced parsley
Dash salt
¹/₂ cup Piñon nuts, toasted
3 Tbsp. freshly grated Parmesan cheese
3 Tbsp. softened butter
3¹/₂ Tbsp olive oil
Spaghetti or homemade pasta

In food processor make paste of garlic, basil, parsley, salt, and Piñon nuts. Gradually add cheese, then blend mixture into butter and oil. Toss with freshly cooked spaghetti or pasta.

PIÑON-CRUSTED TROUT

Serves 4

$^1/_2$ cup roasted Piñon nuts, chopped
$1^1/_2$ Tbsp. sesame seeds, toasted
4 trout, heads and tails removed
$1^1/_2$ Tbsp. butter
2 cloves garlic, minced
$^1/_4$ cup olive oil

Combine Piñon nuts and sesame seeds in small bowl. Open trout (butterfly) and remove bones along spine. Melt butter and add garlic; brush flesh side of trout with mixture, then sprinkle with Piñon–sesame seed mixture, patting to help nuts and seeds to adhere. Chill trout, uncovered, for 30 minutes.

In heavy skillet heat 1 Tbsp. olive oil until hot and sauté each trout, coated side down, for two minutes, adding more oil as needed. Transfer each trout to an oiled baking sheet, coated sides up, and bake in preheated 400°F oven for 10 minutes or until trout just flakes.

PIÑON PIE

Serves 8

Pastry for 9 inch single crust pie
$1^1/_2$ cup toasted Piñon nuts
2 eggs
1 cup sorghum syrup
$^2/_3$ cup brown sugar
2 Tbsp. rum
2 Tbsp. butter

Line pie pan with pastry and crimp the edges. Sprinkle Piñon nuts over pastry. Beat eggs in mixing bowl, then stir in sorghum, sugar, and rum. Pour over Piñon nuts, then dot with butter. Bake in preheated 450°F oven for 10 minutes, reduce heat to 325°F and bake 30 to 35 minutes, or until filling is almost firm in the center. Cool.

PIÑON AND TANGELO FUDGE

1-1/2 lbs.

    2 cups sugar
    1 cup firmly packed brown sugar
 1¹/₄ cups evaporated milk
    2 tsp. freshly grated tangelo zest
    2 Tbsp. butter
  ¹/₂ tsp. pure vanilla extract
 1¹/₂ cups toasted Piñon nuts

In heavy saucepan stir together sugars and milk. Bring to boil over moderate heat, stirring until sugar dissolves and temperature reaches 239°F. Remove from heat and add zest and butter without stirring. Cool to 130°F (approximately 20 minutes). Add vanilla, then beat mixture with a wooden spoon until it begins to lose its gloss and thickens. Beat in Piñon nuts. Pour into a buttered 8 inch square pan and let cool until firm. Cut into squares.

PIÑON TARTS

24 small tarts

    3 eggs
 1¹/₂ cups sorghum
  ¹/₂ cup sugar
    2 Tbsp. flour
    2 Tbsp. butter, melted
    2 Tbsp. rum
  ¹/₄ tsp. vanilla
       Pastry for one 9 inch pie shell
    2 cups roasted Piñon nuts
       Piñon nuts for garnish

Beat eggs slightly. Blend in sorghum, sugar, flour, butter, rum, and vanilla. Roll pastry into 16x20 inch rectangle approximately ¹/₈ inch thick. Cut into 4 inch circles. Fit into 2¹/₂ inch muffin or tart pans, pressing out air bubbles. Sprinkle some Piñon nuts in each tart. Fill with egg–sorghum mixture. Sprinkle a few Piñon nuts on top of each tart. Bake in preheated 325°F oven for 50 minutes or until pastry is golden and filling is set. Cool. Remove from pans.

CHAPTER 18

SALSIFY

(Tragopogon porrifolius)
Also known as
noonday flower, Star of Jerusalem, oyster plant, and goat's beard.

This member of the sunflower family is native to Europe, Asia, and Africa. It's name, *Tragopogon,* came from the Greek word *tragos,* meaning goat, and *pogon,* which translates as beard. The Greek name probably originated from the appearance of the seed heads—fluffy, beard-like seeds bearing tufts resembling a giant dandelion blossom.

Salsify, a biennial and occasionally perennial, was introduced to North America by early colonists as a garden vegetable. The plant has been cultivated for 2,000 years in the Mediterranean. It remains widely cultivated in Europe and parts of the United States and is prized for its unusual flavor which is thought by some to resemble that of an oyster. In cultivation the roots become fairly large resembling those of parsnips, while in its naturalized state Salsify roots are quite small. This versatile vegetable can be substituted for potatoes and parsnips.

In their first year, Salsify leaves are clustered in a rosette at the top of the taproot. During the second year the slender, fleshy taproot produces a light green, hollow stem from one to three feet high, containing a bitter, milky juice. The alternate, grass-like, clasping leaves have curled margins and taper to long, pointed, backward-bending tips. The stem bears a solitary purpose flower head, about one and one-half to two inches in diameter, with ray flowers that unfold early in the morning and close at midday. Salsify blooms from June through September. The blossoms mature to fruits that are seedlike with slender projections bearing parachutes of fuzzy hairs at their tops. Because of the seed's ability to be airborne, Salsify can now be found throughout most of the United States naturalized in moderately dry soil along roadsides and in open fields.

The slender, fleshy taproots of the first year plants are those which are gathered for food, since the roots become unpalatable after the flower stems appear. The roots can be boiled, fried, baked, stewed, or made into soup. Wash and scrape the dug roots and place them in cold water. Add a small amount of lemon juice or vinegar to prevent discoloration. Change water once or twice during cooking to remove any bitterness. The roots may also be roasted in a slow oven until dark brown, ground and used as a coffee substitute. *Tragopogan dubius,* a yellow-flowering Salsify also common to the Rocky Mountains, is edible though its roots are smaller, tougher and more fibrous.

When the top of the root of the first year plant is cut off about three inches below ground level, the resulting leaf crown makes an excellent cooked vegetable rich in vitamins A and C.

FRENCH FRIED SALSIFY

Serves 4

2 lbs. Salsify root, peeled thinly with vegetable peeler and cut into
      3 inch lengths
2 tsp. vinegar
$^1/_2$ tsp. salt
2 peppercorns
1 cup flour
$^1/_2$ tsp. salt
$^2/_3$ cup milk
2 eggs, beaten
     Oil for deep-fat frying

Drop Salsify in cold water to cover. Add vinegar, $^1/_2$ tsp. salt, and peppercorns. Cook, covered, 20 minutes or until tender. Drain and pat dry with paper towels.

Beat together flour, salt, milk, and eggs until smooth batter is formed. Heat oil to 375°F. Dip Salsify in batter and deep-fry, a few at a time, until golden brown. Serve at once.

MOCK OYSTERS

Serves 4

2 lbs. Salsify root, peeled and cooked until tender
3 Tbsp. melted butter
3 lightly beaten eggs
     Salt and pepper
4 Tbsp. melted butter
3 Tbsp. olive oil

Purée cooked Salsify; add 3 Tbsp. butter and beaten eggs. Season with salt and pepper. Blend well. Combine 4 Tbsp. butter with olive oil and heat until bubbly. Drop spoonfuls of Salsify mixture into hot fat and brown on each side. Serve hot.

FRENCH PEASANT SOUP

Serves 12

        1 cup dried white navy beans
    $1^1/_4$ quart water
        8 slices bacon, chopped
        3 onions, sliced
        3 medium heads cabbage, shredded
        1 lb. Salsify root, peeled and cut into 1 inch lengths
        2 carrots, peeled and sliced
        2 leeks, thickly sliced
        4 cloves garlic, minced
        8 new red potatoes, cubed
    $2^1/_2$ quarts water
        2 tsp. salt
        1 tsp. coarsely ground pepper
     $^1/_4$ cup fresh thyme leaves
        1 lb. Polish, Italian, or French sausage

Bring $1^1/_4$ quarts water to boil; add beans and boil 2 minutes. Remove from heat, cover and let stand 1 hour. Simmer beans until tender, 1 to $1^1/_2$ hours.

Cook bacon and add to beans. Cook onions in bacon drippings until lightly browned. Add to beans along with drippings. Add remaining ingredients, except sausage and bring to boil; simmer covered 30 minutes. Add sausage and cook for 20 to 25 minutes longer. Remove sausage, slice and serve separately. Ladle soup into bowls and serve with crusty rolls or hot French bread.

GLAZED SALSIFY

Serves 4

        1 lb. Salsify root, peeled and cooked until tender in 2 changes of water
        6 Tbsp. butter
    $1^1/_2$ Tbsp. light molasses
     $^1/_2$ tsp. coarsely ground pepper
     $^1/_2$ tsp. salt

Combine butter, molasses, salt and pepper in skillet. Add prepared Salsify to pan and stir until coated with mixture. Cook over medium heat until lightly glazed.

SALSIFY AU GRATIN
Serves 6

1$^1/_2$ lbs. Salsify root
1 tsp. vinegar
$^1/_4$ tsp. salt
$^1/_2$ tsp. celery salt
1 egg, beaten
3 Tbsp. butter
3 Tbsp. flour
1$^1/_2$ cups milk
$^2/_3$ cup fresh bread crumbs
2 Tbsp. butter

Peel Salsify and cut into 1 inch lengths. Drop in water to cover along with the vinegar. Add salts, bring to boil and cook, covered, until tender. Drain well and mash. Stir in eggs.

Make white sauce by melting 3 Tbsp. butter in saucepan; add flour and stir until smooth. Gradually add milk; cook and stir over low heat until smooth and thick. Stir in Salsify mixture. Grease 1 quart casserole or 6 large scallop shells; turn Salsify mixture into shells. Melt 2 Tbsp. butter and add crumbs; heat through. Sprinkle over Salsify and broil 5 to 7 inches from heat for 5 minutes; turn off oven and allow to stand 5 minutes in oven. Serve at once.

SALSIFY CAKES
Serves 4

1$^1/_2$ lbs. Salsify root, peeled, cooked and mashed
2 Tbsp. melted butter
  Salt and pepper to taste
1 garlic clove, mashed
  Flour
  Olive oil

Combine Salsify, butter, salt, pepper, and garlic. Form into cakes 3 inches in diameter, dredge in flour and brown in hot olive oil.

SALSIFY CASSEROLE

Serves 6

1¹/₂ lbs. Salsify root, peeled and cut into 1/2 inch slices
1 tsp. vinegar
¹/₂ tsp. salt
2 eggs
6 oz. can evaporated milk
3 oz. canned smoked oysters
1 cup sour cream
1 cup coarse cracker crumbs
Salt and pepper to taste
1 Tbsp. butter
Paprika

Plunge peeled Salsify in cold water containing vinegar to prevent discoloration. Drain. Barely cover with boiling water; add ¹/₂ tsp. salt and cook until tender. Drain and cool.

Beat eggs; add milk, oysters, and sour cream. Place Salsify in greased 1¹/₂ quart casserole. Pour milk mixture over. Fold in crumbs, season to taste with salt and pepper, dot with butter and bake at 350°F for 40 minutes.

SALSIFY SOUP

Serves 4

2 cups sliced, peeled Salsify root
1 quart water
2 Tbsp. butter
1 Tbsp. grated onion
2 Tbsp. flour
1 cup chicken broth
1 cup cream
Salt and pepper to taste
2 Tbsp. chopped fresh parsley

Cook Salsify in 1 quart salted water until tender. Cook onion in butter until soft. Blend in flour, then broth and cream. Cook, stirring constantly, until mixture comes to a boil. Add remaining ingredients along with Salsify and cooking liquid. Serve at once.

SALSIFY WITH CREAM SAUCE

Serves 4

2 lbs. Salsify root, peeled and cut into 2 inch pieces
$^1/_4$ cup butter
$^1/_4$ cup flour
2 cups milk
$1^1/_2$ cups sour cream
  Salt and pepper to taste
2 cups buttered fresh bread crumbs

Butter a 2 quart baking dish and layer half the Salsify in bottom. Make cream sauce by melting butter in skillet. Stir in flour, then slowly add milk. When well combined, stir in sour cream. Cook until thickened. Season with salt and pepper. Spoon half over Salsify in baking dish, then layer remaining Salsify on cream sauce. Spoon over remaining sauce, season with salt and pepper and sprinkle with buttered crumbs. Bake at 350°F for 25 to 30 minutes.

SALSIFY WITH PARMESAN

Serves 4

2 lbs. Salsify root, peeled and cut into 2 inch pieces
1 tsp. vinegar
6 Tbsp. olive oil
2 cloves garlic, crushed
2 Tbsp. lime juice
$^1/_2$ tsp. freshly ground pepper
$^1/_4$ cup freshly grated Parmesan cheese

Cook Salsify in boiling water to which vinegar has been added until Salsify is tender. Drain and rinse. Sauté garlic in olive oil until just wilted. Add Salsify and stir to coat with garlic and oil. Add lime juice and pepper. Spoon into serving dish and sprinkle with Parmesan. Serve at once.

SALSIFY AND POTATOES

Serves 6

2 lbs. Salsify root, peeled, cut into 2 inch pieces, covered with water
    and 1 tsp. vinegar
4 large potatoes, peeled and cut into $1/4$ inch thick rounds
    Butter
    Salt and pepper to taste
    Cream

Butter a 2 quart baking dish. Alternate layers of Salsify and potatoes with dottings of butter in between and salt and pepper to taste. Barely cover with cream and bake at 350°F until Salsify and potatoes are done (approximately 45 to 50 minutes).

Chapter 19

SERVICEBERRY

(Amelanchier alnifolia, A. utahensis, A. pumila)
Also known as
saskatoon berry, Juneberry, sugar plum, and sarvisberry.

Serviceberry is a member of the rose family. There are nineteen species of *Amelanchier* native to North America. *A. alnifolia* being the most common in the Rocky Mountain area. All nineteen species bear palatable fruit. Serviceberry is found throughout the Northwest growing in moist to dry ground along rivers and lakes or in open coniferous forests. Birds and mammals feed on the berries during the summer while deer, moose and elk browse the branches during the winter.

Lewis and Clark noted in their journals that Native Americans crushed the berries, formed them into flat, round patties and dried them to carry on their journeys. Pieces could be broken off from the mass and cooked with meat. Serviceberries were also the principal fruit pounded with dried buffalo meat and fat when making pemmican—a chewy winter staple of Native Americans.

A branching shrub or small tree, the Serviceberry ranges from three to eight feet tall. It has smooth, gray bark. The oval leaves which vary from three-quarters to one and one-half inches in length, are toothed above the middle and smooth along the base. From late April to early June white, sweet smelling flowers form in long, catkin-like clusters. Five flower petals grow from the rim of a tiny cup with twenty stamens protruding from their center.

The vitamin C–rich berries ripen in mid–July through mid–August ascending the stems one by one. The fleshy dark blue fruits are approximately one-quarter of an inch in diameter, have ten seeds each and resemble an apple-like pome rather than a berry. Though sweet and bland in flavor when eaten fresh, the fruit takes on flavor similar to almonds when cooked or dried.

Since the berries grow in clusters, it takes little effort to gather a bucketful in an hour or less. Any tree that is not too large may be bent to the ground without breaking so that the fruit can be easily picked. The berries can be added to pies, muffins, pancakes, and waffles. They are also good made into jams, jellies, syrups, and wine, or used raw on cold cereal with cream. Serviceberries are excellent canned for winter use using a light to medium syrup and processing in a boiling water bath for ten minutes. They also freeze and dry well.

To freeze, spread rinsed berries in a single layer on a cookie sheet lined with waxed paper and place in freezer. When frozen, store them in freezer bags. The frozen berries will keep for six or seven months.

Dried berries have numerous uses when substituting them for dried raisins or currants in recipes. To dry Serviceberries spread them on a cheesecloth which has been stretched over a wooden frame. Sun dry for four to five days. Store in tightly covered containers.

Yearly crops of Serviceberries are not always available. The plant is sometime affected with a rust infestation that can cause the berries to have stunted growth. The fruit can also become infested with insects that cause the berries to dry before they ripen.

Native Americans made a wash for sore eyes, their vision blurred by snow or glare, by simmering the inner bark in rain or spring water.

HARVEST PIE

One 9 inch pie

1 unbaked pie shell
4 cups fresh Serviceberries
3 eggs
1 cup sugar
1 cup canned pumpkin purée
1 cup sour cream
1 tsp. ground cinnamon
$^1/_4$ tsp. ground cloves
$^1/_4$ tsp. ground ginger

In saucepan combine Serviceberries with $^1/_2$ cup water. Simmer 5 minutes. Cool. Beat eggs with electric beater, then add sugar gradually, beating until mixture is thick and pale. Stir in Serviceberries, pumpkin, sour cream, and spices, mixing well. Turn into unbaked pie shell and bake in a preheated 400°F oven for 1 hour or until just set in center. Let cool 30 minutes before cutting.

PEMMICAN

Pound or grind venison jerky to a fine powder. Add approximately half the amount of dried Serviceberries as jerky. Add half the amount of melted suet or marrow fat as pounded meat and dried berries. Mix together thoroughly. Form ingredients into a ball and wrap in heavy muslin then tie ends tightly. Dip bundle into melted bee's wax. This pemmican will keep for years.

SERVICEBERRY BREAKFAST BARS

3/4   cup butter, melted
1/2   cup brown sugar, packed
1/2   cup maple syrup
1/2   tsp. almond extract
1-1/2   cups dried Serviceberries
4   cups quick cooking rolled oats
2/3   cup shelled sunflower seeds
1/2   cup oat bran

Combine all ingredients and mix well. Turn into well oiled 10x15 inch baking pan. Press mixture firmly into even layer. Bake at 400°F for 25 minutes. Cool completely before cutting into bars.

SERVICEBERRY CAKE

8x8 inch pan

2   cups dried Serviceberries
2   cups water
1   tsp. baking soda
$^1/_2$ cup butter
1   cup sugar
$^1/_2$ tsp. ground cloves
$^1/_2$ tsp. ground nutmeg
1   tsp. ground cinnamon
2   cups cake flour
2   eggs, beaten
1   cup pecans, chopped

Simmer Serviceberries in water for 15 minutes. Drain, reserving 1 cup liquid. Cream butter and sugar. Add spices and eggs. Add flour to creamed mixture alternately with Serviceberry water. Fold in berries and nuts. Bake in square cake pan for 25 to 30 minutes in preheated 350°F oven.

SERVICEBERRY CATSUP

$1^1/_2$ quarts fresh Serviceberry pulp
 1 pint vinegar
 1 Tbsp. ground cinnamon
 1 Tbsp. ground cloves
 1 Tbsp. allspice
   Dash cayenne pepper
 4 cups sugar
$^1/_2$ Tbsp. salt

With potato masher, mash enough Serviceberries to make $1^1/_2$ quarts of pulp. Mix with remaining ingredients and cook over slow heat until mixture thickens. Store in refrigerator in covered jars or freeze. Good with game.

SERVICEBERRY CONSERVE

 2 oranges
 5 pints fresh Serviceberries
$^1/_2$ cup lemon juice
 2 cups sugar
 1 cup walnuts, chopped
 1 cup water

Grind oranges. Place in saucepan with remaining ingredients. Simmer over moderate heat for 35 minutes or until thickened. Pour into sterilized jars and seal in boiling water bath for 15 minutes.

SERVICEBERRY MUFFINS

    2 cups flour
    1 tsp. baking soda
    1 tsp. ground cinnamon
  $^1/_2$ tsp. ground cloves
  $^1/_2$ tsp. ground ginger
  $^1/_2$ cup butter
    1 cup brown sugar, firmly packed
    1 egg
    1 cup buttermilk
$1^1/_2$ cups fresh Serviceberries
    1 cup Piñon nuts

Sift together dry ingredients. Cream butter, sugar, and egg until fluffy. Add flour and milk alternately to creamed mixture. Beat smooth. Fold in berries and nuts. Fill well-oiled muffin tins $^2/_3$ full and bake at 350°F for 35 to 40 minutes.

SERVICEBERRY NUT STUFFING

Stuffs 2 quail or 1 chicken

    2 cups dried bread crumbs
  $^1/_3$ cup melted butter
    1 cup fresh Serviceberries
  $^1/_2$ cup Piñon nuts
  $^1/_4$ tsp. salt
  $^1/_4$ tsp. pepper
  $^1/_2$ tsp. ground sage

Combine ingredients and mix well.

SERVICEBERRY SAUCE FOR VENISON
4 pints

    4 quarts Serviceberries
    2 cups minced onion
2$^1/_2$ cups sugar
    2 cups chopped raisins
    2 cups white wine vinegar
1$^1/_2$ tsp. salt
    1 Tbsp. ground cloves
    1 Tbsp. ground cinnamon
    1 Tbsp. ground allspice
    1 Tbsp. celery seed
    2 Tbsp. grated orange rind

Combine Serviceberries, onion, and 2 cups water. Cover and simmer 10 minutes. Purée mixture in blender. Combine purée with sugar, raisins, vinegar, and seasonings. Bring to boiling, reduce heat and simmer 25 minutes, stirring frequently. Remove from heat. Skim foam. Ladle mixture into hot jars to within $^1/_2$ inch of rim. Adjust lids and seal in boiling water bath for 7 minutes.

STEAMED SERVICEBERRY PUDDING
Serves 4

1$^1/_2$ cups fresh Serviceberries
    1 cup sliced peaches
 $^1/_2$ cup granulated sugar
    1 tsp. cinnamon
 $^1/_2$ cup biscuit mix
 $^1/_3$ cup granulated sugar
 $^1/_3$ cup milk

Mix together berries, peaches, $^1/_2$ cup sugar and cinnamon. Spoon into 4 large custard cups. Make batter from biscuit mix, $^1/_3$ cup sugar, and milk. Drop onto fruit. Place in large kettle on racks with enough water to reach bottom of custard dishes. Cover tightly and steam on medium heat for 45 minutes.

STEAMED SERVICEBERRY PUFF WITH LEMON SAUCE

Serves 4

$^1/_2$ cup butter
3 Tbsp. sugar
2 eggs
2 cups flour
2 tsp. baking powder
1 cup milk
1 cup fresh Serviceberries

Cream together butter and sugar. Beat in eggs, one at a time. Sift together flour and baking powder. Add alternately to creamed mixture with milk. Fold in Serviceberries. Pour into oiled pudding mold. Steam on rack in covered kettle, with water touching bottom of mold, for 30 minutes.

Lemon Sauce:

$^1/_2$ cup sugar
1 Tbsp. cornstarch
1 cup water
2 Tbsp. butter
1 tsp. grated lemon rind
2 Tbsp. fresh lemon juice

Combine sugar, cornstarch, and water. Cook over moderate heat until sauce thickens. Remove from heat and stir in butter, rind, and juice. Serve over steamed puff.

STEWED SERVICEBERRIES

2 cups dried Serviceberries
1 stick cinnamon
$^1/_2$ tsp. whole cloves
2 Tbsp. fresh lime juice
$^1/_3$ cup honey

Place Serviceberries in saucepan and cover with water. Tie spices in bag and place in saucepan. Simmer, covered, 45 minutes. Add lemon juice and honey. Serve warm or chilled.

VENISON MINCEMEAT

  4 lbs. venison meat with bones (trimmed of fat)
  3 lbs. dried Serviceberries
  1 lb. golden raisins
$^3/_4$ lb. beef suet
  4 lbs. tart apples, peeled and cored
$^1/_2$ Tbsp. salt
  1 Tbsp. ground cinnamon
  1 Tbsp. ground ginger
  1 Tbsp. ground cloves
  1 Tbsp. ground nutmeg
$1^1/_2$ Tbsp. ground allspice
  2 quarts apple cider
  1 lb. brown sugar
$^1/_2$ cup fresh lime juice
  3 Tbsp. grated orange rind

Cover venison with water. Simmer until meat is tender. Chill venison in liquid overnight. Remove fat from liquid. Remove meat from bones and put through meat grinder using coarsest blade. Grind suet and apples. Add to large kettle along with venison cooking liquid, venison, and remaining ingredients. Simmer 2 hours over medium heat, stirring often. Pack in hot sterilized jars, tighten lids and process 20 minutes at 10 lbs. pressure (240°F).

CHAPTER 20

SHEEP SORREL

(Rumex acetosella)

Also known as red sorrel, sour dock, and sourgrass.

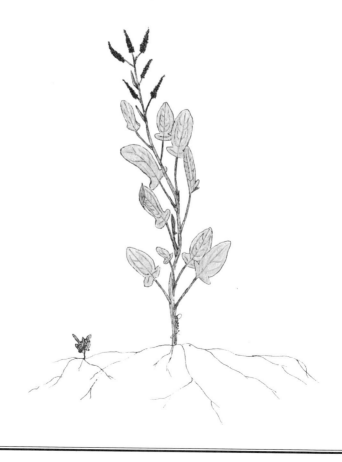

The pleasant–tasting perennial is a European native which escaped the gardens of early colonists and spread throughout the United States. It is very rich in vitamin A and C. The lemony flavor of Sheep Sorrel is imparted by a salt—binoxalate of potash.

Sheep Sorrel can be found from sea level to elevations of 8,000 feet. It is common in fields, gardens, lawns, as well as along roadsides and streams. Domestic sheep, cattle, and horses have managed to distribute Sheep Sorrel throughout the Rocky Mountains via manure.

Sheep Sorrel grows up to eighteen inches tall from long, slender, creeping roots. The plant is easily identified by its arrow-shaped, pale green leaves. The lower lobes point strongly outward and the center lobe is slender and lance-shaped. The leaves are between one and six inches long. They have a thirst quenching effect when chewed in the field. A refreshing drink similar to lemonade can be prepared by steeping the leaves in hot water, sweetened with honey or sugar and chilled. A liquid prepared by boiling a large quantity of leaves in water, discarding spent solids, can be used like rennet to convert milk to pudding or junket.

From June to August inconspicuous bright red to rust colored flowers are borne in dense whorls on branches at the upper end of the stem. The red pigment which colors the flowers sometimes colors the leaves as well. The tiny flowers form small three-winged fruits approximately one-twenty-fourth of an inch long. These seeds can be gathered and added to other wild seeds and grains to be eaten as an emergency food source. They may also be cooked as a porridge.

The leaves and stems can be gathered for use any time the plant is available but they are at their peak during early spring before the flower stalks appear. After collecting, discard flower stalks and rinse the herb in cold water, shaking moisture from the leaves.

Sheep Sorrel is tasty raw or cooked. It makes an excellent addition to salads and soups. French cooks have long used Sheep Sorrel as a seasoning in omelets, soups, and stews. In fact, their famous green fish sauce is merely chopped Sheep Sorrel leaves simmered in clarified butter. Many European chefs not only cook regularly with Sheep Sorrel, but also use it as an attractive garnish for gourmet dishes. The herb can be dried and mixed with bland wild herbs for tea or used in place of lemon for regular tea. Fresh greens may be cooked in a small amount of boiling water for five to six minutes and seasoned to taste with salt, pepper, and butter for a quick economical vegetable.

Sheep Sorrel has been used in European medicine as a diuretic, blood purifier, a refrigerant for cooling fevers, and as a wound cleanser.

POTATO AND SHEEP SORREL SOUP

Serves 4

5 medium potatoes, cooked but not peeled
2 cups packed Sheep Sorrel leaves
1 Tbsp. butter
$^1/_2$ cup cream
4 cups water
   Salt and pepper

Chop potatoes very fine. Add along with other ingredients to kettle and cook 2 minutes to heat through, but do not boil.

SALMON SPREAD WITH SHEEP SORREL

3 cups

$1^1/_2$ lbs. poached salmon, boned and skinned
$1^1/_2$ cups butter
$^1/_2$ tsp. Worcestershire sauce
$1^1/_2$ Tbsp. Dijon-style mustard
1 tsp. catsup
$^1/_4$ cup lemon juice
$^1/_8$ tsp. hot sauce
$^1/_8$ tsp. freshly ground nutmeg
$^1/_4$ tsp. curry powder
1 Tbsp. finely mined onion
$^1/_2$ cup minced Sheep Sorrel

Purée salmon in food processor with the butter. Add remaining ingredients except Sheep Sorrel. Process to spread consistency by pulsating the food processor until all ingredients are blended. Add Sheep Sorrel and run machine to just blend. Keeps up to 1 week refrigerated.

SHEEP SORREL CAKE

$^1/_2$ cup butter
1$^1/_2$ cups sugar
1 egg
2 cups Sheep Sorrel
2 tsp. baking soda
$^2/_3$ cup boiling water
2$^1/_2$ cups cake flour
$^1/_4$ tsp. salt
$^1/_2$ tsp. each ground cinnamon, cloves, and allspice
1 cup dried currants
1 cup chopped walnuts

Purée Sheep Sorrel in blender with $^1/_3$ cup boiling water. In mixing bowl cream sugar, butter, egg, and puréed Sheep Sorrel. Combine soda with remaining boiling water and add alternately with remaining dry ingredients Fold in nuts and currants. Pour into 8x12 inch square baking pan and bake at 350°F for 1 hour.

SHEEP SORREL–ENDIVE SALAD

Serves 6

3 cups Sheep Sorrel leaves
4 heads endive, torn
2 cups cooked beets, cut in julienne strips
$^1/_2$ cup pecans
$^1/_2$ cup cubed tofu
1 Tbsp. honey
$^1/_2$ cup yogurt
1 Tbsp. minced tarragon
2 tsp. freshly squeezed lemon juice

In bowl, combine Sheep Sorrel leaves, endive, beets, pecans, and tofu. Chill. In small bowl combine honey, yogurt, tarragon, and lemon juice. Mix well. Add salt and pepper to taste. Toss with salad just before serving.

SHEEP SORREL PIE

8 cups chopped Sheep Sorrel leaves
3 Tbsp. freshly squeezed lime juice
1¼ cups packed brown sugar
6 Tbsp. flour
¼ tsp. salt
½ tsp. freshly grated nutmeg
3 Tbsp. butter
   Pastry for double-crust 9 inch pie

Put Sheep Sorrel in pastry-lined pie plate and sprinkle with lime juice. Combine brown sugar, flour, salt, and nutmeg and sprinkle over top of Sheep Sorrel. Dot with butter. Adjust top crust and crimp edges. Bake in preheated 425°F oven for 20 minutes, then reduce heat to 350°F and bake 35 to 40 minutes longer.

SHEEP SORREL PURÉE

Serves 4

2 cups Sheep Sorrel
¼ cup water
4 cups milk
½ cup grated onion
1 Tbsp. butter
2 Tbsp. flour

Slowly cook Sheep Sorrel in ¼ cup water in covered pan for 20 minutes. Cool slightly, then whirl in blender along with grated onion until smooth. In saucepan, melt butter over medium-high heat, then stir in flour. Slowly add milk, stirring constantly until thickened. Add Sheep Sorrel purée and heat thoroughly. Do not boil. Serve at once.

SHEEP SORREL SAUCE

3-1/2 cups

 1 egg
 2 cups tightly packed Sheep Sorrel greens
 1 tsp. lemon juice
 $^1/_2$ tsp. white pepper
 $1^1/_2$ Tbsp. red wine vinegar
 2 cups olive oil

Place egg, Sheep Sorrel, lemon juice, pepper, and vinegar in a food processor and pulse it on and off until greens are chopped. With the machine running, add the oil very slowly until the sauce has a mayonnaise consistency.

Sauce keeps 1 week refrigerated.

SMOKED SALMON AND SHEEP SORREL TART

Serves 6

 $1^1/_4$ cups all-purpose flour
 6 Tbsp. cold butter, cut into small bits
 2 Tbsp. cold vegetable shortening
   Uncooked beans for weighting the pie shell
 1 cup chopped Sheep Sorrel leaves
 3 eggs
 1 cup heavy cream
 $^1/_4$ lb. thinly sliced smoked salmon
 $^1/_4$ cup plain yogurt
 2 Tbsp. capers

In bowl blend flour, butter, and vegetable shortening until mixture resembles fine meal. Add 3 Tbsp. ice water and toss the mixture with two forks. Form into a ball and knead lightly. Dust ball with flour, wrap in wax paper and chill 1 hour.

Roll dough on lightly floured surface and fit into an 8 inch tart pan with removable fluted rim. Prick shell and chill for 30 minutes. Line shell with foil and fill $^3/_4$ full with beans. Bake in preheated 425°F oven for 10 minutes. Carefully remove foil with beans and continue baking for 6 to 8 minutes longer, or until light brown.

Spread Sheep Sorrel evenly in shell. In bowl whisk together eggs and cream. Pour over Sheep Sorrel and bake in preheated 350°F oven for 25 minutes or until set in center. Arrange salmon on top and bake for 3 minutes longer. Drizzle with yogurt and sprinkle with capers. Serve warm.

SWAMP SODA

      6 cups water
  1¹/₂ cups sugar
      6 cups Sheep Sorrel, chopped
         Club soda

Bring first three ingredients to a boil; turn off heat and allow to stand for 3 to 4 hours. Strain liquid through cheesecloth. Fill glasses ¹/₃ full of Sheep Sorrel syrup, add a few ice cubes and fill with soda.

TANSY

      9 inch unbaked pie shell
      7 eggs, separated
      1 pint cream
   ¹/₂ cup Sheep Sorrel juice
      1 tansy leaf, pulverized
      2 cups soda cracker crumbs
   ³/₄ cup honey
      1 cup dry white wine
         Freshly grated nutmeg

To make Sheep Sorrel juice, put 3 pints of leaves in food processor with ¹/₄ cup water and purée. Strain through several layers of cheesecloth and measure out ¹/₂ cup.

Beat egg yolks. Add cream, Sheep Sorrel juice, tansy, cracker crumbs, honey, and wine. Beat egg whites until stiff. Carefully fold into yolk mixture. Pour into pie crust and bake in preheated 400°F oven for 15 minutes, then reduce heat and bake at 325°F until custard is firm and a golden color.

CHAPTER 21

STINGING NETTLE

(Urtica dioico, U. procera)

Also known as nettle.

Caesar's troops introduced the Stinging Nettle (*U. dioico*), into Britain because they thought that they would need to flail themselves with Nettles to keep warm. Beating the flesh with Stinging Nettles was a standard remedy for increasing blood circulation and for treating arthritis and rheumatism. In an Anglo–Saxon herbal of the tenth Century, Nettle was also listed as one of the nine sacred herbs used to combat "evils."

Thomas Campbell, the British poet, stated, "In Scotland I have eaten nettle, I have slept in nettle sheets, I have dined off a nettle tablecloth." As bizarre as this may sound, stalks of mature Stinging Nettles do yield a valuable textile fiber when processed like flax. In Scotland, where Nettle linen was once made, the mountain people claimed that it was more beautiful and durable than linen made from flax. Nettle fiber also played a part in World War I. During 1916, when Germany's cotton and flax supply was low, Germans collected nearly six million pounds of Stinging Nettle, using the fiber to make uniforms. Archaeologists found Nettle fabric wrapped around a body in a Bronze Age burial site in Denmark.

The first seeds of *U. dioico* were brought to the United States from England by a horticulturist named John Jossely and the plant quickly naturalized throughout North America. There are nearly five hundred species of Urticaceae, the generic name being derived from the Latin *uro*, meaning to burn. *Urtica procera* is one of the more common Native American Stinging Nettles found throughout the Rocky Mountains. It is very similar to the common naturalized *U. dioico*, but its leaves are narrower.

Stinging Nettles are found along streams, valleys, marshes, and damp spots, from sea level to 10,000 feet but are most common above 4,000 feet. They prefer soil rich in nitrogen.

A perennial, Stinging Nettles grow from underground rhizomes. As soon as the weather turns warm in the spring tender young shoots appear. The opposite heart-shaped leaves are finely toothed on the margins and taper to points. Stinging Nettles often look bushy since each plant can send out underground roots that generate new stalks, resulting in a dense cluster. The single stems are square, stout, and usually reach one to two feet in height. However, they may reach as high as five feet along rich stream banks. Small, inconspicuous, green flowers are borne in July through September on branched clusters that grow from the axils of the leaves. They mature to small winged seeds. The entire plant is downy and covered with stiff stinging hairs. Each hair is actually a sharp hollow spine that rises from a slightly swollen base. This swelling contains formic acid, histamine and acetylcholine that is released through the spine whenever the plant is brushed. The stinging elements are destroyed by heat.

Nettles take minerals, including iron, from the soil and are therefore a good tonic for anemia; their high vitamin C content ensuring that the iron is properly absorbed. Also high in vitamins A and B, plant protein and chlorophyll, Stinging Nettles are one of the most nutritious foods in the plant kingdom.

The early spring shoots are harvested for food. They are a popular ingredient in French, European, and Scottish cuisine. Wear leather or heavy cotton gloves while gathering Nettles, picking those which are from four to eight inches in height. As the plant matures, so do those flax-like fibers! After the herb has been gathered it should be washed in cold water. A pair of kitchen tongs will be of considerable help when removing the washed greens from the water.

Rennet can be made from Stinging Nettles by boiling the fresh leaves in water to make a strong tea. The tea is then mixed with salt in the ratio of two parts salt to every three parts tea. One to two teaspoons of this solution are usually sufficient to convert one quart of warm milk into rennet pudding or junket.

Nettle tea is a popular item in natural food stores and can be easily made at home. Hang bundles of Nettle greens in a warm, airy place. Allow four to five days of drying time before crumbling leaves and stems. Store the dried herb in a tightly covered container. When brewing the tea use two teaspoons of dried herb per cup of boiling hot water. Homeopathic remedies use Nettle tea to treat inflammation of the kidneys and to expel phlegm from the lungs.

Native Americans made a yellow dye by boiling the rhizomes.

CREAM OF STINGING NETTLE SOUP

Serves 4

   1 lb. young Stinging Nettle shoots
   1 cup chicken broth
   1 minced onion
$^1/_2$ cup chopped cilantro
   1 cup milk
   2 Tbsp. fresh chopped tarragon
$^1/_4$ tsp. freshly grated nutmeg
   2 cloves crushed garlic
$^1/_2$ tsp. salt
$^1/_2$ tsp. pepper
   1 cup heavy cream

Combine first 9 ingredients and simmer for 30 minutes. Cool for 10 minutes then purée in food processor. Return to pot and stir in heavy cream; heat but do not boil. Serve at once.

LENTIL SOUP WITH STINGING NETTLE AND LEMON

Serves 6

$1^1/_2$ cups lentils
   2 lbs. young Stinging Nettle greens
$^1/_2$ cup olive oil
   1 cup chopped onion
   4 cloves garlic, crushed
      Salt
$^1/_4$ cup chopped celery
   1 cup lemon juice
$1^1/_2$ tsp. flour
      Chopped chives

Cover lentils with cold water and cook until tender. Chop Stinging Nettles and add to lentils along with 1 cup water. Cover and simmer 12 to 15 minutes. Heat olive oil in skillet and sauté onion, garlic and celery until soft. Season with salt and add mixture to lentils. Mix lemon juice with flour and stir into soup. Cook gently, stirring occasionally, until soup has thickened. Chill. Serve in chilled bowls and garnish with chives.

STINGING NETTLE ALE

8 quarts young Stinging Nettle greens
4 gallons water
2 lemons, thinly sliced
3 limes, thinly sliced
3 oz. fresh gingerroot, grated
4 cups light brown sugar
2 pkg. baker's yeast

Boil first 4 ingredients in large open kettle for 45 minutes. Strain through several layers of cheesecloth, then add sugar. Cool to lukewarm. Dissolve yeast in 2 cups of ale liquid, then stir back into remaining ale. Bottle and cap. Allow to stand at least 1 week before using. Serve well chilled.

NETTLE FRITTATA

Serves 6

2 cloves garlic, finely chopped
1 onion, thinly sliced
4 Tbsp. olive oil
2 cups cooked, chopped Stinging Nettles
$1/4$ cup salt
$1/2$ tsp. freshly ground pepper
$1/4$ tsp. freshly grated nutmeg
8 medium-sized eggs
$1/2$ cup freshly grated Parmesan cheese

In 10 inch cast iron skillet sauté garlic and onion in olive oil until just wilted. Add Stinging Nettles and heat through. Beat together eggs, seasonings, and cheese. Pour over ingredients in skillet. Put skillet in preheated 350°F oven and bake for 45 minutes or until eggs are set. Cut into slices and serve hot.

STINGING NETTLE CANNELLONI
Serves 6

3 cups cooked, coarsely chopped Stinging Nettle
4 Tbsp. minced onion
2 Tbsp. minced basil
  Dash freshly grated nutmeg
2 Tbsp. minced fresh parsley
$^1/_2$ cup butter
$^1/_2$ cup finely-chopped baked ham
1$^1/_4$ cups Ricotta cheese
$^1/_2$ cup freshly-grated Parmesan cheese
$^1/_2$ cup freshly-grated Swiss cheese
2 egg yolks
1 lb. lasagna noodles
  Pasta sauce

Cook lasagna noodles in boiling salted water for 5 minutes. Drain and rinse in cold water. Set aside.

Squeeze out excess liquid from cooked Stinging Nettles. Melt butter and sauté onion in butter until onion is light in color. Remove from heat. Add basil, nutmeg, parsley, and ham. Stir in Stinging Nettles, Ricotta, and egg yolks. Stir in other cheeses. Put a generous amount onto the end of a lasagna noodle and roll up. Place flap side down in buttered baking dish. Cover with a layer of pasta sauce, sprinkle with extra Parmesan and bake at 400°F until hot and browned on top (approximately 30 minutes).

NETTLE GREENS
Serves 4

2 lbs. Stinging Nettle greens
  Melted butter
1 Tbsp. freshly squeezed lemon juice
  Salt and freshly ground pepper

Wash greens well, then put in heavy kettle, cover tightly and cook over medium heat until just wilted and tender. Drain well. Dress with butter, lemon juice, salt, and pepper.

NETTLE DESSERT PUDDING

2$^1/_2$ lbs. Stinging Nettles
$^1/_2$ cup milk
$^1/_2$ cup cream
3 egg yolks
$^1/_4$ cup sugar
1 Tbsp. orange liqueur
1 tsp. finely grated lemon peel

Rinse Stinging Nettles, then cook in pan with just the water which clings to the leaves, for 3 to 4 minutes. Drain well. Purée in food processor or blender. In top of double boiler combine milk, cream, egg yolks, and sugar; cook over simmering water until mixture coats a metal spoon, stirring constantly. Combine with puréed Stinging Nettles, liqueur, and lemon rind. Transfer into buttered quart baking dish. Bake at 350°F for 30 to 35 minutes. Serve warm.

NETTLE GREENS WITH BACON DRESSING

Serves 4

$^1/_2$ lb. bacon, cut into 1/2 inch pieces
3 cloves garlic, finely chopped
$^1/_2$ cup chopped fresh mint
3 Tbsp. red wine vinegar
3 quarts Stinging Nettle greens, washed and coarsely chopped
    Salt and freshly ground pepper

Sauté bacon with garlic. When bacon is cooked, but not crisp, add remaining ingredients and cook, stirring, until Nettles are wilted. Serve at once.

NETTLE NOODLES

1 cup young Stinging Nettle greens
$^1/_4$ cup water
1 large egg, beaten
$^1/_4$ tsp. salt
2 cups all-purpose flour

Cook Nettles in water in covered pan for 10 minutes. Purée in blender or food processor. Measure $^1/_4$ cup purée. Cool. Add purée to egg and salt; gradually stir in flour. Knead dough until smooth. Roll dough into paper thin sheet, spread on dry cloth and allow to dry slightly. Roll sheet up and cut into thin shreds with knife. Toss apart and allow to dry thoroughly. Store in covered containers in moisture free area. To cook, boil desired amount in salted water for 15 to 20 minutes. Use as regular noodles.

NETTLE SOUFFLE

Serves 4

3 Tbsp. butter
3 Tbsp. flour
$^3/_4$ cup milk, scalded
$^1/_4$ tsp. salt
   Freshly ground pepper to taste
   Dash Tabasco
4 egg yolks
1 cup cooked, puréed Stinging Nettles
$^1/_4$ cup freshly grated Parmesan cheese
6 egg whites
$^1/_2$ tsp. cream of tartar

Melt butter and combine with flour. Cook several minutes to blend thoroughly. Add the hot milk and stir until the mixture is thickened. Add salt and pepper. Remove from heat, cool slightly, and add the egg yolks. Return to heat and stir for a minute or two. Add Nettles and cheese, blending well. Beat egg whites until stiff but not dry, adding cream of tartar when eggs begin to foam.

Thoroughly blend in approximately $^1/_3$ of the beaten whites with egg yolk mixture, carefully folding with a spatula. Carefully fold in remaining whites, then pour into a buttered $1^1/_2$ quart soufflé dish. Bake in preheated 375°F oven for 35 minutes or until soufflé is brown and puffy.

STINGING NETTLE PIES

Serves 4

1 lb. chopped young Stinging Nettle shoots, blanched and drained
3 eggs
$^1/_2$ lb. Ricotta cheese
2 tsp. fresh chopped tarragon
2 Tbsp. fresh chopped mint leaves
$^1/_2$ cup chopped chives
1 tsp. salt
$^1/_2$ tsp. pepper
2 Tbsp. melted butter
1 lb. phyllo dough
   Additional melted butter

Beat eggs and stir in Ricotta, tarragon, mint, chives, salt, and pepper. Combine with Stinging Nettles and 2 Tbsp. melted butter.

Cut phyllo dough into $4^1/_2$ inch wide strips. Use two sheets for each pie. Brush with melted butter. Place a tablespoon of the Stinging Nettle filling onto the sheet and fold as you would a flag to create a triangle. Crimp edges. Brush with more melted butter and bake at 375°F for 20 minutes or until crisp and brown.

NETTLE PURÉE

Serves 4

2 quarts young Stinging Nettle greens
$^1/_4$ cup water
2 Tbsp. butter
$^1/_4$ tsp. salt
3 Tbsp. sour cream
   Pepper to taste

With kitchen sheers snip greens into saucepan. Add water and simmer, covered, for 12 minutes. Cool 10 minutes, then place in blender or food processor and purée. Add butter, salt, sour cream, and pepper and heat over low heat until warmed through. Serve immediately.

Chapter 22

WATERCRESS

(Rorippa-nasturtium-aquaticum)

Also known as water nasturtium.

Watercress, an aquatic, perennial plant was among the earliest European plants introduced to North America. It quickly naturalized throughout the United States and Canada. This pungent, peppery-flavored member of the mustard family is rich in vitamins A and B. It also contains vitamins B and B^2, iron, manganese, sulfur, calcium, and copper, making the plant an excellent remedy for anemia.

The plants form thick beds in cold, moving water such as brooks, streams, springs, and ditches throughout much of the Rocky Mountain region. Its jointed stems float in water and send out roots from the joints that anchor it to drift in a suitable spot. These white roots are visible hanging from the floating stems. The stems are from six to eighteen inches long and often extend two to four inches above the water.

The leaves form thick mats of floating vegetation. They are glossy and deep green in color with smooth edges with a slightly irregular outline. The leaves have three to nine leaflets, the terminal leaflet always the largest and the most irregularly shaped.

The small white blossoms appear from April through October. They are borne in clusters at the ends of the stems and have four petals arranged in the shape of a cross. The flowers mature in small, slim, seed-filled pods approximately one-half to one inch in length. Each pod contains two parallel rows of tiny seeds. There are approximately 150,000 watercress seeds per ounce.

The lower parts of the stems get tough, so only the leafy leading ends should be collected. They can be snapped off without disturbing the plant. Should a plant become dislodged during harvesting the freely rooting stems should be replaced whenever possible to encourage regrowth. Caution should be taken when gathering Watercress since it often thrives in polluted water. Avoid any found growing in stagnant or still water, or any thriving near stock yards. It is safest harvested near the mouth of a fenced-in spring or from a stream with a sandy bottom where it is less likely to come into contact with pollutants or contamination. Watercress is available in its fresh state throughout most of the year. In milder climates where the streams do not freeze, it is available the entire year.

Watercress is best used as a raw salad green but it also makes an excellent potherb that requires only brief cooking. It is frequently used as a garnish, or added to soups, stews, and sandwiches. The leaves can be dried, ground and used on top of other foods as a mild seasoning.

COTTAGE CHEESE AND WATERCRESS SANDWICH

4 sandwiches

1¹/₂ cups cottage cheese
¹/₃ cup finely chopped Watercress
1 Tbsp. finely chopped chives
1 Tbsp. finely chopped pimento stuffed green olives
    Mayonnaise
8 slices bread

Mix cottage cheese with Watercress, chives, and olives. Spread bread slices with mayonnaise and sandwich filling between slices.

GREEN GODDESS SALAD DRESSING

2 cloves garlic, crushed
1 oz. anchovy paste
¹/₄ cup finely chopped chives
¹/₄ cup freshly squeezed lime juice
¹/₃ cup white wine vinegar
1 cup sour cream
2 cup mayonnaise
1 cup chopped Watercress
¹/₂ tsp. freshly grated pepper

Combine all ingredients in food processor or blender and blend until liquefied. Chill. Serve over tossed green salad.

LENTIL–WATERCRESS SOUP

Serves 10

 1 lb. washed lentils
10 cups water
 2 cups chopped onions
 1 cup diced celery
 4 cloves garlic, crushed
 1 tsp. salt
 $^1/_2$ tsp. freshly grated pepper
 2 chicken bouillon cubes
 4 cups packed chopped Watercress
 1 Tbsp. freshly squeezed lemon juice

Bring to boil in large kettle the lentils, water, onions, celery, garlic, salt, pepper, and bouillon. Cover and simmer for 3 hours, stirring occasionally. Add Watercress. Cover and simmer 30 minutes. Stir in lemon juice. If soup becomes too thick, stir in some boiling water.

POTATO–WATERCRESS SOUP

Serves 4

 2 cups water
 3 large potatoes, peeled and diced
 1 medium-sized onion, diced
 1 cup Watercress, chopped
 2 stalks celery, diced
 $^1/_2$ tsp. salt
 2 strips bacon, fried crisp then crumbled
 2 cups milk

Cook potatoes, onion, and celery in salted water until potatoes are tender. Cool slightly then add to food processor along with Watercress and purée. Return to saucepan, add milk and heat thoroughly, stirring. Do not allow mixture to boil. Serve hot with a sprinkling of bacon.

WATERCRESS AND ENDIVE SALAD

Serves 4

    1 cucumber, thinly sliced
$^1/_2$ lb. Watercress
    2 endive, cut into long strips
    1 Tbsp. chopped cilantro
    1 Tbsp. chopped fresh oregano
    1 Tbsp. chopped fresh tarragon
      Salt and pepper to taste
      Several large white mushrooms, sliced
    1 cup olive oil
$^1/_2$ cup red wine vinegar
    1 Tbsp. sugar
    2 hard-cooked eggs, riced
    8 cherry tomatoes

Combine herbs, oil, salt, pepper, vinegar, and sugar. Mix and allow to stand 1 hour. Add $^1/_3$ of the dressing to cucumber, $^1/_3$ to the Watercress, and $^1/_3$ to the endive, tossing each well. Arrange the Watercress, endive, and cucumbers attractively on four individual plates. Top with sliced mushrooms, riced eggs, and cherry tomatoes.

WATERCRESS JELLY

3 pints

      6 cups sugar
      1 cup white wine vinegar
      2 cups Watercress leaves, tightly packed
$1^1/_2$ cups water
        Green food coloring, if desired
      1 pkg. powdered pectin

In large saucepan combine sugar, vinegar, Watercress, and water. Bring to boiling and boil hard 1 minute. Let stand 5 minutes. Pour through cheesecloth and discard solids. Add coloring, if desired.

Return to kettle and bring to boiling. Add pectin and boil hard 1 minute, stirring constantly. Remove from heat and pour into sterilized jars. Adjust lids and seal in boiling water bath 7 minutes.

WATERCRESS AND SARDINE PASTE ON RYE

1 cup Watercress
1¹/₂ cups sardines, drained and mashed
2 Tbsp. sour cream
1 Tbsp. freshly squeezed lemon juice
1 Tbsp. grated onion
  Rye toast

Mix ingredients together and spread on rye toast. Broil under oven broiler until hot.

WATERCRESS VINEGAR

Fresh Watercress leaves
White wine vinegar
Garlic cloves, peeled
Additional Watercress leaves

Pack glass jars with Watercress leaves. Pour wine vinegar over leaves, cover jars and place in cool dark place for 3 weeks. Strain vinegar, discarding leaves. Pour vinegar into decorative bottles. Add a branch of fresh Watercress and a peeled garlic clove to each. Cap tightly.

WATERCRESS WITH WILD VIOLET FLOWERS

Serves 4

7 cups Watercress leaves
6 slices bacon
1 Tbsp. freshly squeezed lemon juice
3 hard-cooked eggs, riced
2 cups wild violet flowers

Sauté bacon until crisp. Crumble and set aside. Sauté Watercress in ¹/₃ cup drippings until Watercress wilts. Toss with lemon juice, crumbled bacon, egg, and violet flowers. Serve at once.

WATERCRESS TEA SANDWICHES

1 loaf soft white bread
4 seeded and finely chopped cucumbers
2 cups chopped Watercress leaves
3 oz. softened cream cheese
$^1/_2$ tsp. salt
$^1/_2$ tsp. white pepper
1 bunch Watercress
$^1/_2$ cup butter at room temperature

Add salt and pepper to cucumbers and Watercress; place in strainer and allow to drain for 1 hour. Mash cream cheese into Watercress mixture. Trim crusts from bread slices. Spread butter onto one side of bread. Spoon Watercress mixture down center of bread then turn one side of the bread over mixture and then the other side of the bread over the first, pressing so that the butter will adhere to the bread. Turn folded side down on platter so that the sandwiches won't pull open. Push a fresh sprig of Watercress into the end of each sandwich. Garnish platter with Watercress, cover with plastic wrap and chill.

WATERCRESS WITH WHITE BEANS AND GRUYERE

Serves 5

1 lb. dried Great Northern beans
4 cups chopped onion
$^1/_4$ cup olive oil
1 Tbsp. wine vinegar
$^1/_2$ tsp. salt
2 cups packed Watercress
   Additional sprigs of Watercress for garnish
$1^1/_2$ cups fresh bread crumbs
$1^1/_2$ cups grated Gruyere
2 cloves garlic, minced

Cook beans in water to cover until tender. Drain, reserving liquid. Cook onions in olive oil until onions are tender. Boil cooking liquid until it is reduced to $1^1/_2$ cups. Purée 1 cup beans and add to liquid along with cooked onions, vinegar, salt, and Watercress. Stir into beans.

Toss together crumbs, Gruyere, and garlic. Put beans in baking pan and sprinkle crumb mixture over top. Bake in preheated 425°F oven for 20 minutes. Divide among dinner plates and garnish with additional Watercress sprigs.

CHAPTER

23

WILD CURRANT

(Ribes aureum, R. inebrians, R. pumilum, R. cereum)

Also known as Squaw currant, bear currant, and wax currant.

The three to eight foot shrubs are one of the first to show leaves in the spring. The regional Indians gathered the young leaves and ate them with venison fat. The leaves are maple-shaped with two to four lobes and veined with edges that have coarse teeth. These leaves are arranged alternately, occurring in clusters on short lateral branches that are in their first year of growth. Younger branches are slate gray in color, while the older branches are somewhat roughened and nearly black in color. Flowers are borne on drooping stalks that rise from the stems at the bases of the leaf stalks. Berries form in clusters and mature in mid–July through August. All currants retain part of the flower at the tip of the fruit.

There are numerous species of currants in the Rocky Mountains. The species most popular with Native Americans and early explorers was *R. aureum,* a currant widespread in the Rocky Mountain area. It was collected by Captain Lewis on the Lewis and Clark Expedition across the continent in 1805. Several times in their journal there was mention of feasting on this Wild Currant. The Grandall currant, a popular form cultivated for its fruit, was developed from this species. Of all our regional currants, *R. aureum* is the best to use in pies, james, jellies, syrups, and wines. Regional Indians frequently used the dried currants in pemmican. The dried wild berries resemble commercial dried currants, but there is a noticeable seed.

R. aureum shrubs produces a bright yellow blanket of trumpet-shaped flowers, one-quarter to one-half inch long, with a spicy fragrance. The blossoms often contain such an abundance of nectar that some people enjoy eating the flowers right off the bush. The smooth, globe-shaped flavorful fruits are relatively large (one-quarter to three-fifths inch wide) and occur in clumps of up to ten. Their color is most often black but may sometimes be red, yellow, or orange. When eaten raw in quantity the berries are emetic, though there is no problem if they are cooked.

Ribes inebrians, R. pumilum, and *R. cereum* are very similar to one another. All three species are smaller than *R. aureum,* with leaves three-eighths to one and one-half inches wide and pink to white flowers ranging from one-quarter to one-half inches long. The berries are one-quarter to one-half inches in diameter, usually smooth, globe-shaped and are most often red in color. They have a sticky surface and an aromatic odor that some find unpleasant. The fruits are not very juicy and lack the flavor of *R. aureum.* In fact, *R. cereum* has a rather acrid and bitter flavor.

These three species are found from 5,000 to 9,000 feet in elevation from

South Dakota and Nebraska to Idaho, Colorado, New Mexico, Arizona, and California. Like *R. aureum*, they prefer moist areas of pine forests, growing near other trees and bushes, or at the base of cliffs. Their fruit makes an acceptable jam or jelly when mixed with berries such as Wild Gooseberry or Serviceberry.

APPLE–WILD CURRANT BREAD

$^1/_2$ cup butter
  1 cup sugar
  1 egg
  2 cups all-purpose flour
  1 tsp. baking soda
  1 tsp. ground cinnamon
$1^1/_2$ cups chopped, cored, and peeled tart apples
$^1/_2$ cup milk
$^1/_2$ cup Wild Currants
$^1/_2$ cup chopped walnuts

Cream butter and sugar. Add egg, beating well. Add apples, Wild Currants and walnuts. Sift together dry ingredients and add to batter alternately with milk. Bake in buttered bread pan at 350°F for 45 minutes to 1 hour, or until a toothpick inserted comes out clean.

Cool bread in pan before removing.

PEMMICAN

  6 cups jerky, ground into a powder
  4 cups dried Wild Currants, chopped
$^1/_3$ cup melted marrow

Mix first two ingredients well. Gradually add hot fat until mixture is moist enough to stick together. Form into small balls.

Dried Wild Currant–Poppy Seed–Almond Muffins

12 muffins

     1 cup buttermilk
    $^2/_3$ cup dried Wild Currants
    $^1/_4$ tsp. ground cinnamon
    $^1/_8$ tsp. ground ginger
    $^1/_4$ cup butter, cut into bits
    $1^1/_2$ cups all-purpose flour
    $^2/_3$ cup sugar
    $^1/_4$ cup wheat bran
     2 tsp. baking powder
     2 Tbsp. poppy seeds
    $^1/_2$ cup slivered almonds, toasted
     1 tsp. almond extract

Add Wild Currants, cinnamon, and ginger to milk. Heat over moderate heat until milk is hot but not boiling. Remove from heat and set aside. Add butter and stir until butter has melted. Put dry ingredients in bowl. Beat egg into milk mixture. Add poppy seeds, almonds, and extract. Pour over dry ingredients and stir batter until all particles are moistened (do not over-mix). Spoon into 12 buttered muffin tins. Bake in preheated 350°F oven for 20 to 25 minutes.

Spiced Wild Currants

2 pints

     3 quarts ripe Wild Currants, washed and stemmed
     1 tsp. ground cloves
     2 tsp. ground cinnamon
    $^1/_4$ cup water
    $^1/_4$ cup cider vinegar
     5 cups sugar
    $^1/_2$ bottle liquid pectin

In large saucepan combine currants, spices, water, and vinegar. Bring to boiling over medium heat, stirring constantly. Lower heat and simmer, covered, 10 minutes. Add sugar and increase heat; boil hard 1 minute, stirring constantly. Remove from heat and stir in pectin. Stir and skim alternately for 5 minutes. Ladle into hot sterilized jars, filling to $^1/_4$ inch from rim. Seal in boiling water bath for 7 minutes.

FILLED WILD CURRANT COOKIES

4-1/2 dozen

Filling:

- $1^1/_2$ cups Wild Currant purée
- 2 Tbsp. honey

Dough:

- 1 cup butter, softened
- $1^1/_2$ cups brown sugar
- 2 eggs, beaten
- 2 tsp. vanilla
- 3 cups all-purpose flour
- 3 tsp. baking powder
-   Dash salt

To make purée whirl stemmed fresh Wild Currants in food processor until smooth. Add honey and mix well. Set aside.

Cream butter and sugar; add eggs and vanilla. Sift dry ingredients. Add to creamed mixture and blend well. Chill 2 to 3 hours. Roll out a small amount of dough (keeping remainder chilled). Cut rolled dough into rounds with cookie cutter. Place $^1/_2$ tsp. filling on half the cookies. Top with other cookie halves and seal around edges with tines of fork. Bake at 350°F for 12 to 15 minutes.

GLAZED ACORN SQUASH WITH WILD CURRANTS

Serves 6

- 3 acorn squash, halved and seeded
- $^1/_4$ cup butter
- $^1/_2$ cup pure maple syrup
- $^1/_4$ tsp. freshly grated nutmeg
- $^1/_3$ cup dried Wild Currants

Butter each squash half and salt and pepper to taste. Place in large baking pan, cut side down. Add enough water to reach $^1/_4$ inch up the sides of squash halves. Bake at 400°F for 35 minutes.

Combine remaining butter with remaining ingredients and heat over low heat until butter has melted and Wild Currants are plumped. Remove squash from oven and divide maple mixture among the six halves, brushing mixture up sides of squash. Return to oven and continue baking for 25 to 30 minutes, occasionally basting with maple mixture in squash cavities.

WILD CURRANT CAKE

$^3/_4$ cup softened unsalted butter
$^1/_2$ cup sugar
$^1/_4$ cup honey
 3 eggs, well beaten
 2 cups Wild Currants
 1 cup chopped black walnuts
 3 cups sifted cake flour
$^1/_2$ tsp. ground cinnamon
$^1/_4$ tsp. ground cloves
$^1/_4$ tsp. freshly grated nutmeg
 1 tsp. baking powder
$^1/_2$ cup sherry

Cream butter; gradually add sugar and honey; beat until light. Beat in eggs. Add Wild Currants and nuts. Sift together dry ingredients, then add to batter alternately with sherry, beating well after each addition.

Grease and flour a 9 inch tube pan. Line bottom with waxed paper. Pour batter into prepared pan and bake in preheated 300°F oven for $1^1/_2$ hours. Cool 5 minutes. Turn cake onto rack and peel off paper. Cool completely. Wrap and store in tightly covered container for at least 2 weeks before slicing. Keeps 1 month refrigerated or 6 months frozen.

WILD CURRANT LIQUEUR

   Zest from 1 small lemon
 6 cups Wild Currants
 3 cups sugar
 1 fifth vodka

Combine zest, Wild Currants, sugar, and vodka in gallon jar. Invert jar daily until sugar dissolves (approximately 6 days). Place in cool dark place and allow to stand for 6 weeks. Strain through several layers of cheesecloth. Pour into bottles; cork. After 4 weeks, siphon clear liquid into decorative bottles and seal.

WILD CURRANT PIE

Pastry for two-crust 9 inch pie
1¹/₂ cups dried Wild Currants
1¹/₂ cups water
  3 Tbsp. flour
 ³/₄ cup brown sugar
  2 Tbsp. fresh lemon juice
  2 tsp. grated lemon rind
 ¹/₂ tsp. ground cinnamon
 ¹/₄ tsp. freshly grated nutmeg
 ¹/₄ tsp. ground allspice
2¹/₂ Tbsp. butter

Simmer Wild Currants in water for 5 minutes. Mix together flour and sugar; slowly stir in some of the hot cooking liquid. When well combined, add Wild Currants and cook, stirring, until thickened. Add remaining ingredients. Cool to room temperature. Turn into pastry-lined pan, trim and moisten edge, then top with pastry. Trim and crimp the edges. Bake at 425°F for 15 minutes, reduce heat to 350°F and bake 30 minutes longer.

WILD CURRANT–RASPBERRY PUDDING

Serves 4

Thin slices white bread with crusts removed
1¹/₂ pints raspberries
 ³/₄ pint Wild Currants
1¹/₄ cups sugar
  Whipped cream

Line 1¹/₂ quart pudding mold or bowl with bread slices. Combine fruit and sugar in saucepan and simmer over low heat for 5 minutes. Cool. Pour into lined mold or bowl and top with slices of bread. Cover with a plate which will fit inside mold or bowl and weight it well. Let mold stand in refrigerator overnight. To serve, unmold in a deep dish and garnish with whipped cream.

WILD CURRANT PUDDING WITH SHERRY SAUCE

8x8 inch pan

1   cup sifted flour
1   tsp. baking soda
    Dash salt
$^1/_4$ tsp. ground cinnamon
1   cup seedless raisins
1   cup chopped walnuts
1   cup sugar
$1^1/_2$ cups puréed Wild Currants
1   Tbsp. melted butter
1   tsp. vanilla
$^3/_4$ cup milk
    Sherry Sauce (recipe follows)

Sift together dry ingredients; combine with raisins and nuts. Add sugar to Wild Currant purée, then mix in butter and vanilla. Combine dry ingredients with Wild Currant mixture and milk, blend thoroughly. Spoon into greased 8x8 inch pan and bake in 325°F oven for 1 hour. Serve warm with sherry sauce.

Sherry Sauce:

3   egg yolks
2   cups sugar
1   cup Sherry wine
$^1/_2$ cup butter

Beat eggs well in top of double boiler. Mix in sugar. Stir in sherry and butter. Cook over simmering water, stirring constantly, until fairly clear and thickened. Serve hot.

CHAPTER 24

WILD GOOSEBERRY

(Ribes inerme, R. leucaderme, R. montigenum)

Also known as
Prickly Currant

Ribes, is a name from the ancient Arabic. The specific name, *inerme,* means unarmed, but don't be fooled by the name—this Gooseberry is armed, as are all of the eighty species of Wild Gooseberries growing in North America. The branches are loaded with one-quarter to one-half inch thorns. The thorns are particularly evident at the point where the leaves attach to the stems.

There are several species of Wild Gooseberries widely distributed throughout the Rocky Mountains. They are all very similar. *Ribes inerme* and *R. leucoderme* have smooth berries, while the berries of *R. montigenum* are covered with hairs.

These three to five foot tall shrubs grow in moist areas in pine forests, preferring flood plains, stream banks, and cool ravines at elevations from 5,000 to 9,000 feet. They are very hardy, doing best in cold climates. Frost never bothers the blossoms and winter cold doesn't harm the plants.

Wild Gooseberries, members of the saxifrage family, bloom in May having white to pink colored trumpet-shaped flowers in saucer-shaped racemes. The small flowers each have five petals and five sepals. The clusters of leaves are arranged alternately on young, slender, reclining branches that are in their first year of growth. The leaves have three to five lobes and resemble rounded maple leaves; the lobes being irregular and toothed.

The thin skinned berries ripen in mid–July to mid–August, turning from green to reddish or deep purple in color. The green berries have white lines running lengthwise, but as they ripen the lines become less distinct. The round fruits develop on short stems and average three-eighths of an inch in diameter. The Gooseberry flower has an inferior ovary, located beneath the floral parts, which expands when fertilized, forcing the dried blossom part to the top of the fruit. The retained part resembles a pigtail.

Wild Gooseberries, like the domestic fruits, are great for pies, jams, jellies and syrups. The wild are not as numerous as the domestic, so they take longer to gather, averaging one quart per hour. Several tribes native to the Rocky Mountains not only used the fruit as a food source but also consumed the cooked berries to relieve fevers and chills.

Wild Gooseberries and Wild Currants, both members of the *Ribes,* are likely carriers of blister rust, a disease that is fatal to five-needled pines. Blister rust does not affect the *Ribes.* Massive efforts have been made by the Forest Service to destroy the *Ribes* in order to protect the timber producing pines. All efforts have failed.

POACHED GOOSEBERRIES
Serves 4

- 2 cups sugar
- $^1/_2$ cup water
- 3 slices lemon
- $^1/_4$ tsp. cinnamon
- 2 pints Wild Gooseberries
- 2 Tbsp. Cointreau

Combine sugar, water, lemon, and cinnamon and boil for 8 to 10 minutes. Add Wild Gooseberries and simmer 4 to 5 minutes. Allow to cool in syrup. When cool stir in Cointreau. Serve with whipped cream, if desired.

SPICED WILD GOOSEBERRY JAM
3 pints

- 2 quarts Wild Gooseberries
- 4 cups brown sugar
- 1 cup cider vinegar
- 3 sticks cinnamon
- 10 whole cloves
- 3 whole allspice
- $^1/_2$ cup water

Combine sugar, vinegar, spices, and water. Bring to boiling. Boil 5 minutes. Add Wild Gooseberries, reduce heat and cook for 25 minutes (or until syrup has thickened). Remove cinnamon sticks, cloves, and allspice. Ladle into sterilized jars and seal.

WILD GOOSEBERRY FOOL
Serves 4

- $1^1/_2$ pints Wild Gooseberries
- $1^1/_4$ cups sugar
- 1 cup water
- $1^1/_2$ cups heavy cream

Combine sugar and water and bring to boil. Add Wild Gooseberries and simmer 8 to 10 minutes. Cool. Drain well, then purée in food processor. Whip cream until stiff; sweeten with a little sugar, if desired. Fold in Gooseberry purée. Serve chilled.

WILD GOOSEBERRY LIQUEUR

4 cups Wild Gooseberries
6 inch piece cinnamon stick
2 Tbsp. apple juice
2 cups sugar
3 cups dry white wine
2 cups brandy

In food processor, finely chop Wild Gooseberries. Put in saucepan with apple juice and cinnamon and simmer, covered, 5 minutes. Stir in sugar until dissolved; cool. Combine Wild Gooseberry mixture with wine and brandy. Pour into glass jar, cover, and store in cool place for 4 to 6 weeks. Strain through several layers of cheesecloth. Pour into decorative containers. Cap tightly.

WILD GOOSEBERRY SYRUP

4 half pints

3 cups ground Wild Gooseberries
$^1/_2$ cup water
$2^1/_2$ cups sugar
1 cup clover honey
2 Tbsp. powdered pectin

Simmer Wild Gooseberries in water for 10 minutes. Pour into jelly bag and squeeze out juice. Place in large kettle and bring to boil. Add remaining ingredients and cook 4 minutes. Pour into sterilized jars or bottles and seal in boiling water bath for 10 minutes.

WILD GOOSEBERRY STREUSEL

Serves 4

$2^1/_2$ pints Wild Gooseberries
Juice of 2 limes
$^3/_4$ cup firmly packed brown sugar
$^1/_2$ cup flour
$^1/_3$ cup butter

Combine Wild Gooseberries with lime juice and let stand for 30 minutes. Blend together sugar and flour, then cut in butter until mixture is crumbly. Place Wild Gooseberry mixture in a 6 cup baking dish and top with streusel mixture. Bake at 400°F for 30 to 35 minutes or until golden brown. Serve with whipped cream.

WILD GOOSEBERRY ICE CREAM

1   quart Wild Gooseberries
1   Tbsp. freshly squeezed lemon juice
1   quart heavy cream, scalded
1$^1/_2$ cups sugar
1   cup water

Combine sugar and water; add Wild Gooseberries and simmer, without stirring, for 8 to 10 minutes. Cool. Pour cream into ice cream freezer and follow manufacturer's directions for freezing. When cream turns mushy, add Wild Gooseberry mixture and continue freezing until thoroughly frozen.

WILD GOOSEBERRY BASTING SAUCE

1-1/2 cups

1   onion, chopped
3   cups chopped Wild Gooseberries
1   Tbsp. vegetable oil
1   tsp. dry mustard
2   Tbsp. fresh lime juice
1   Tbsp. Dijon-style mustard
2   tsp. soy sauce
2   Tbsp. sugar
$^1/_2$ cup water

Cook onion and Wild Gooseberries in oil over moderately low heat until onion is softened. Stir in mustards, lime, soy sauce, sugar, and $^1/_2$ cup water. Bring mixture to boil and simmer, stirring occasionally, for 25 minutes or until very thick. Use to baste chicken, ribs, or shrimp during last third of cooking time.

WILD GOOSEBERRY MARGARITAS

Serves 8

   1 cup firmly packed light brown sugar
1¹/₂ cups apple juice
   1 lb. Wild Gooseberries
   2 tart green apples, peeled and sliced
   6 cups ice cubes
1¹/₂ cups tequila
   6 Tbsp. triple sec
 ¹/₂ cup liquid whiskey-sour mix
 ¹/₂ cup fresh lime juice

In heavy saucepan combine brown sugar and 1 cup apple juice, bring to boiling, stirring, then add Wild Gooseberries. Boil mixture for 2 to 3 minutes, stirring. Reduce heat and simmer mixture for 8 minutes longer, stirring occasionally. Cool to room temperature, then purée in food processor along with remaining apple juice and the two apples.

In blender purée ice with remaining ingredients, then add Wild Gooseberry mixture and purée until smooth. Serve at once.

WILD GOOSEBERRY PIE

   4 cups Wild Gooseberries
   1 cup sugar
 ¹/₄ cup cornstarch
   1 egg yolk
   2 Tbsp. heavy cream
      Crust for two-crust 9 inch pie
   3 Tbsp. butter

Line 9 inch pie pan with pie crust. Add Wild Gooseberries, sugar, and cornstarch, then dot with butter. Cover with top crust. Crimp edges, vent for steam and brush top of crust with beaten egg yolk. Bake in preheated 450°F oven for 10 minutes, reduce heat and bake at 325°F for 35 to 45 minutes.

CHAPTER
25

WILD MINT

(Mentha arvensis)
Also known as field mint, poleo mint, and Indian mint.

The goddess Persephone discovered that Pluto adored the beautiful Minthe. In a fit of jealousy she turned Minthe into a lowly plant. Pluto couldn't undo Persephone's spell, but he did have the power to add one of his own. He bestowed upon Minthe a fragrance that would grow sweeter and more enticing whenever she was trod upon. Over time the name Minthe was changed to Mentha and become the genus of mint.

Mentha arvensis is the only native true mint in the Rocky Mountains. There are, however, numerous naturalized mints growing in the Rocky Mountain region including *M. aquatica* (water-mint), *M. longifolia* (horse-mint), *M. piperita* (peppermint), and *M. spicata* (spearmint). All mints have similar characteristics and uses.

Mints are square stemmed perennials, averaging one and one-half to two feet in height, which send up new plants from their spreading roots. The leaves grow opposite along the stem and are simple, toothed and very fragrant. The plants are a light green when found growing in sunny areas and darker when growing in shade. Tiny, bell-shaped pale pink to lavender flowers bloom from July through September each maturing into four smooth ovoid nutlets.

Naturalized mint flowers grow on spikes. Our native mint, however, forms flowers around the plant stem just above the pairs of leaves. Also, unlike naturalized mints which rise on single, unbranched stems, *M. anvensis* frequently branches, particularly in late summer. It's scent is a cross between peppermint and pennyroyal.

Wild mint is found in wet places, such as along streams, ditches, and moist meadows, from 5,000 to 9,000 feet throughout the Rocky Mountains. Being rich in vitamins A, B, and C, mints make a delicious and healthful addition to vegetables, salads, soups, and beverages. Some chefs have even used the fresh leaves to line cake tins to impart their delightful flavor to the baked product. Though some naturalists claim that mint is best picked before the flowers appear, I have found the plant delightful to use during all stages of its development.

Dried mint makes excellent tea. Peppermint and spearmint came to North America with the colonists who used them medicinally as a tea for headaches, heartburn, indigestion, and to induce sleep. It is important that mint be dried slowly to retain its flavor. Hang bundles of mint in a warm area, out of direct sunlight. After three to four days, when the leaves and stems are dry and brittle, crumble them into a container which can be tightly sealed. To brew Wild Mint tea, pour boiling water over two teaspoonfuls of dried herb and allow to steep for several minutes.

CHILLED PEA SOUP WITH WILD MINT

Serves 6

1¹/₂ cups green split peas
   4 cups water
   4 cups chicken broth
   1 small onion, sliced
   3 cloves garlic, crushed
   4 sprigs Wild Mint
     Salt to taste
   2 cups heavy cream
     Fresh Wild Mint leaves, finely chopped

Add peas to water in kettle and bring to boiling. Cook for 5 minutes. Remove from heat and let stand 1 hour. Drain. Add chicken broth to peas and bring to a boil. Add onion, garlic, Wild Mint, and salt. Reduce heat, cover, and simmer until peas are tender. Remove Wild Mint and purée pea mixture. Chill overnight. Just before serving stir in heavy cream. Serve in chilled bowls and garnish with chopped Wild Mint.

FRENCH DRESSING WITH WILD MINT

   2 cloves garlic, crushed
   1 cup white wine vinegar
   2 tsp. dry mustard
   1 Tbsp. sugar
   2 tsp. salt
   1 tsp. paprika
¹/₂ tsp. freshly ground pepper
   2 cups olive oil
¹/₄ cup chopped Wild Mint

Mix all ingredients together in food processor or blender. Store in covered container in the refrigerator.

Stuffed Leg of Lamb with Wild Mint

Serves 6

    Leg of lamb, boned, with shank bone left in
6 cloves garlic, minced
$^2/_3$ cup chopped Wild Mint
$^1/_4$ cup chopped cilantro
2 tsp. freshly ground pepper
2 tsp. brown sugar
1 Tbsp. fresh lime juice
$^1/_2$ cup red wine
$^1/_2$ cup melted butter

Combine garlic, Wild Mint, parsley, pepper, brown sugar, and lime juice. Spread mixture over inner surface of lamb, then roll and tie it. Place on rack in roasting pan and roast at 325°F, basting with mixture of wine and butter which have been added to pan juices. Serve with pan juices.

Tabbouleh

Serves 4

1 cup bulgar wheat
1 onion, chopped
3 red tomatoes, chopped
2 yellow tomatoes, chopped
$^1/_2$ cup finely chopped Wild Mint
$^1/_4$ cup chopped parsley
$^1/_4$ cup fresh lime juice
$^1/_2$ cup olive oil
    Freshly ground pepper
    Wild Mint leaves for garnish

Cover bulgar with 2 cups water and let stand for $1^1/_2$ hours. Drain bulgar. Add remaining ingredients and chill. Serve garnished with fresh Wild Mint leaves.

Turkish Yogurt Soup with Wild Mint

Serves 6

6 cups chicken broth
$^1/_2$ cup long-grain rice
2 cups yogurt
2 egg yolks
$^1/_4$ cup finely chopped fresh Wild Mint

In large saucepan combine broth and rice. Simmer gently 20 minutes or until rice is tender. In bowl whisk together yogurt and yolks. Whisk in 1 cup hot broth, then add to remaining broth in saucepan, whisking to keep smooth. Cook over moderately low heat, stirring, until slightly thickened. Add Wild Mint and salt and pepper to taste.

Wild Mint Butter

$^1/_2$ cup butter
2 Tbsp. fresh squeezed lime juice
1 tsp. curry powder
$^1/_2$ cup Wild Mint, finely chopped

Soften butter and mix with remaining ingredients. Good served with lamb or pork.

Wild Mint Cordial

2 pints

$1^1/_2$ pints water
3 cups sugar
5 cups chopped Wild Mint
$1^1/_2$ cups gin

Combine sugar with water and bring to boiling. Boil hard 2 minutes, then cool. Add Wild Mint and gin. Let stand for 4 weeks. Strain. Pour into an attractive bottle and cork or cap securely.

WILD MINT JELLY

3 pints

6 cups apple juice
3 cups torn Wild Mint leaves
$^3/_4$ cup water
$3^1/_2$ cups sugar

In saucepan combine Wild Mint, water, and 1 cup sugar. Let stand 4 hours. Heat to boiling; remove from heat and let stand 1 hour. Strain and discard leaves.

Bring apple juice to boiling. Add remaining sugar and boil hard for 4 minutes. Stir in strained Wild Mint liquid. Cook until mixture has reached jelly point. Remove from heat and skim. Ladle into sterilized jars, adjust lids and seal in boiling water bath for 7 minutes.

WILD MINT JULEP

In bottom of each tall, chilled glass put 1 tsp. sugar and 1 tsp. water; mix well. Add 2 tsp. fresh Wild Mint leaves and grind into sugar–water mixture with back of spoon. Fill glasses with crushed ice. Pour bourbon over ice and stir well. Garnish with Wild Mint sprigs.

WILD MINT–LEMON COOLER

Serves 2

2 lemons
12 sprigs Wild Mint
$^1/_3$ cup granulated sugar
4 cups cold water

Squeeze juice from lemons; add Wild Mint and sugar. Mash with potato masher to extract flavor from mint. Let mixture set for 30 minutes. Stir in water. Pour over cracked ice and serve.

WILD MINT SHERBET

2 cups milk
2¹/₂ cups chopped Wild Mint leaves
1¹/₂ cups sugar
¹/₂ cup light corn syrup
2 cups light cream
Few drops green food coloring (optional)

Heat Wild Mint in milk over double boiler, mashing with potato masher to extract mint flavor. When milk starts to bubble, remove from heat. Let cool, then strain to remove spent leaves. Add sugar, syrup, and cream to milk. Add food coloring, if desired. Beat with electric mixer until smooth. Freeze in ice cream freezer, following the manufacturer's directions.

WILD MINT AND YOGURT MARINADE

1 cup

¹/₃ cup minced fresh Wild Mint leaves
1 tsp. honey
1 tsp. minced garlic
1 Tbsp. fresh lime juice
2 Tbsp. olive oil
1 cup plain yogurt

In bowl mash Wild Mint, sugar, and garlic together with fork. Stir in remaining ingredients. Add salt to taste. Use to marinate lamb or chicken. Cover and chill overnight.

CHAPTER
26

WILD PLUM

(Prunus americana)

Also known as
Cherry Plum

Immigrants traveling The Oregon Trail often wrote in their diaries of the wonderful sweet-tart Wild Plums found along the trail in late summer. The fruit was also enjoyed extensively by the Native Americans who often dried them for winter use by slitting the plums, removing the pits, then spreading the fruit in the sun to dry.

Wild Plums are one of the first flowering shrubs to bloom in the spring, displaying a profusion of fragrant white blossoms in late April and early May. The delicate flowers, which appear before the leaves, resemble cherry blossoms, each with five spreading petals surrounding fifteen to twenty stamens. Unfortunately, the danger of frost has not always passed when the Wild Plum blooms, so often the crop is lost by a late cold snap.

The three to ten foot bushes are most often found growing clumped together in thickets. These thickets are irregularly scattered in the Rocky Mountain area, usually at lower elevations. They grow on rolling plains, foothills, draw, canyons, and flood plains, preferring east slopes. The bark of the branches vary, the older branches being a glossy gray with thorns or spines at the tips, while the younger branches are a dark brown. Leaves, which appear as the blossoms fade, are two or four inches long, spear-shaped and have a serrated margin.

In late August through September the fruit of the Wild Plums ripen and will remain on the bush until mid–October. They vary from the size of a marble to that of a cherry tomato, one-half to one and one-half inches in diameter, depending on how fertile the soil is and the amount of moisture received. The pulpy fruits are round to oval in shape, having rather tough skin and a flattened pit. When ripe, their hue can vary from deep pink to pale yellow. Wild Plums also vary in flavor from tree to tree so it is best to sample a few to find one which best suits your taste. Many cultivated varieties have been developed from the Wild Plum.

Insects can invade the green fruit, causing them to swell, turn black and drop off the bush. Therefore, if the frost doesn't bite the blossoms and the insects don't infest the fruit, you have a good chance of beating the birds, deer, and bear to the harvest.

The green fruit of the Wild Plums can be eaten when cooked with sugar and honey or used in chutney. Most people prefer the ripened fruit for use in jams, jellies, sauces, syrups, chutneys, and wine. The fresh fruit is also delightful eaten off the bush.

Wild plums are easy to freeze by rinsing and draining them, then placing the fruit in gallon freezer bags and freezing. They will keep up to six months. Thawed plums are easier to pit since the seed slips out when the softened fruit is gently squeezed. Another method of pitting is to gently simmer the fruit in a small amount of water until the skins begin to break, cool, then gently squeeze out the pits. If you desire to use the fresh fruit pitted, most Wild Plums will fit through the opening of a hand-cranked cherry pitter.

The pits of Wild Plums contain high levels of toxic hydrocyanic acid, or cyanide. The nutlike core of the pits should not be eaten raw. Cyanide is destroyed by heat and the inner core of the pits may be eaten as a survival food if roasted.

PIQUANT WILD PLUM

2 cups

2 cups pitted Wild Plums
$^1/_2$ cup honey
$^1/_2$ cup water
$^1/_3$ cup cider vinegar
3 Tbsp. rum
$^1/_2$ Tbsp. minced onion
1 Tbsp. fresh rosemary
1 tsp. soy sauce

Boil honey and water for 1 minute. Add the remaining ingredients except the Wild Plums. Stir well. Pour the mixture over Wild Plums and let them marinate for 3 to 4 hours or overnight. Serve as an appetizer with toothpicks.

WILD PLUM BUTTER

1 quart

1 quart sieved cooked Wild Plums
1 cup honey
1 tsp. powdered ginger

Combine ingredients and mix well. Put into a baking pan and bake at 300°F until thick, stirring every 30 minutes. Spoon into hot sterilized jars and seal in boiling water bath 10 minutes.

SPICED WILD PLUM BRANDY

6 quarts

3 gallons ripe Wild Plums
2 lbs. sugar
2 Tbsp. whole cloves
4 inch piece stick cinnamon
2 quarts brandy

Mash Wild Plums to release juice. Put in large kettle and bring to boiling. Reduce heat and simmer 5 minutes. Pour plums into clean pillow case and hang over large kettle overnight. Discard solids in pillow case.

Bring juice, sugar, and spices to a boil. Skim carefully; cool completely. Add brandy and mix well. Pour into decorative bottles and cork.

WILD PLUM CHUTNEY

4 quarts

$1^1/_2$ cups cider vinegar
$2^1/_2$ cups firmly packed brown sugar
5 cups pitted and chopped Wild Plums
1 lemon, seeded and finely chopped
3 cloves garlic, crushed
1 seeded green bell pepper, chopped
1 seeded red bell pepper, chopped
$^1/_2$ cup grated fresh gingerroot
$1^1/_2$ cups raisins
1 tsp. salt
$^1/_2$ tsp. cayenne pepper
1 large onion, chopped

Bring vinegar and brown sugar to a boil. Add Wild Plums and simmer 10 minutes. Add remaining ingredients and simmer another 10 minutes. Fill sterilized jars with hot mixture and seal in boiling water bath for 10 minutes.

WILD PLUM CURRY SAUCE

1 pint

       6 Tbsp. butter
    $^3/_4$ cup finely chopped onion
    $^3/_4$ cup finely chopped pitted Wild Plums
    $^1/_4$ cup finely chopped celery
       2 tsp to 1 Tbsp. curry powder, depending on taste
    $^1/_4$ tsp. hot pepper sauce
          Salt to taste
    $1^1/_2$ cups chicken broth
          Beurre manié
       2 Tbsp. chutney
          Grated lime rind

Melt butter in saucepan, add onion and Wild Plums and cook slowly until soft. Add celery and cook 5 minutes longer. Blend in curry and cook 4 more minutes. Add pepper sauce, salt, and broth. Cook 5 minutes, then thicken with beurre manié. Add chutney and a little grated rind just before serving.

WILD PLUM–HORSERADISH SAUCE

3 cups

    $^3/_4$ cup freshly grated horseradish (may use prepared)
       3 cups pitted, chopped Wild Plums
    $^1/_2$ cup brown sugar, firmly packed

Cook together Wild Plums and brown sugar until plums are very soft. Put through a sieve. Stir in horseradish and chill. Serve with pork or poultry. Keeps 1 month.

WILD PLUM LEATHER

       3 pints cooked, sieved Wild Plums
       2 cups brown sugar, firmly packed

Add sugar to sieved Wild Plums and simmer over moderate heat until thickened (approximately 45 minutes). Spread $^1/_4$ inch thick on sheets of plastic wrap and place in sunny spot until dry and leather-like. Peel from plastic wrap, roll, and wrap in fresh plastic.

WILD PLUM MARMALADE

2$^1/_2$ lbs. sugar
1$^1/_4$ cups water
2$^1/_2$ lbs. Wild Plums, pitted and chopped
1 cup orange juice
$^1/_2$ cup orange rind, very thinly sliced
3 Tbsp. lemon rind, very thinly sliced
$^1/_4$ cup freshly squeezed lemon juice

Bring sugar and water to boil. Add remaining ingredients and simmer 1$^1/_2$ hours over medium heat. Ladle into sterilized jars and seal.

WILD PLUM PAN DOWDY

Serves 8

5 cups pitted and sliced Wild Plums
1$^1/_2$ cups sorghum
1 tsp. freshly grated nutmeg
1 tsp. ground cinnamon
$^1/_4$ tsp. ground cloves
$^1/_2$ tsp. ground ginger
Pastry for one-crust 9 inch pie

Put Wild Plums into a buttered 9x9 inch baking dish. Cover with sorghum and spices. Top with pastry and bake at 350°F for 1 hour. Serve warm with crust down and Wild Plum mixture on top. Add vanilla ice cream or whipped cream, if desired.

WILD PLUM PIE

5 cups pitted and chopped Wild Plums
1$^1/_4$ cups sugar
2 Tbsp. cornstarch
Dash salt
$^1/_2$ tsp. freshly grated nutmeg
1$^1/_2$ Tbsp. butter
Pastry for two-crust 9 inch pie

Combine Wild Plums with cornstarch, salt, sugar, and nutmeg. Line 9 inch pie pan with pastry and spoon fruit into crust. Dot with butter, adjust top crust and crimp edges to seal. Bake in preheated 425°F oven for 10 minutes; reduce heat to 350°F and bake 35 to 45 minutes longer.

WILD PLUM SOUP

Serves 6

2 lbs. pitted Wild Plums, chopped
2 cups water
2 inch piece cinnamon stick
3 cloves
  Dash salt
2 cups Sherry wine
$^1/_2$ cup sugar
2 egg yolks, well beaten

Cook Wild Plums in water with cinnamon, cloves, and salt until they are soft. Remove cinnamon and cloves and purée in food processor or blender. Stir in sherry and sugar. Mix a small amount of soup mixture with yolks, then stir into soup. Cook over medium heat, stirring, until soup thickens. Cool and chill. Serve cold as a first course or dessert.

WILD PLUM UPSIDE-DOWN CAKE

1 cup butter
2 cups sugar
3 cups sifted cake flour
4 eggs
4 tsp. baking powder
  Dash salt
1 cup milk
2 tsp. pure vanilla extract
$^1/_2$ cup melted butter
1 cup brown sugar
4 cups sliced Wild Plums
1 cup coarsely chopped filberts
1 Tbsp. finely chopped candied ginger

Make batter of first seven ingredients, beating until smooth batter is formed. Melt butter in bottom of 10x14x2 inch sheet cake pan. Sprinkle sugar over melted butter, then sprinkle Wild Plums, ginger, and walnuts over the sugar. Top with batter.

Bake at 350°F for 45 minutes. Loosen edges and quickly invert cake onto foil covered baking sheet. Serve hot or cold.

Chapter 27

WILD ROSE

(Rosa woodsii, ssp.)
Also known as
Brier Hip

Wild Roses grow around the world from Greenland to Tasmania, from Siberia to India. There are more than one hundred species of *Rosa* growing wild in North America and since they easily hybridize with one another even botanists have difficulty keeping them straight. Several species of Wild Rose grow in the Rocky Mountains, these species range in elevation from 4,000 to 9,000 feet. Some types are found growing in pine forests, some along streams and others in dry rocky places.

All of our regional roses, however, have some of the same characteristics—fragrant flowers, approximately $^1/_2$ inch across, with five pink petals, five sepals, numerous yellow stamens, hips, thorns, and prickles. Though some species may reach four feet in height, others don't exceed a foot. All have alternate, pinnately compound leaves with five to nine serrated leaflets.

Wild Roses bloom from June to July, depending on elevation. Many delicious foods can be made from the fresh petals. Where the shrubs grow densely an ambitious harvester can gather a plastic bag filled with petals within an hour. The white base of the petal must be removed before the petals are used since this portion contains a disagreeable bitter flavor. Snip off the white base with a pair of kitchen shears. The petals can be added to salads, pancakes, muffins, and omelets. Native Americans combined the petals with bear grease to cure mouth sores. Powder made from the dried petals was applied to fever sores and blisters. They also soaked the petals in rain water and used the solution to bathe sore eyes.

The flower petals are attached to the edge of an urn-shaped receptacle that is a swelling at the end of the stem supporting the flower. After the petals fall, the receptacle becomes more fleshy as hard seeds form inside. As the fruit matures the receptacles begin to modify in color, changing from green to orange or red as autumn approaches. These elliptical or globular shaped fruits, called Rosehips, ripen in late August through September. Since Rosehips need cold weather to mature they are best harvested following a heavy frost, often being found still clinging to the bush well after snow fall. The fruits can reach up to one inch in length.

Ounce for ounce ripe Wild Rosehips contain approximately sixty times more vitamin C than lemons and twenty-five times that of oranges; a single hip averaging ten milligrams—the highest concentration of vitamin C of all fruits. These berry-like fruits are also rich in vitamin A, B, and K. The seeds, which have fine hairs attached, are extremely rich in vitamin E. During

World War II, when Britain found itself without enough oranges for the children, Rosehip syrup was substituted. In 1943 approximately five hundred tons of Rosehips were collected to make what was called "National Rose Hip Syrup."

Wild Rosehips can be split, the seeds removed and the pulp eaten raw or cooked. The fresh, seeded Rosehips may be used as a substitute for cranberries in sauces and relishes. They can also be dried and kept for long periods of time. Native Americans would grind the dried Rosehips, seeds and all, into meal.

Even the inner bark and roots of the Wild Rose has had its uses. Rocky Mountain Indians drank a tea made from the roots for fevers and cold symptoms. The inner bark was applied to boils.

ROSEHIP CAKE

```
 1  cup butter
 2  cups sugar
 1  tsp. ground cinnamon
1/2 tsp. freshly grated nutmeg
 1  tsp. grated orange rind
 4  eggs
 2  cups finely chopped, seeded Wild Rosehips
1/2 cup chopped black walnuts
2 1/2 cups sifted flour
 3  tsp. baking powder
    Dash salt
1/3 cup warm water
```

Cream butter and sugar until light and fluffy. Add spices and rind and beat well. Add eggs, one at a time. Stir in Wild Rosehips and nuts. Sift together dry ingredients. Add to Rosehip mixture along with water, folding until all is well moistened. Turn into greased and floured 11x15x2 inch cake pan and bake at 350°F for 45 to 50 minutes. Cool. Ice with penuche, butter, or cream cheese frosting. Best if allowed to stand a day or two before serving.

ROSEHIP COOKIES

$^3/_4$ cup butter
$^3/_4$ cup sugar
$1^1/_2$ cups finely chopped, seeded Wild Rosehips
1 egg
3 tsp. grated orange rind
$2^1/_4$ cups sifted flour
  Dash salt
2 tsp. baking powder
$^1/_2$ tsp. freshly grated nutmeg

Cream together butter and sugar, beat in Wild Rosehips and egg. Mix in rind and dry ingredients. Drop by teaspoonfuls onto greased baking sheet and bake at 375°F for 12 to 15 minutes.

ROSEHIP PUDDING

2 cups finely chopped, seeded Wild Rosehips
$1^1/_2$ cups fine bread crumbs
1 tsp. freshly grated nutmeg
1 tsp. cinnamon
  Dash salt
6 eggs
$^3/_4$ cup sugar
2 Tbsp. butter, melted

Combine Wild Rosehips, crumbs, and spices. Beat eggs with sugar until they are thick and blend into Rosehip mixture along with the butter. Bake pudding in buttered $2^1/_4$ quart baking dish at 350°F for 50 to 55 minutes, or until set. Serve warm with custard or lemon sauce.

ROSEHIP LIQUEUR

1 fifth

1 fifth vodka
$^2/_3$ cup sugar
$^1/_2$ cup water
3 lbs. Wild Rosehips, seeded

Bring sugar and water to boiling. Cool. Add vodka along with Wild Rosehips and allow to stand in covered jug for 8 weeks, shaking every 2 weeks. Strain through several layers of cheesecloth (Rosehips may be saved by drying them and using them in tea). Pour liqueur into decorative bottles; cap or cork securely.

ROSEHIP SOUP

Serves 4

$2^1/_2$ cups Wild Rosehips, halved and seeded
4 cups water
$^1/_2$ cup honey
1 Tbsp. cornstarch
$1^1/_2$ cups water

Simmer Wild Rosehips in 4 cups water for 35 minutes. Cool. Purée. Add cornstarch to $1^1/_2$ cups water in saucepan, then stir in honey and purée. Simmer 5 minutes. Serve at once as a dessert, topped with whipped cream, if desired.

ROSE PETAL BLANCMANGE

(as an accompaniment with wild berries or fruit)

$^3/_4$ cup sugar
$^1/_4$ cup cornstarch
$^1/_4$ tsp. salt
3 cups milk
3 cups Wild Rose Petals
1 tsp. pure vanilla extract
Fresh Wild Rose Petals for garnish

Combine Wild Rose Petals with milk and heat over double boiler for 1 hour. Strain, discarding petals. In saucepan combine sugar, cornstarch, and salt. Blend in the milk. Bring mixture to boil over moderate heat, stirring constantly. Cook 1 minute. Remove the pan from heat and add vanilla. Pour mixture into serving dishes, cover and let pudding cool. To serve, spoon huckleberries or other wild or domestic fruit onto blancmange. Garnish with fresh petals.

SPICED ROSEHIP JAM

Six 6 oz. jelly jars

5 cups seeded Wild Rosehips
4 cups apple juice
$1^1/_4$ cups sugar
$^1/_4$ cup honey
1 tsp. ground cinnamon
$^1/_4$ tsp. ground cloves
$^1/_4$ tsp. freshly grated nutmeg

Combine Rosehips and juice in saucepan. Bring to boiling over medium heat. Reduce heat and simmer, covered, 30 minutes. Purée cooked pulp in blender or food mill. Add sugar, honey, and spices. Return to heat and simmer until fairly thickened. Pour into jelly jars, adjust lids and seal in boiling water bath for 10 minutes.

WILD ROSE CUSTARD PIE

4 eggs, separated
1 cup sugar
1$^1/_2$ Tbsp. flour
$^1/_4$ tsp. powdered ginger
3 cups milk, scalded
$^1/_2$ cup Wild Rose Petals (white part removed)
2 Tbsp. sugar
9 inch pastry shell, unbaked

Combine yolks with 2 egg whites and beat. Mix together sugar, flour, and ginger. Add to eggs; stir in 2 cups milk, gradually. Purée petals in blender with 1 cup milk. Slowly stir into egg mixture. Pour into pastry shell and bake at 450°F for 10 minutes, then reduce heat and bake at 350°F for 30 minutes longer. Beat remaining 2 egg whites stiff, fold in sugar and frost over baked custard. Brown in 300°F oven.

WILD ROSE ICE CREAM

4 cups light cream
3 cups heavy cream
1 cup milk
1 cup sugar
1 cup Wild Rose Petals (white portion removed)
  Dash salt
1 tsp. pure vanilla extract
3 drops red food coloring (optional)

Purée Wild Rose Petals in 1 cup milk. Mix all ingredients together. Freeze in ice cream freezer following manufacturer's instructions.

WILD ROSE PETAL JAM

5 pints

  7 cups Wild Rose Petals, picked in midmorning just after the dew
           evaporates
  4 cups warm water
$5^1/_2$ cups sugar
  1 Tbsp. lemon juice
  1 bottle liquid pectin

Snip white portion from base of Wild Rose Petals. Pour water over petals in saucepan and simmer over medium heat 10 minutes. Lift out petals and set aside. Add sugar and bring to boiling. Boil hard 1 minute. Add petals and simmer 5 minutes. Increase to boiling and add pectin and lemon juice, boil 1 minute. Tint a light pink with food coloring, if desired. Pour into sterilized jars, adjust lids. Seal in boiling water bath 7 minutes.

WILD ROSE SODA

  2 cups sugar
  1 cup light corn syrup
$1^1/_4$ cup water
  1 cup Wild Rose Petals (white part removed)
  1 tsp. freshly squeezed lime juice
  2 drops red food coloring (optional)
      Vanilla ice cream
      Soda water

Simmer sugar, syrup, and $^3/_4$ cup water in saucepan. Purée Wild Rose Petals with $^1/_2$ cup water. Add to cooled sugar-syrup mixture along with lime juice. Mix in coloring, if desired. Pour 3 Tbsp. of syrup in bottom of an 8 oz. glass. Add a scoop of ice cream. Fill with soda water.

WILD ROSE VINEGAR

2 pints

    Wild Rose Petals
  2 pints white wine vinegar

Snip off white portion of Wild Rose Petals. Pack petals in glass jars. Pour vinegar over. Secure lid and allow to infuse in direct sunlight for 2 weeks. Strain vinegar, discarding petals. Pour into bottles and cap tightly.

CHAPTER

28

YAMPA

(Perideridia gairdneri)

Also known as wild caraway, ipo, and squawroot.

Yampa was a favorite root food among Rocky Mountain tribes and has often been mentioned as the one they liked the best. In fact, John C. Fremont, declared Yampa to be the finest of all Indian foods. Pioneer travelers and settlers of the Northwest traded flour and meal for the sweet, nutty, parsnip-flavored root gathered by the regional Indians. Lewis and Clark also mentioned Yampa and its value as a native food in their journals.

This plant, closely related to the commercial caraway, is found from British Columbia to Southern California, east to the Black Hills, Colorado, and New Mexico. Yampa is found in open meadows, valleys, on sunlit slopes, or in partial shade and is often very abundant in the Rocky Mountain area. The Yampa River valley in Northwestern Colorado was one of the Rocky Mountain regions where Native Americans annually gathered to harvest the root. According to J.F. Dawson, author of *Place Names in Colorado,* when names were considered for the new state, "Yampa" was a popular choice and ran close competition with the selected name of "Colorado."

This biennial, and sometimes perennial, plant produces a taproot during the first year of growth. It sends up a single stem one to three and one-half feet tall with few leaves which are pinnate with three to seven narrow leaflets. The upper leaves are small and undivided. The tender young plants can be harvested and cooked as a potherb or used fresh as an addition to tossed green or fruit salads, soups, and stews. By the time Yampa flowers, the narrow, grass-like leaves have usually dried up. The blossoms appear in May and June, a compound umbel of small white to yellowish flowers forming rays of unequal length similar to those of a blooming carrot.

The finger-like roots grow deep and sometimes form in groups of two or three. The roots tend to taper both ways and are fairly small, five-eighths of an inch in diameter being a typical size. They are covered with a thin, brown skin. Some of the regional Indians gathered the roots in the spring or early summer then placed them in large baskets set in running water and trod on them with bare feet to remove the outer skin. I have found the brown skin tender and therefore unnecessary to remove. Yampa roots, rich in sugar and starch, may be eaten raw or cooked. They do not store well fresh but will keep indefinitely dried.

Some Native Americans sun-dried the roots then ground them into meal for porridge or for use in breads, soups, and stews. Others steamed them in earth pits covered with wet leaves, grasses, and soil. When the roots had cooked, the covering was removed and the Yampa was mashed and formed into patties which were then set in the sun to dry. Early settlers used the roots as they would potatoes or parsnips.

The seeds are about one-eighth of an inch long and can be used to season soups and stews. The seeds are ripe when they turn brown. To collect the seeds snip the stalk before the seeds fall, then tie the stalks in bundles and hang them upside down in a warm, airy place. Let the seeds drop onto a clean cloth and store them in an airtight container. Since Yampa seeds become bitter during prolonged cooking, the crushed seeds should be added during the last five minutes. Crushed seeds are also good added to biscuits and breads. Native American mothers chewed the seeds to promote the secretion of milk and fed their infants a tea made of the crushed seeds to relieve colic.

BARLEY, YAMPA, AND CABBAGE SOUP
Serves 12

  1 quart boiling water
1¹/₂ cups barley
  2 quarts turkey stock
  4 cups shredded Yampa roots
  4 cups finely diced red or green cabbage
  2 cups cubed turkey
 ¹/₄ tsp. coarse black pepper

Pour water over barley and let stand for 1 hour. Drain. Place barley in kettle and add stock. Bring to boil, reduce heat and simmer for 30 minutes. Add Yampa and cabbage and enough water to cover vegetables with 2 inches to spare. Simmer 15 minutes. Add turkey and pepper and simmer 5 minutes longer. Remove from heat and allow to stand 1 hour to blend flavors. Reheat just prior to serving.

GINGERED YAMPA

Serves 4

30 Yampa roots, peeled
1 tsp. salt
$^1/_4$ tsp. pepper
2 Tbsp. finely chopped candied ginger
$^1/_4$ cup butter
$^1/_4$ cup evaporated milk
$^1/_2$ cup slivered toasted almonds
3 Tbsp. corn flake crumbs

Cook Yampa in covered pot in small amount of boiling water until tender. Drain and mash well. Add remaining ingredients, except nuts and corn flake crumbs. Mix well then turn into a 1 quart buttered casserole. Sprinkle with almonds and crumbs. Bake at 370°F for 25 minutes.

LAMB STEW WITH YAMPA

Serves 6

3 lbs. cubed lamb
Flour
3 Tbsp. olive oil
$^1/_4$ cup butter
Boiling water
1 tsp. salt
6 medium onions, peeled
20 Yampa roots, peeled
5 cloves garlic, crushed
$^1/_4$ cup chopped celery tops
12 small new potatoes, cooked until just tender
2 lbs. frozen peas, thawed
$^1/_4$ cup chopped parsley
$1^1/_2$ tsp. freshly ground pepper

Coat lamb cubes with flour and brown in small amounts of olive oil and butter. Add more oil and butter, if necessary. Transfer meat to heavy kettle or Dutch oven. Rinse the pan with enough boiling water to barely cover lamb and add to pot. Stir in salt and simmer, covered 1 hour. Add onions, Yampa, garlic, and celery tops. Cook until Yampa is tender. Add potatoes, peas, parsley, and pepper. Heat until potatoes are warm.

Mashed Potatoes with Yampa and Horseradish

Serves 4

15 Yampa roots, peeled and cut in half
 1 lb. russet potatoes, peeled and cubed
$^1/_4$ cup cream
$^1/_4$ cup butter
 2 Tbsp. horseradish

Cook Yampa and potatoes in boiling salted water until tender. In saucepan heat cream, butter, and horseradish. Drain, then cook over high heat in dry pan for 30 seconds to evaporate any excess liquid. Remove from heat. Add cream mixture and mash with potato masher until they are smooth. Season to taste with salt and pepper.

Roast Lamb with Yampa

Serves 4

   1 Tbsp. olive oil
   3 lb. rack of lamb
$1^1/_2$ lbs. Yampa roots, scrubbed and peeled, and cut into 1 inch pieces
   1 cup butter
   1 cup heavy cream
   2 canned mild green chilies
   2 Tbsp. salsa
   1 cup dry white wine
   1 cup white wine vinegar
   1 Tbsp. cream
   2 Tbsp. finely chopped shallot

Brown rack of lamb in olive oil. Season with salt and pepper, then place in roasting pan, rib side down, and roast in preheated 400°F oven for $1^1/_2$ hours. Allow to stand 15 minutes, then cut into slices.

As lamb roasts, in steamer set over boiling water, steam Yampa until very tender. Then purée with 1 Tbsp. butter and 1 cup cream; transfer to metal bowl, season with salt and pepper and keep warm.

Purée chilies and salsa; set aside. In heavy skillet simmer wine and vinegar with shallot until liquid is just evaporated. Stir in 1 Tbsp. cream and remaining butter, 2 tablespoons at a time, swirling skillet with each addition. The sauce should not get hot enough to liquefy. Stir in chili mixture.

Divide Yampa purée among 4 heated plates, top each with lamb and spoon sauce over top. Serve at once.

SAUTEED YAMPA

Serves 4

20 Yampa roots, scraped and cut into thin strips
6 Tbsp. butter
   Salt and pepper to taste

Parboil Yampa in salted water for 8 minutes. Drain well. Again cook in salted water for 8 minutes. Drain. Put butter in saucepan and heat until bubbling, then add Yampa and sauté quickly over fairly high heat, stirring, until Yampa is lightly browned. Season with salt and pepper and serve at once.

YAMPA AND APPLE PURÉE

Serves 6

2 lbs. Yampa roots, scraped and cut into 1 inch pieces
1 cup finely chopped onion
2 large Granny Smith apples, peeled, cored, and thinly sliced
2 Tbsp. butter
3 Tbsp. sour cream
$^1/_2$ tsp. freshly grated nutmeg
   Salt and pepper to taste

Cook Yampa in salted water for 12 minutes. Drain and rinse well. In large skillet cook onion and apples in butter over moderate heat until apples are very tender. Add to food processor along with drained Yampa and purée until smooth. Add cream, nutmeg, and salt and pepper to taste. Heat and serve.

YAMPA FRITTERS

Serves 4

1 lb. Yampa roots, scraped
1 cup milk
2 eggs
1 tsp. baking powder
$^1/_4$ tsp. salt
   Flour
   Oil for deep-frying

Cook roots in boiling salted water until tender. Drain. Combine remaining ingredients, adding enough flour to make a batter the consistency of pancakes. Dip Yampa in batter and deep-fry, a few at a time, at 375°F until golden brown.

YAMPA WITH HERBS

Serves 6

1¹/₂ lbs. Yampa roots, scraped
1 tsp. white wine vinegar
¹/₂ tsp. salt
¹/₄ cup butter
1 Tbsp. chopped parsley
2 tsp. chopped chives
1 tsp. chopped dill weed
¹/₄ tsp. salt
Flour
1 Tbsp. lemon juice

Cover Yampa with cold water. Add vinegar and ¹/₂ tsp. salt, then bring to a boil. Cook, covered, 20 minutes. Drain. Melt butter. Add herbs. Dredge Yampa lightly with flour; add to butter mixture and cook until lightly browned. Add lemon juice just before serving.

YAMPA PURÉE

Serves 8

3 lbs. Yampa, scraped
1 tsp. salt
1¹/₂ tsp. sugar
¹/₂ cup butter, melted
¹/₄ cup heavy cream
¹/₃ cup Madeira
Buttered bread crumbs

In salted water boil Yampa until tender. Drain. Purée in food processor, then add salt, sugar, butter, cream, and Madeira. Spoon into 1 quart baking dish, sprinkle with bread crumbs and bake at 350°F for 25 to 30 minutes.

BIBLIOGRAPHY

Angier, Bradford, *Field Guide to Medical Wild Plants*. Pennsylvania: Stackpole Books, 1978.

Angier, Bradford, *Skills for Taming the Wilds*. Pennsylvania: Stackpole Books, 1967.

Audubon Society Field Guide to North American Trees: Western Region. New York: Alfred A. Knopf, 1980.

Boren, Marjorie D., and Boren, Robert R., *Mountain Wildflowers of Idaho*. Idaho: Sawtooth Publishing Company, 1989.

Cummings, Elsie J., Charlton, Wavie J., *Survival: Pioneer, Indian and Wilderness Lore*. Montana: Wavie J. Charlton, 1971.

Dawson, Adele G., *Health, Happiness, and the Pursuit of Herbs*. Vermont: The Stephen Greene Press, 1980.

Gibbons, Euell, *Stalking the Healthful Herbs*. New York: David McKay Company, Inc., 1970.

Hall, Alan, *The Wild Food Trail Guide*. New York: Rinehart and Winston, 1976.

Harrington, H.D., *Edible Native Plants of the Rocky Mountains*. New Mexico: University of New Mexico Press, 1967.

Krumm, Bob, *The Rocky Mountain Berry Book*. Montana: Falcon Press, 1991.

Lincoff, Gary H., *The Audubon Society Field Guide to North American Mushrooms*. New York, Alfred A. Knopf, 1981.

Lust, John, *The Herb Book*. New York: Bantam Books, 1974.

Medsger, Oliver Perry, *Edible Wild Plants*. New York: Collier Books, 1972.

Moore, Michael, *Medicinal Plants of the Mountain West*. New Mexico: Museum of New Mexico Press, 1979.

Niethammer, Carolyn, *American Indian Food and Lore*. New York: Collier Books, 1974.

Ody, Penelope, *The Complete Medicinal Herbal*. New York: Dorling Kindersley, 1993.

Olsen, Dean, *Outdoor Survival Skills*. Utah: Brigham Young University Press, 1967.

Randall, W.R., Keniston, R.F., Bever, D.N., *Manual of Oregon Trees and Shrubs*. Oregon: O.S.U. Books, Inc., 1976.

Rodale's Illustrated Encyclopedia of Herbs. Pennsylvania: Rodale Press, 1987.

Spellenberg, Richard, *The Audubon Society Field Guide to North American Wildflowers: Western Range*. New York: Alfred A. Knopf, 1992 edition.

Sweet, Muriel, *Common Edible and Useful Plants of the West*. California: Naturegraph Publishers, 1976.

Underhill, J.E., *Wild Berries of the Pacific Northwest*. Seattle: Superior Publishing Company, 1974.

Williamson, Darcy, *How to Prepare Common Wild Foods*. Oregon: Maverick Publications, 1979.

Williamson, Darcy, *Wild Foods of the Desert*. Oregon: Maverick Publications, 1987.

INDEX

Acorn Squash with Currants, Glazed, 197
Ale, Nettle, 181
Almandine, Fireweed, 80
Almond Muffins, Dried Wild Currant with
      Poppy Seed, 196
Almonds, Milkweed with, 116
Alsatian Stew, 97
Amelanchier alnifolia, 161
Amelanchier pumila, 161
Amelanchier utahensis, 161
Anchovy Salad, Cattail Shoot, Pepper, 29
Angel Pie, Elderberry, 62
Apple Butter, Chokecherry–, 44
Apple Crisp, Huckleberry, 87
Apple Purée, Yampa and, 234
Apple–Wild Currant Bread, 195
Arctium minus, 13
ARROWHEAD
    Campfire Stew, 9
    Chicken Stir-Fry, and, 4
    Chowder, 3
    Creamed, 9
    Egg Vinaigrette, with, 5
    Garlic Dressing, with, 5
    Garlic Puréed, 10
    Field Preparation of, 3
    Leek and Canadian Bacon Soup, 6
    Millet Soup, 10
    Molded Tofu Salad, 11
    Nettle Spread, 11
    Lime and Dill, with, 6
    Pickles, 7
    Shredded Salad, 12
    Tarragon Salad, 7
    Venison Kabobs, 12
    Vinaigrette, with, 8

Watercress Soup, 8

Asclepias speciosa, 112
Au Gratin, Salsify, 157

Bacon Dressing, Nettle Greens with, 183
Bacon, Wilted Lamb's Quarters–
      Watercress Salad with, 109
Baked Morels with Sour Cream, 130
Barley, Yampa and Cabbage Soup, 231
Basil, Lamb's Quarters with, 110
Basting Sauce, Wild Gooseberry, 205
Batter, Fireweed in Buttermilk, 80
Batter-Fried Fiddleheads, 71
Bean Sprouts, Chickweed Salad with, 37
Beans, Greens and, 39
Beans (White) and Gruyere, Watercress
      with, 192
Beef Salad, Miner's Lettuce Roast, 124
Beer Battered Milkweed, 115
Belgium Red Cabbage, 98
Biscuits, Cattail Pollen–Poppy Seed, 29
Biscuits, Dandelion Flower, 54
Biscuits, Lamb's Quarters Seed Drop, 110
Blancmange, Rose Petal, 226
Blue Cheese Piñon Spread, Brandied, 147
Blue Cornmeal Griddle Cakes, Piñon–, 149
Bourbon Filling, Huckleberry Tort with, 92
Braised Burdock, 15
Braised Fireweed, 79
Brandied Blue Cheese–Piñon Spread, 147
Brandy, Spiced Wild Plum, 217
Bread
    Apple–Wild Currant, 195
    Huckleberry Nut, 9
    Cattail Flour Batter, 27

Cattail Corn, 26
Indian Flat, 99
Oat with Lamb's Quarter Seed, 111
Navajo Juniper Corn, 102
Pauper's, 102
Bread Sticks, Cattail Pollen, 28
Breakfast Bars, Serviceberry, 164
Brottorte, Piñon, 150
Buckwheat Pancakes, Cattail, 26
BURDOCK
Braised, 15
Fritters, 16
Candied, 18
Carrots and Red Peppers, Pickled, 21
Chicken Cantonese with, 19
Egg Drop Soup with, 21
Gobo Maki, 20
Greens, Herbed, 22
Greens with Monterey Jack, 16
Japanese Stir-Fry Burdock, 22
Mold, 17
Relish, 18
Soup with Smoked Steelhead, Cream of, 20
Burgoo, Fiddlehead, 72
Butter
Chokecherry, 44
Chokecherry–Apple, 44
Roast Grouse with Juniper, 103
Wild Mint, 211
Wild Plum, 216
Buttermilk Batter, Fireweed in, 80
Buttermilk Pancakes with Dandelion Flowers, 52
Buttermilk Pancakes, Huckleberry, 87

Cabbage, Belgium Red, 98
Cabbage Soup, Barley, Yampa, 231
Cake
Huckleberry, 88
Rosehip, 223
Serviceberry, 164
Sheep Sorrel, 173
Snake River Moonshine, 33

Sunshine, 28
Wild Currant, 198
Wild Plum Upside-Down, 220
Cakes, Salsify, 157
Campfire Stew, Arrowhead, 9
Canadian Bacon Soup, Arrowhead, Leek and, 6
Candied Burdock, 18
Candy, Chokecherry, 45
Cannelloni, Nettle, 182
Cantonese Chicken with Burdock, 19
Carrots and Red Peppers, Pickled Burdock with, 21
Casserole, Salsify, 158
Catsup, Serviceberry, 165
CATTAIL
Batter Bread, 27
Buckwheat Pancakes, 26
Corn Bread, 26
Creamed Shoots with Tarragon and Tomato, 32
Homestead Pudding, 32
Pancake Mix, 27
Pollen Bread Sticks, 28
Pollen–Poppy Seed Biscuits, 29
Shoot, Pepper, Anchovy Salad, 29
Shoot Soup, 30
Shoots with Wild Mint, 30
Snake River Moonshine Cake, 33
Sprout Pickles, 33
Sprouts with Whole Wheat Fettuccine, 31
Sprouts with Wild Greens, 31
Sunshine Cake, 28
Celery Seed Dressing, Miner's Lettuce, 123
Cerastium arvense, 34
Cerastium vulgatum, 34
Cheddar and Parmesan, Fireweed with, 81
Cheese Ball with Piñon, Gourmet, 147
Cheese, Chickweed with Swiss, 38
Cheese, Fiddleheads with, 73
Cheese–Piñon Spread, Brandied Blue, 147
Cheesecake, Huckleberry, 88
Chenopodium album, 104

Chenopodium berlandieri, 104
Chicken Breasts, Ricotta Stuffed with
    Morel Sauce, 136
Chicken, Juniper, 99
Chicken and Morel Mushroom Soup, 131
Chicken Stir-Fry, Arrowhead and, 4
CHICKWEED
    Egg Salad with, 38
    Lamb's Quarters, and, 36
    Greens and Beans, 39
    Herbed Chickweed, 41
    Mixed Wild Greens Salad, and, 36
    Molded Cottage Cheese Salad, 40
    Russian Sandwiches, 36
    Salad, 37
    Salad with Bean Sprouts, 37
    Smoked Salmon Sandwich with, 40
    Sorrel Greens, and, 38
    Swiss Cheese, with, 38
    Vegetable Soup, Chilled, 39
Chilled Chickweed–Vegetable Soup, 39
Chilled Huckleberry Soup, 86
Chilled Pea Soup with Wild Mint, 209
Chocolates, Huckleberry, 89
CHOKECHERRY
    Apple Butter, 44
    Butter, 44
    Candy, 45
    Dumplings, 45
    Jam, 46
    Liqueur, 46
    Mousse, 47
    Sauce for Wild Fowl, 47
    Sherbet, 48
    Spiced Cordial, 49
    Syrup, 48
    Whip, 49
Chops, Morel Stuffed Lamb, 135
Chowder, Arrowhead, 3
Chowder, Fiddlehead, 73
Chowder, Milkweed Bud, 114
Chutney, Wild Plum, 217
Coffee, Dandelion Root, 57
Cookies, Filled Wild Currant, 197

Cookies, Rosehip, 224
Cooler, Frosted Oregon Grape, 140
Cooler, Wild Mint Lemon, 212
Conserve, Serviceberry, 165
Cordial, Elderberry, 62
Cordial, Spiced Chokecherry, 49
Cordial, Wild Mint, 211
Corn Bread, Cattail, 26
Corn Bread, Navajo Juniper, 102
Corn and Tomatoes, Milkweed with, 117
Cottage Cheese Salad, Molded
    Chickweed–, 40
Cottage Cheese with Watercress
    Sandwiches, 188
Crab Stuffed Morels, 132
Cream of Burdock Soup with Smoked
    Steelhead, 20
Cream, Fiddleheads in, 74
Cream of Milkweed Soup, 115
Cream of Nettle Soup, 180
Cream Sauce, Salsify with, 159
Creamed Arrowhead, 9
Creamed Cattail Shoots with Tarragon and
    Tomato, 32
Creamed Lamb's Quarters with Onions,
    106
Creamed Morels and Oysters, 133
Creole Gumbo with Milkweed Pods, 116
Crepes, Dandelion, 53
Crusted Trout, Piñon, 157
Curry Sauce, Wild Plum, 218
Curried Fireweed, 79
Custard Pie, Wild Rose, 227

DANDELION
    Buttermilk Pancakes with Flowers, 52
    Crepes, 53
    Duchess Soup, 54
    Flower Biscuits, 54
    Freezing of, 57
    Greens, 55
    Greens, Southern Style, 55
    Root Coffee, 57
    Salad with Guacamole Dressing, 56

Scalloped Greens, 58
Sheep Sorrel Salad, 56
Tuna and Greens Salad, 57
Wine, 58
Dill, Arrowhead with Lime and, 6
Dilled Fiddlehead Pickles, 71
Dipping Sauce, Milkweed Tempura with
    Gingered, 119
Dressing
    Dandelion Salad with Guacamole,
      56
    French with Wild Mint, 209
    Garlic, Arrowhead with, 5
    Green Goddess Salad, 188
    Huckleberry, 89
    Miner's Lettuce with Celery Seed,
      123
    Miner's Lettuce with Spicy Lime,
      126
    Nettle Greens with Bacon, 183
Dried
    Morels in Olive Oil, 137
    Morels and Rice, 131
    Wild Currant–Poppy
      Seed–Almond Muffins, 196
Dumplings, Chokecherry, 45

Egg Drop Soup with Burdock, 20
Egg Mustard Sauce, Fiddleheads with, 74
Egg Salad with Chickweed, 38
Egg Vinaigrette, Arrowhead with, 5
ELDERBERRY
    Angel Pie, 62
    Blossom Fritters, 65
    Blossom Muffins, 66
    Blossom Pancakes, 66
    Cordial, 62
    Jelly, 63
    Sauce, 63
    Slump, 63
    Soufflé, 64
    Spiced, 67
    Syrup, 64
    Tapioca, 65

Endive Salad, Sheep Sorrel–, 173
Endive Salad, Watercress and, 190
Epilobium angustifolium, 77
Escarole Salad with Piñon Nuts, 147

Fettuccine, Cattail Sprouts with Whole
    Wheat, 31
Fettuccine with Morels, 133
Field Preparation of Arrowhead, 3
FIDDLEHEAD
    Batter Fried, 71
    Burgoo, 72
    Cheese, with, 73
    Chowder, 73
    Cream, in, 74
    Dilled Pickles, 71
    Egg Mustard Sauce, with, 74
    Gumbo, Shrimp, 76
    Morels, with, 75
    Oriental Style, 75
    Parmesan, 76
Filled Wild Currant Cookies, 197
FIREWEED
    Almandine, 80
    Braised, 79
    Buttermilk Batter, in, 80
    Cheddar and Parmesan, with, 81
    Curried, 79
    Orange Sauce, with, 81
    Purée, 82
    Soup, Spring Lamb, 83
    Stir-Fried, 83
    Tomatoes, with, 82
Flat Bread, Indian, 99
Fool, Wild Gooseberry, 203
Foil-Roasted Quail with Juniper, 98
Freezer Jam, Oregon Grape, 141
French Dressing with Wild Mint, 209
French Fried Salsify, 155
French Peasant Soup, 156
Frittata, Nettle, 181

Fritters
    Burdock, 16

Elder Blossom, 65
Morel, 133
Yampa, 234
Frosted Oregon Grape Cooler, 140
Frosting, Huckleberry Tort with Bourbon, 92
Fudge, Piñon Tangelo, 152

Garlic Dressing, Arrowhead with, 5
Garlic Puréed Arrowhead, 10
Ginger Dipping Sauce, Milkweed Tempura with, 119
Gingered Yampa, 232
Glaze, Oregon Grape, 141
Glazed Acorn Squash with Wild Currants, 197
Glazed Salsify, 156
Gobo Maki, 20
Gravy for Wild Game, Juniper, 100
Green Goddess Dressing, 188
Green Onion Tart, Lamb's Quarters and, 107
Green Rice, 123
Greens
Beans and (Chickweed), 39
Burdock with Monterey Jack, 16
Cattail Sprouts with, 31
Chickweed Sorrel, 38
Dandelion, 55
Dandelion, Southern Style, 55
Herbed Burdock, 22
Nettle, 182
Nettle with Bacon Dressing, 183
Scalloped Dandelion, 58
Griddle Cakes, Lamb's Quarter Seed, 108
Griddle Cakes, Piñon–Blue Cornmeal, 149
Ground Lamb Kabobs with Piñon, 148
Gourmet Cheese Ball with Piñon, 147
Grouse with Juniper Butter, Roast, 103
Guacamole Dressing, Dandelion Salad with, 56
Gumbo, Creole, with Milkweed Pods, 116
Gumbo, Shrimp–Fiddleheads, 76

Gruyere, Watercress with White Beans and, 192

Harvest Pie, 163
Hazelnuts, Lamb's Quarters with, 106
Herbed Burdock Greens, 22
Herbed Chickweed, 41
Herbs, Yampa with, 235
Homestead Pudding, 32
Horseradish, Mashed Potatoes and Yampa with, 223
Horseradish Sauce, Wild Plum, 218
HUCKLEBERRY
Apple Crisp, 87
Buttermilk Pancakes, 87
Cake, 88
Cheesecake, 88
Chocolates, 89
Dressing, 89
Jam, 90
Nut Bread, 90
Pie, 90
Pudding with Lemon Sauce, 91
Soup, Chilled, 86
Sour Cream Muffins, 94
Syrup, 92
Tort with Bourbon Frosting, 92
Truffles, 93
Uncooked Pie, 94
Waffles, 93
Hummus with Piñon Nuts, 148

Ice Cream, Oregon Grape, 142
Ice Cream, Wild Gooseberry, 205
Ice Cream, Wild Rose, 227
Indian Flat Bread, 99

Jam
Chokecherry, 46
Huckleberry, 90
Oregon Grape Freezer, 141
Spiced Rosehip, 226
Spiced Wild Gooseberry, 203
Wild Rose Petal, 228

Japanese Stir-Fry Burdock, 22
Jelly
    Elderberry, 63
    Oregon Grape, 142
    Watercress, 190
    Wild Mint, 212
Julep, Wild Mint, 212
JUNIPER
    Alsatian Stew, 97
    Belgium Red Cabbage, 98
    Chicken, 99
    Foil-Roasted Quail with, 98
    Gravy for Wild Game, 100
    Indian Flat Bread, 99
    Leg of Lamb with Sauce, 101
    Leg of Pork with, 101
    Marinade for Wild Game, 100
    Navajo Juniper Corn Bread, 102
    Pauper's Bread, 102
    Roast Grouse with Juniper Butter, 103
Juniperus scopulorum, 95

Kabobs, Ground Lamb with Piñon, 148
Kabobs, Venison and Arrowhead, 12

Lamb
    Ground Kabobs, with Piñon, 148
    Lebanese Lamb and Rice, 149
    Leg of, with Juniper Sauce, 101
    Morel Stuffed Chops, 135
    (Spring), Fireweed Soup, 83
    Stew with Yampa, 232
    Stuffed Leg of, with Wild Mint, 210
    with Yampa, Roast, 233
LAMB'S QUARTERS
    Basil, with, 110
    Chickweed and, 36
    Creamed with Onions, 106
    Green Onion Tart, and, 107
    Hazelnuts, with, 106
    Lentil Stew with, 109
    Oat Bread with Seed, 111
    Piñon Salad, 108
    Pot Likker, with, 108

Seed Drop Biscuits, 110
Seed Griddle Cakes, 108
Siciliani, 106
Soup, 107
Watercress Salad with Bacon,
    Wilted, 109
Leather, Wild Plum, 218
Lebanese Lamb and Rice, 149
Leek and Canadian Bacon Soup,
    Arrowhead, 6
Leg of Lamb with Juniper Sauce, 101
Leg of Lamb, Stuffed, with Wild Mint, 210
Leg of Pork with Juniper, 101
Lemon Cooler, Wild Mint–, 212
Lemon, Lentil Soup with Nettle and, 180
Lemon Sauce, Huckleberry Pudding with,
    91
Lemon Sauce, Steamed Serviceberry Puff,
    91
Lentil Soup with Nettle and Lemon, 180
Lentil Stew with Lamb's Quarters, 109
Lentil–Watercress Soup, 189
Lime and Dill, Arrowhead with, 6
Lime Dressing, Miner's Lettuce with Spicy,
    126
Liqueur
    Chokecherry, 46
    Oregon Grape, 143
    Wild Currant, 198
    Wild Gooseberry, 204
    Wild Rosehip, 225

Mahonia repens, 138
Maki, Gobo, 20
Margaritas, Wild Gooseberry, 206
Marinade for Wild Game, Juniper, 100
Marinade, Wild Mint and Yogurt, 213
Marmalade, Wild Plum, 219
Mashed Potatoes and Yampa with
    Horseradish, 233
Mentha arvensis, 207
MILKWEED
    with Almonds, 116
    Beer Battered, 115

Chowder, 114
with Corn and Tomatoes, 117
Cream Soup, 115
Creole Gumbo, 116
with Mustard, 118
Pie, 118
Sautéed, 120
Sesame Seeds, 117
Tempura with Gingered Dipping
Sauce, 119
Millet–Arrowhead Soup, 10
Mincemeat, Venison, 169
MINER'S LETTUCE
with Celery Seed Dressing, 123
Green Rice, 123
Mushroom Salad, and, 124
Roast Beef Salad, 124
Salad, 124
Salad with Peanuts, 124
with Spicy Lime Dressing, 126
Spring Mold, 126
Tomato Salad, and, 127
Yogurt Salad–,127
Mock Oysters, 155
Mold, Burdock, 17
Mold, Miner's Lettuce Spring, 126
Molded Arrowhead Tofu Salad, 11
Molded Chickweed–Cottage Cheese Salad,
40
Monterey Jack, Burdock Greens with, 16
Montia perfoliata, 121
Moonshine Cake, Snake River, 33
Morchella angusticeps, 128
MOREL MUSHROOM
Baked with Sour Cream, 130
Chicken and Morel Soup, 131
Crab Stuffed, 132
Creamed with Oysters, 132
Dried Morels and Rice, 131
Dried in Olive Oil, 137
Fettuccine with, 133
Fiddleheads with, 75
Fritters, 133
Paté, 134

Piñon and Wild Currant Stuffing, 135
Ricotta Stuffed Chicken Breasts with
Sauce, 136
Rotelle with Sauce, 137
Sautéed with Piñon Nuts, 136
Stuffed Lamb Chops, 135
Wild Rice Soup, 137
Mousse, Chokecherry, 47
Muffins
Dried Wild Currant–Poppy
Seed–Almond, 196
Elder Blossom, 66
Serviceberry, 166
Sour Cream Huckleberry, 94
Mushroom Salad, Miner's Lettuce–, 124
Mustard Sauce, Milkweed Shoots with, 118

Navajo Juniper Corn Bread, 102
Nettle and Arrowhead Spread, 11
Noodles, Nettles, 184
Nut Stuffing, Serviceberry, 166

Oat Bread with Lamb's Quarter Seed, 111
Oatmeal Pancakes with Oregon Grape
Syrup, 140
Olive Oil, Dried Morels in, 137
Onions, Creamed Lamb's Quarters with,
106
Orange Sauce, Fireweed with, 81
OREGON GRAPE
Cooler, 140
Freezer Jam, 141
Glaze, 141
Ice Cream, 142
Jelly, 142
Liqueur, 143
Oatmeal Pancakes with Syrup, 140
Sherbet, 143
Vinegar, 143
Oriental Style, Fiddleheads, 75
Oysters, Creamed Morels and, 133
Oysters, Mock, 155

Pan Dowdy, Wild Plum, 219

Pancake Mix, Cattail Flour, 27

Pancakes
    Buttermilk, with Dandelion
        Flowers, 52
    Cattail Buckwheat, 26
    Cattail Flour Mix, 27
    Elder Blossom, 66
    Huckleberry, 87
    Oatmeal with Oregon Grape
        Syrup, 140
Parmesan, Fiddleheads, 76
Parmesan, Fireweed with Cheddar and, 81
Parmesan, Salsify with, 159
Paté, Morel, 134
Pauper's Bread, 102
Pea Soup with Wild Mint, Chilled, 209
Peanuts, Miner's Lettuce Salad with, 125
Pemmican, 195
Pemmican, Serviceberry, 163
Perideridia gairdneri, 228
Pesto, 150
Pickled Burdock with Red Peppers and
    Carrots, 21
Pickles, Arrowhead, 7
Pickles, Cattail Sprout, 33
Pickles, Dilled Fiddlehead, 71
Pie
    Elderberry Angel, 62
    Harvest, 163
    Huckleberry, 90
    Huckleberry, Uncooked, 94
    Milkweed, 118
    Nettle, 185
    Piñon, 151
    Sheep Sorrel, 174
    Wild Currant, 199
    Wild Gooseberry, 206
    Wild Plum, 219
    Wild Rose Custard, 227
PIÑON NUTS
    Blue Cornmeal Griddle Cakes, 149
    Brandied Blue Cheese Spread, 147

Brottorte, 150
Crusted Trout, 151
Escarole Salad with, 147
Gourmet Cheese Ball, 147
Ground Lamb Kabobs, 148
Hummus, 148
Lamb's Quarters–Piñon Salad, 108
Lebanese Lamb and Rice, 148
Morel and Wild Currant Stuffing, 135
Pesto, 150
Pie, 151
Sautéed Morels with, 136
Tangelo Fudge, 152
Tarts, 152
Pinus edulis, 144
Piquant Wild Plum, 216
Poached Gooseberries, 203
Poppy Seed Biscuits, Cattail Pollen, 29
Poppy Seed–Almond Muffins, Dried Wild
    Currant, 196
Pot Likker, Lamb's Quarters with, 108
Potato and Sheep Sorrel Soup, 172
Potato–Watercress Soup, 189
Potatoes and Yampa with Horseradish,
    Mashed, 233
Potatoes, Salsify and, 160
Prunus americana, 215
Prunus demissa, 42
Prunus melanocarpa, 42
Prunus virginiana, 43
Pteretis pensylvanica, 68
Pudding
    Homestead, 32
    Huckleberry with Lemon Sauce, 91
    Nettle Dessert, 183
    Rosehip, 224
    Serviceberry, Steamed, 167
    Wild Currant–Raspberry, 199
    Wild Currant with Sherry Sauce,
        200
Puff with Lemon Sauce, Steamed
    Serviceberry, 168
Purée
    Fireweed, 82

Nettle, 185
Sheep Sorrel, 174
Yampa, 235
Yampa and Apple, 235
Puréed Arrowhead, Garlic, 10

Quail with Juniper, Foil-Roasted, 98

Raspberry Pudding, Wild Currant–, 199
Red Peppers, Burdock Pickled with
    Carrots and, 21
Relish, Burdock, 18
Ribes aureum, 193
Ribes inebrians, 193
Ribes inerme, 201
Ribes leucaderme, 201
Ribes montigenum, 201
Ribes pumilum, 193
Rice, Green, 123
Rice, Lebanese Lamb and, 149
Rice, Dried Morels and, 131
Rice and Morel Soup, Wild, 137
Ricotta Stuffed Chicken Breasts with Morel
    Sauce, 136
Roast Beef Salad, Miner's Lettuce, 125
Roast Grouse with Juniper Butter, 103
Roast Lamb with Yampa, 233
Rorippa-nasturtium-aquaticum, 186
Rosa woodsii, 220
Rotelle with Morel Sauce, 137
Rumex acetosella, 170
Russian Sandwiches, Chickweed, 36
Rye, Watercress and Sardine Paste on, 191

Sagittaria latifolia, xi
Salad
    Arrowhead–Tarragon, 7
    Arrowhead with Vinaigrette, 8
    Arrowhead with Egg Vinaigrette, 5
    Cattail Shoot Pepper, Anchovy, 29
    Cattail Sprouts and Wild Greens,
      31
    Chickweed, 37
    Chickweed with Bean Sprouts, 37

Chickweed and Wild Mixed
    Greens, 36
Dandelion with Guacamole
    Dressing, 56
Dandelion–Sheep Sorrel, 56
Eggs with Chickweed, 38
Escarole with Piñon Nuts, 147
Lamb's Quarters–Piñon, 108
Miner's Lettuce, 124
Miner's Lettuce with Celery Seed
    Dressing, 123
Miner's Lettuce–Mushroom, 124
Miner's Lettuce with Peanuts, 124
Miner's Lettuce–Roast Beef, 124
Miner's Lettuce with Spicy Lime
    Dressing, 126
Miner's Lettuce Spring Mold, 126
Miner's Lettuce and Tomato, 127
Miner's Lettuce–Yogurt, 127
Molded Arrowhead Tofu, 11
Molded Chickweed–Cottage
    Cheese Salad, 40
Sheep Sorrel–Endive, 173
Shredded Arrowhead, 12
Tuna and Dandelion Greens, 56
Watercress and Endive, 190
Wilted Lamb's
    Quarters–Watercress, 109
Salmon Sandwich with Chickweed,
    Smoked, 40
Salmon and Sheep Sorrel Tart, Smoked,
    175
Salmon Spread with Sheep Sorrel, 172
SALSIFY
    Au Gratin, 157
    Cakes, 157
    Casserole, 158
    with Cream Sauce, 159
    French Fried, 155
    French Peasant Soup, 156
    Glazed, 156
    Mock Oysters, 155
    with Parmesan, 159
    and Potatoes, 160

Soup, 158
Soup, French Peasant, 156
Sambucus cerulea, 59
Sambucus glauca, 59
Sandwich, Smoked Salmon with
    Chickweed, 40
Sandwich, Cottage Cheese with
    Watercress, 188
Sandwiches, Chickweed Russian, 36
Sandwiches, Watercress Tea, 192
Sardine Paste on Rye, Watercress and, 191
Sauce
    Chokecherry for Wild Fowl, 47
    Egg Mustard, Fiddleheads with, 74
    Elderberry, 63
    Leg of Lamb with Juniper, 101
    Lemon, Huckleberry Pudding
      with, 91
    Lemon Sauce, Steamed
      Serviceberry Puff, 168
    Milkweed Shoots with Mustard,
      118
    Milkweed Tempura with Gingered
      Dipping, 119
    Orange, Fireweed with, 81
    Ricotta Stuffed Chicken Breasts
      with Morel, 136
    Rotelle with Morel, 137
    Salsify with Cream, 159
    Serviceberry for Venison, 167
    Sheep Sorrel, 175
    Wild Currant Pudding with Sherry,
      200
    Wild Gooseberry Basting, 205
    Wild Plum Curry, 218
    Wild Plum Horseradish, 218
Sautéed Milkweed, 120
Sautéed Morels with Piñon Nuts, 136
Sautéed Yampa, 234
Scalloped Dandelion Greens, 58
Sesame Seeds, Milkweed Buds with, 117

SERVICEBERRY
    Breakfast Bars, 164

    Cake, 164
    Catsup, 165
    Conserve, 163
    Harvest Pie, 163
    Muffins, 166
    Nut Stuffing, 166
    Pemmican, 163
    Sauce for Venison, 167
    Steamed Pudding, 167
    Steamed Puff with Lemon Sauce, 168
    Stewed, 168
    Venison Mincemeat, 169
SHEEP SORREL
    Cake, 173
    Chickweed and, 38
    Dandelion Salad, 56
    Endive Salad, 173
    Pie, 174
    Potato Soup, 172
    Purée, 174
    Salmon Spread with, 172
    Sauce, 175
    Smoked Salmon Tart, 175
    Swamp Soda, 176
    Tansy, 176
Sherbet
    Chokecherry, 48
    Orange Grape, 143
    Wild Mint, 213
Sherry Sauce, Wild Currant Pudding with,
    200
Shredded Arrowhead Salad, 12
Shrimp–Fiddlehead Gumbo, 76
Siciliani, Lamb's Quarters, 106
Slump, Elderberry, 63
Smoked Salmon Sandwich with
    Chickweed, 40
Smoked Salmon and Sheep Sorrel Tart, 175
Smoked Steelhead, Cream of Burdock
    Soup with, 20
Snake River Moonshine Cake, 33
Soda
    Swamp, 176
    Wild Rose, 228

Soufflé, Elderberry, 64
Soufflé, Nettle, 225
Soup
    Arrowhead, Leek and Canadian
      Bacon, 6
    Arrowhead with Watercress, 8
    Barley, Yampa and Cabbage, 231
    Cattail Shoot, 30
    Chicken and Morel Mushroom, 131
    Chilled Chickweed–Vegetable, 39
    Chilled Huckleberry, 86
    Chilled Pea with Wild Mint, 209
    Cream of Burdock with Smoked
      Steelhead, 20
    Cream of Milkweed, 115
    Cream of Nettle, 180
    Dandelion Duchess, 54
    Egg Drop with Burdock, 21
    Fiddlehead Chowder, 73
    French Peasant, 156
    Lamb's Quarters, 107
    Lentil with Nettle and Lemon, 180
    Lentil–Watercress, 189
    Milkweed Bud Chowder, 114
    Millet–Arrowhead, 10
    Potato and Sheep Sorrel, 172
    Potato–Watercress, 189
    Salsify, 158
    Spring Lamb–Fireweed, 83
    Turkish Yogurt with Wild Mint,
      211
    Wild Plum, 220
    Wild Rice and Morel, 137
    Wild Rosehip, 225
Sour Cream, Baked Morels with, 130
Sour Cream Huckleberry Muffins, 94
Southern Style, Dandelion Greens, 55
Spiced Chokecherry Cordial, 49
Spiced Elderberries, 67
Spiced Rosehip Jam, 226
Spiced Wild Currants, 196
Spiced Wild Gooseberry Jam, 203
Spiced Wild Plum Brandy, 217

Spicy Lime Dressing, Miner's Lettuce with,
    126
Spread, Brandied Blue Cheese–Piñon
    Spread, 147
Spread, Nettle and Arrowhead, 11
Spread, Salmon with Sheep Sorrel, 172
Spring Lamb–Fireweed Soup, 83
Squash with Wild Currants, Glazed Acorn,
    197
Steamed Serviceberry Pudding, 167
Steamed Serviceberry Puff with Lemon
    Sauce, 168
Steelhead, Cream of Burdock Soup with
    Smoked, 20
Stellaria media, 34
Stew, Alsatian, 97
Stew, Arrowhead Campfire, 9
Stew, Lentil with Lamb's Quarters, 109
Stew with Yampa, Lamb, 232
Stewed Serviceberries, 168
STINGING NETTLE
    Ale, 181
    Cannelloni, 182
    Cream Soup, 180
    Dessert Pudding, 183
    Frittata, 181
    Greens, 182
    Greens with Bacon Dressing, 183
    Lentil Soup with Lemon, 180
    Noodles, 184
    Pies, 185
    Purée, 185
    Soufflé, 184
Stir-Fried Fireweed, 83
Stir-Fry Burdock, Japanese, 22
Streusel, Wild Gooseberry, 204
Stuffed Lamb Chops, Morel, 135
Stuffed Leg of Lamb with Wild Mint, 210
Stuffed Morels, Crab, 132
Stuffing, Morel, Piñon and Wild Currant,
    135
Stuffing, Serviceberry Nut, 165
Swamp Soda, 176
Swiss Cheese, Chickweed with, 38

Syrup
  Chokecherry, 48
  Elderberry, 64
  Huckleberry,.92
  Oregon Grape, Oatmeal Pancakes
    with, 140
  Wild Gooseberry, 204

Tabbouleh, 210
Tangelo Fudge, Piñon and, 152
Tansy, 176
Tapioca, Elderberry, 65
Taraxacum officinale, 50
Tarragon Salad, Arrowhead–, 7
Tarragon and Tomato, Creamed Cattail
    Shoots with, 32
Tart, Lamb's Quarters and Green Onion,
    107
Tart, Smoked Salmon and Sheep Sorrel,
    175
Tarts, Piñon, 152
Tea Sandwiches, Watercress, 192
Tofu Salad, Molded Arrowhead, 11
Tomato, Creamed Cattail Shoots with
    Tarragon and, 32
Tomato Salad, Miner's Lettuce and, 127
Tomatoes, Fireweed with, 82
Tomatoes, Milkweed with Corn and, 117
Tort with Bourbon Frosting, Huckleberry,
    92
Tuna and Dandelion Greens Salad, 57
Tragopogon porrifolius, 153
Trout, Piñon Crusted, 157
Truffles, Huckleberry, 93
Turkish Yogurt Soup with Wild Mint, 211
Typha latifolia, 23

Upside-Down Cake, Wild Plum, 220
Urtica dioico, 177
Urtica procera, 177

Vaccinium globlare, 84
Vaccinium membranaceum, 84
Vegetable Soup, Chilled Chickweed, 39

Venison and Arrowhead Kabobs, 12
Venison Mincemeat, 169
Venison, Serviceberry Sauce for, 167
Vinegar
  Oregon Grape, 143
  Watercress, 191
  Wild Rose, 228
Vinaigrette, Arrowhead with Egg, 5
Vinaigrette, Arrowhead with, 8

Waffles, Huckleberry, 93
WATERCRESS
  Arrowhead Soup, and, 8
  Endive Salad, 190
  Green Goddess Salad Dressing, 188
  Jelly, 190
  Lentil Soup, 189
  Potato Soup, 189
  Sandwich, Cottage Cheese with, 188
  Sardine Paste on Rye, 191
  Soup, Arrowhead with, 8
  Tea Sandwiches, 192
  Vinegar, 191
  White Beans and Gruyere, 192
  Wild Violet Flowers, and, 191
  Wilted Lamb's Quarters Salad, 109
White Beans and Gruyere, Watercress
    with, 192
Whip, Chokecherry, 48
Whole Wheat Fettuccine, Cattail Sprouts
    with, 31
WILD CURRANT
  Apple Bread, 195
  Cake, 198
  Dried, –Poppy Seed–Almond Muffins,
    196
  Filled Cookies, 196
  Glazed Acorn Squash with, 196
  Liqueur, 198
  Morel, Piñon, and Stuffing, 130
  Pemmican, 195
  Pie, 199
  Pudding with Sherry Sauce, 200
  Raspberry Pudding, 199

Spiced, 196
Stuffing, Morel, Piñon and, 135
Wild Fowl, Chokecherry Sauce for, 47
Wild Game, Juniper Gravy for, 100
Wild Game, Juniper Marinade for, 100
WILD GOOSEBERRY
Basting Sauce, 205
Fool, 203
Ice Cream, 205
Liqueur, 204
Margaritas, 206
Pie, 206
Poached, 203
Spiced Jam, 203
Streusel, 204
Syrup, 204
Wild Greens, Cattail Sprouts with, 31
WILD MINT
Butter, 211
Cattail Shoots with, 30
Chilled Pea Soup, 209
Cordial, 211
French Dressing, 209
Jelly, 212
Julep, 212
Lemon Cooler, 212
Sherbet, 213
Stuffed Leg of Lamb, 210
Tabbouleh, 210
Turkish Yogurt Soup, 211
Yogurt Marinade, 213
WILD PLUM
Butter, 216
Chutney, 217
Curry Sauce, 218
Horseradish Sauce, 218
Marmalade, 219
Leather, 218
Pan Dowdy, 219
Pie, 219
Piquant, 216
Upside-Down Cake, 220
Soup, 220
Spiced Brandy, 217

Wild Rice and Morel Soup, 137

WILD ROSE
Petal Blancmange, 226
Petal Custard Pie, 227
Petal Ice Cream, 227
Petal Jam, 228
Petal Soda, 228
Rosehip Cake, 223
Rosehip Cookies, 224
Rosehip Liqueur, 225
Rosehip Pudding, 224
Rosehip Soup, 225
Spiced Rosehip Jam, 226
Vinegar, 228
Wild Violet Flowers, Watercress and, 191
Wilted Lamb's Quarters–Watercress Salad,
109
Wine, Dandelion, 58

YAMPA
Apple Purée and, 234
Barley and Cabbage Soup, 231
Fritters, 234
Gingered, 232
Herbed, 235
Lamb Stew with, 232
Mashed Potatoes with Horseradish,
233
Purée, 235
Roast Lamb with, 233
Sautéed, 234
Yogurt Marinade, Wild Mint and, 213
Yogurt Salad, Miner's Lettuce, 127
Yogurt Soup with Wild Mint, Turkish, 211